THE THEORY OF A. R. LURIA

Functions of Spoken Language
in the
Development of Higher Mental Processes

THE THEORY OF A. R. LURIA

Functions of Spoken Language
in the
Development of Higher Mental Processes

DONNA R. VOCATE

University of Colorado, Boulder

LEA LAWRENCE ERLBAUM ASSOCIATES, PUBLISHERS
1987   Hillsdale, New Jersey   London

Lawrence Erlbaum Associates, Inc., Publishers
365 Broadway
Hillsdale, New Jersey 07642

Library of Congress Cataloging in Publication Data
Vocate, Donna R.
  The theory of A. R. Luria.

  Bibliography: p.
  Includes index.
  1. Psycholinguistics. 2. Intellect. 3. Neurolinguistics. 4. Luria, A. R. (Aleksandr Romanovich),
1902-   . I. Luria, A. R. (Aleksandr Romanovich),
1902-   . II. Title. [DNLM: 1. Language. Mental
Processes—physiology. BF 455 V872t]
BF455.V63 1987   153   86-16568
ISBN 0-89859-709-9

Printed in the United States of America

10   9   8   7   6   5   4   3   2   1

CONTENTS

Preface

When Dr. Vocate first approached me to inquire if I would write a preface to her book about Alexander Luria's research on language and human psychological processes, my reaction was one of curiousity and misgiving. I was curious about the kind of book that would result from a meticulous study of Luria's translated work, and I doubted strongly that I could add anything of value to readers' experience of her account. When I first read through the manuscript my curiousity was satisfied. In the pages to follow you will find an exceedingly thorough exposition of Luria's work over more than half a century, gleaned from an amazing range of sources. But my misgiving remained. I was uncertain what I could add to Dr. Vocate's scholarship.

However, as time passed I found myself in odd moments letting my mind wander over the incredible canvas of the man's work. Phrases and paragraphs written as many as 50 years apart from each other juxtaposed themselves in my mind, and I was assailed (not for the first time) by a strong sense of wonder at the richness of the insights that Alexander Luria's work contains for contemporary studies of human nature. As these pages testify, I eventually agreed that perhaps it would not be useless for me to comment on the book for English-speaking readers. Whether this judgment was correct or not, those readers must decide for themselves.

Alexander Romanovich Luria began his career prior to the Russian Revolution, while still an enthusiastic teenager, imbued with the ideals of Russian activist humanism and burning with a desire to apply science to the improvement of his countrymen. He died a world famous professor in his country's most prestigious university more than half a century later. In the interim he published a large number of books (more than a dozen of which have been translated into English) and hundreds of research papers. His subject matter included experimental studies of the relation between cognition and affect, the impact of cultural and social conditions on cognitive development, the role of genetic influences in development, mental retardation, aphasia, the restoration of function following brain lesions, and the psychophysiology of mind. More important than the variety of his efforts was their unity; the scientific goals he set himself as a young man remained those he was pursuing when he died.

Notice that in creating the list of topics in the previous paragraph, the word "language" is not included. To someone totally unfamiliar with Luria's work, this omission might be taken as a signal that I was saving the topic of the present book for last as a means of highlighting it. After all, this is a book about Luria's view of language and human nature. But to anyone familiar with his work, it quickly will be recognized that the topic, *language,* need not (perhaps *can* not) be separated from the topics just listed. Language was there at the beginning and it was there at the end providing substantive unity to his far-flung work.

Dr. Vocate's book, sampling as it does from all phases of Luria's career, provides an excellent overview of his intellectual journey. In this preface, I attempt to provide a map of the route in the hope that a little prior orientation may deepen the reader's enjoyment of the trip.

As a teenager, Alexander Romanovich (as his students referred to him) was drawn to the recently created discipline of psychology, but dissatisfied with the form in which he inherited it. The discipline was divided into two branches. One branch asserted that psychology could be an *experimental* science, modeled on the precise, objective methods of the physical sciences. Its champion was Wilhelm Wundt, generally acknowledged as the "father of scientific psychology" in American textbooks. The other branch, whose champion was Wilhelm Dilthey, asserted that psychology is ineluctibly a part of the *humane* sciences, the goal of which is the description of consciousness.

Luria, first intuitively and then self-consciously, rejected this division of psychology and set out to create a science that could unify its descriptive and experimental branches. In reading this book, and in reading Luria's work more generally, it is important to remember that despite changes in the specific topics of research, this goal was never relinquished; it simply underwent a variety of transformations as a consequence of the scientific and historical circumstances in which the man and his work found themselves.

Luria's first guess at a new psychological synthesis drew heavily on Sigmund Freud's theory of the psychodynamics of individual experience. Especially attractive to Luria was Freud's insistence on the long-term action of basic motives and his promise of a method to uncover the hidden psychological processes of individual human beings. However, Luria soon grew sceptical of the subjectivity of Freud's methods, although he retained an interest in his theoretical claims. He resolved to retain the virtues of Freud's psychodynamic insights, but to provide an objective methodology upon which to base further theorizing.

In Luria's first attempts to overcome the division of psychology through the creation of a synthetic methodology, language loomed large as both the key element in his methods and as the medium within which mind itself is constituted. The first major work to come out of this period was *The Nature of Human Conflicts,* in which the idea of language-as-method is combined with the idea of language-as-medium.

The basic problem in this early work was to find an objective approach to the study of mind, the "hidden psychological processes" of the individual subject. The impediments to this project loomed large. "The structure of the organism," Luria wrote, "presupposes not an accidental mosaic, but a complex organization of separate systems . . . . [which] unite as very definite parts into an integrated functional structure" (1932a, p.6). The problem was to discover the structure of this non-accidental mosaic.

The solution was called the "combined motor method." For a long time I was puzzled by this strange name for Luria's methodology. What was being combined, and how did language enter into it? What was being combined was a smoothly flowing, highly organized, voluntary response structure set up by the experimenter on the one hand and the subject's past history on the other.

The basic technique was to teach the subject to hold one hand perfectly steady while the other hand was used to respond as fast as possible by pushing a button in response to an acoustic stimulus (such as a pure tone or the word "press"). After some practice, when this response system was well established, more complex language stimuli were substituted for the tone or the simple instruction. These stimuli were selected to map onto the hypothetical structure of the subject's past experience, making thoughts accessible to objective analysis even if the subject did not want to reveal them. For example, a suspected murderer was taught the preparatory phase and at a crucial juncture, Luria introduced the word "towel" into the stream of word signals for pressing the button. The selective *disruption* of the subject's motor response became the warrant for claiming access to his hidden thoughts. The same technique was used to study a wide variety of subject populations and psychological states.

As Luria explained it, the combination of motor response and the subject's thought processes "stimulate in our subject two systems of activity which are connected with each other so closely that they are set in motion by two simultaneously occurring activities of one and the same process" (1932a, p.23). The medium within which these two processes interacted was human language, within which the patterned mosaic of individual consciousness could be discerned.

One major shortcoming of the combined motor method as a cornerstone of Luria's dreamed-for unified psychology was the absence of a way to link the psychological experiences of individuals to the socio-cultural-historical circumstances in which they lived their lives. In the years from 1925–1934, in collaboration with L. S. Vygotsky and A. N. Leontiev, Luria worked to fill in this essential gap through research with children growing up in a variety of circumstances.

During this period he replicated and extended the techniques of influential developmental psychologists from Western Europe and America such as Jean Piaget, Wolfgang Kohler, Kurt Koffka, Kurt Goldstein, Heinz Werner, and many others. He also studied the word associations of children growing up in different socio-cultural circumstances as a way of untangling the experience-language-mind nexus and wrote prolifically about the laws of cognitive development and their implications for Soviet pedagogy.

One of his most original lines of research during this time was the comparison of language and cognitive development among fraternal and identical twins as part of a mammoth project to study the interrelationship of biology and experience on cognitive development. Only small parts of his work survived to be published, but enough to solidify his claim to the mutability of human cognitive processes through the organization of children's linguistic and cognitive experiences. Before long the work on twins was terminated as a consequence of the USSR's internal political disputes, but not before Luria had managed to collect unique information.

Well before this line of work came to an end, Luria was conducting research on the cultural history of language and mind in Central Asia. A little known aspect of this work that indicates something of the incredible ambitions underlying Luria's project was his hope that by uncovering the specific dynamics of thought in pre-literate societies, he could collaborate in a program of film-mediated education that would bring Soviet peasants a richer understanding of their historical circumstances, the better to guide their own destinies. His partner in this effort, Sergei Eisenstein, had been experimenting with the way in which visual images could be artfully combined to evoke emergent generalizations in the viewers of his films, even though they could not read and the films were silent. Luria hoped that his work would aid this effort by revealing the cognitive dynamics of pre-industrial peoples as a basis for arranging the sequence of film images.

From the mid-1930s to virtually the end of his life, Luria pursued a different side of the language-experience-thought nexus. His work with twins and peasants was highly suspect in the politically perilous atmosphere of Joseph Stalin's purges. Cut off from productive pursuit of his research on the socio-historical underpinnings of mind, Luria turned instead to a study of the anatomical and physiological substrata of mind. This research, which is covered in some detail in this volume, is among his best known work in the United States. Combining the insights of Vygotsky and other Soviet scholars with the work of Jackobsen, Head, and a variety of Western scholars, Luria fashioned a theory of aphasia that served as a practical guide to therapeutic medical practice when the Nazi invasion of the USSR decimated a generation of Soviet citizens.

Following the war, with the exception of a few years of research on language and thought disturbances of mentally retarded children (in which variations on the combined motor method were the core of his methodology), Luria pursued his research on the neuropsychology of mind and wrote up volumes of war-time and pre-war research that had gone unpublished as a consequence of the political and war-time upheavals through which he had passed.

When I first came to know him in the early 1960s Alexander Luria was a senior statesman of 20th century psychology who still hung tenaciously to his dream of a unified science of psychology built upon the principal that language and culture render human-kind distinctively different from all the earth's other creatures. The very scope of his theoretical ambitions rendered him something of an anomaly. From time to time one of his books would appear in translation. If it was on a topic unusual for Western European readers, it was likely to win praise for its originality. If it was on a topic that Western European psychologists considered their own, it was likely to be subjected to guarded praise and pointed criticism.

One issue that came up time and again in the dialogue between Luria and his American readers was the nature of psychological theory and the role of methodology. Luria believed, and did not hesitate to state, that he thought Western psychologists, Americans in particular, were "a-theoretical." This judgement evoked howls of disbelief and counter-charges that Luria's methods were outmoded. In my own view, very few Western psychologists had any inkling of the continuity and breadth of Luria's work. They believed his neuropsychological methods to be no more than a hodgepodge of tests from bygone eras. Without statistical verification of their properties when used on selected patient populations, it was difficult for Americans to take much stock in the claimed results.

In one respect, Luria's critics among American quantitative neuropsychologists were correct. There is no doubt that he lacked high speed computers to assist him in complex factor analyses of neuropsychological symptoms, and that the diagnostic value of many of his tests was rendered moot by modern brain scanning techniques. On the other hand, very few of his critics understood or appreciated the fact that his neuropsychological techniques were far from a hodgepodge made up specifically for purposes of neuropsychological diagnosis. Instead they represented a highly selected set of tools fashioned from his early research on hidden psychological processes or the dynamics of cognitive development. Their validity derived in part from the intricate pattern of the whole, woven from an unprecedented span of observations, into which they fit.

In the pages to follow, a very original 20th century psychologist's ideas about language and human nature have been summarized. Whether one agrees with particular formulations or not, American scholars owe Dr. Vocate a vote of thanks for bringing together the far-flung ideas of a remarkable psychologist whose thoughts can instruct us still.

Michael Cole

Foreword

In the course of my military service in the United States Army, I was exposed to a number of courses dealing with Soviet political thought and practice. Embedded in some of the lectures were numerous allusions to the work of Ivan Petrovich Pavlov. This introduction to Dr. Pavlov and his intellectual descendants was the most significant benefit of my time in uniform. I must frankly admit that I became fascinated with Pavlov, his person, his thought, his research, his school. It was clear to me that Pavlov, in his work on the second signal system, was perceptively analyzing the role of spoken language in human development. My interest in Russian and Soviet contributions to the study of spoken language started at that time and persists even now. It would be impossible to have such an interest without becoming an admirer of the contributions of Aleksandr Romanovich Luria.

I never had the pleasure of meeting Luria. I knew him only through his publications, a few letters, and students whom we both taught. From these sources I developed a deep respect for his insights and methods, and a liking for his obvious kindness and humane concerns. On my office wall hangs a small framed snapshot of Luria with one of his patients. Luria had just made a therapeutic breakthrough, and both he and his patient are looking at the camera and smiling. It's a nice picture and it always helps me to remember the man in the writings.

Donna Vocate's excellent analytical presentation of Luria's work as it bears on how spoken language suffuses higher mental processes brings both the man and his work within easy reach of English speaking scholars of spoken language. This is a valuable contribution to the literature, and to the resources of those of us committed to the study of spoken language.

It is a source of constant amazement to me that so many scholars and other interested parties find it difficult, if not impossible, to appreciate and understand the importance of the fact that in its genesis human language is spoken. I find it easy to assert that spoken language forms the mind. Luria provides essential support for this assertion. As Dr. Vocate points out, Luria saw in the relationship between spoken language and higher mental processes an avenue of continuing hope for improvement of the individual and social human condition. Spoken language, as Luria noted, is the most easily affected of the higher mental processes and thus affords us the easiest access to benign change. Of course, as in all such instances, we cannot allow ourselves to forget that the same instrument of spoken language is also as easily accessible to malignant influence.

In the field of speech communication, which houses some of those scholars interested in the study of spoken language, there is a sub-area labeled *speech science.* The work of A. R. Luria is essential to the literature of that area.

One of the knottiest problems in spoken language and its study is the problem of meaning. This question of "meaning" is so perplexing that many choose simply to ignore it. And yet, meaning suffuses the entire enterprise of communication through spoken language. I found Dr. Vocate's comments on the role of the word "mean" in summarizing Luria's work peculiarly appropriate and illuminating given the importance of meaning. The fact that spoken language is the means by which higher mental processes are formed as well as the means by which higher mental processes are given form in expression both make this book an important contribution to the understanding of the meaning of spoken language.

Frank E.X. Dance

THE THEORY OF A. R. LURIA

Functions of Spoken Language
in the
Development of Higher Mental Processes

Nec manus nuda, nisi intellectus sibi permissus,
multum valent: instrumentis et auxilibus res perticitur.
(Neither bare hand, nor intellect by itself, are worth
much: things get done with the aid of tools and means.)
—Bacon

1 Theoretical Foundations

Any definitive explanation of the relationship between mind and speech has been precluded by the fact that there has been no integrating perspective available to reconcile the conflicting theories about mind and speech produced in isolation from each other. Failure to attain a conclusive explanation of the mind/speech relationship has not resulted from a lack of effort. Our attempts to explain the relationship date back to Heraclitus (Sokolov, 1972). It is the thesis of this book, however, that such a synthesizing perspective is available in the work of one man, Alexander Romanovich Luria, (1902–1977), whose theory encompasses explanations of mind, speech, and the relationship between them.[1]

In Russia, prior to the 1920s, psychologists espoused dualism and concerned themselves with whether or not psychic and physiological activities (mind and brain) were parallel or interactive occurrences (Luria, 1978d). Commencing in the 1920s, the naturalistic approach become dominant in the Soviet Union, and psychologists concerned themselves with demonstrating that mental activity was a complex of properties of solely physiological origin common to man as well as to other animals. This approach sufficed for elementary mental activities such as involuntary attention, but it faltered before the task of explicating the mechanism of intentional mental acts in humans. The solution offered at the time was the creation of an idealistic, descriptive psychology that rejected any scientific, concrete analysis of mentality.

Another approach developing in the Soviet Union during this period differed radically from the popular view, and would eventually permeate

---

[1]Because of that thesis, it is beyond the scope of this book to attempt a synopsis of the history of Soviet Psychology. Readers interested in a more holistic review of trends in Russian psychology would be well advised to refer to two excellent works in that area: Alex Kozulin's *Psychology in Utopia* (1984), and T. R. Payne's *S. L. Rubinstejn and Soviet Psychology* (1968). More consonant with the mind/speech focus of this text is the overview of Soviet psychology provided by Luria's book, *The Making of Mind: A Personal Account of Soviet Psychology* (1979). Yet, that source also provides more historic detail than is noted here in the mere identification of the major views of mind that existed prior to Vygotsky.

Soviet psychology. This was the view of L. S. Vygotsky that higher mental processes originated neither in the psychic nor in the physical, but rather

> outside the individual human organism in objective *social history* .... The formation of language during the process of social development provided him (mankind) not only with a new, previously unknown method of communication but also with a new tool for ordering his mental processes. The higher mental functions that originated in social labor and speech enabled man to rise to a new level of organization in his activity. By adapting the methods created for verbal communication to his own needs, he developed forms of intelligent perception, voluntary attention, active recall, abstract thought, and voluntary behavior that had never existed in the animal world and that have never, to any extent, been demonstrated to be primordial properties of the "spirit." (Luria, 1978d, p. 275).[2]

Prior to his association with Vygotsky, Luria had attempted his own synthesis of the psychic/physical dichotomy by elaborating on Jung's method of free-association and linking it with voluntary motor activity research to produce the "combined motor method," which Cole explains in the Preface of this text. However, as a result of extensive interaction with Vygotsky during the period from 1924 to 1934, Luria retained the methodology while dropping Freudian theory, and gradually substituted Vygotsky's theories as the underlying philosophic base for his own work on human mental functioning.

Attempts by theorists to explicate the ontogenesis of spoken language have resulted in positions almost as polemical as those produced by considerations of human mental functioning. While scholars considering human mentality have divided over the psychic/physical dichotomy, those considering spoken language acquisition have split over internal/ external causation. The internal cause position holds that humans are biologically prewired with a deep-syntax language structure that is

> one of the faculties of the mind, common to the species, . . . a faculty of language that serves the two basic functions of rationalist theory: it provides a sensory system for the preliminary analysis of linguistic data, and a schematism that determines, quite narrowly, a certain class of grammars. Each grammar is a theory of a particular language, specifying formal and semantic properties of an infinite array of sentences. These sentences, each with its particular structure, constitute the language generated by the grammar. The languages so generated are those that can be "learned" in the normal way .... This knowledge can then be used to understand what is heard and to produce discourse as an expression of thought within the constraints of the

---

[2]All of the emphases occurring in excerpted material throughout the book existed in the original source.

internalized principles, in a manner appropriate to situations as these are conceived by other mental faculties, free of stimulus control. (Chomsky, 1975, pp. 12–13)

The rules that Chomsky outlined covering the transformation of such deep structures into the surface structure utilized in the overt production of spoken language laid the foundation for the area of study now known as transformational generative grammar. Luria included this grammar in a book-length discussion of neurolinguistics; and commented that he found Chomsky's ideas interesting, but that the transformational rules are limited analogies rather than accurate descriptions of the real processes involved in the formation and decoding of speech (Luria, 1974a).

The opposing external cause position holds that humans acquire spoken language as a result of behavioral conditioning so that

A child acquires verbal behavior when relatively unpatterned vocalizations, selectively reinforced, gradually assume forms which produce appropriate consequences in a given verbal community. In formulating this process we do not need to mention stimuli occurring prior to the behavior to be reinforced. It is difficult, if not impossible, to discover stimuli which evoke specific vocal responses in the young child. There is no stimulus which makes a child say b or ă or ē, as one may make him salivate by placing a lemon drop in his mouth or make his pupils contract by shining a light into his eyes. The raw responses from which verbal behavior is constructed are not "elicited." In order to reinforce a given response we simply wait until it occurs. (Skinner, 1957, p. 31)

Thus Skinner views the child as the passive subject of operant conditioning in whom randomly occurring behavior is selectively reinforced, and rejects classical conditioning which would require that a specific behavior first be elicited and then reinforced.

One possible synthesis of this internal/external dichotomy is the position of most Soviet scholars that the causes of spoken language acquisition are *both* internal and external, and that the child is an active participant:

Language learning is seen as an active process in which the child develops speech in order to communicate with adults and get them to satisfy his needs—both physical and intellectual. Soviet psychologists have found that almost from the beginning of life, words call forth orienting reactions from the child. (Slobin, 1966, p. 137)

This synthesizing position has been facilitated by the philosophic world view of the Soviets that resulted from the influence of continental philosophers such as Kant, Schopenhauer, and Leibnitz, and that emphasizes

> the *active* part played by the subject (and especially the conscious human subject) in *structuring* his own environment and his own experience, in contrast to the traditional (though perhaps weakening) Anglo-Saxon insistence on a *passive* organism, in which associations were formed by the interplay of processes (such as temporal contiguity), and successful *adaptation to* the environment. (Gray, 1966, p. 2)

Our focus is on one particular Soviet scholar, A. R. Luria, who constitutes a unique resource for consideration of the relationship between higher mental processes and spoken language for four reasons: (1) By viewing higher mental processes from the philosophic perspective of Vygotsky, Luria does not dismiss either psychic or physical components of mental functioning from consideration and thus maintains a more comprehensive perspective than would be possible if he had endorsed either the psychic or physical reductionist positions. (2) By embodying the position of Soviet scholarship that spoken language acquisition is *both* internally and externally caused, Luria is again removed from the limitations of the extreme positions, and is therefore able to consider any internal and/or external factor that might influence spoken language or its acquisition. (3) Luria began his specialization in neurology upon receipt of his M.D. in 1937, and concluded his formal neurological education with a second, higher medical degree in 1943. Because of this training, Luria is capable of linking his theories on higher mental processes or spoken language to concrete evidence manifested in anatomical or neuronal characteristics of the human organism. (4) Because Luria's theory includes explanations of both higher mental processes *and* spoken language, his consideration of the relationship between these two phenomena avoids the difficulty of attempting to reconcile two conflicting perspectives.

Autobiographies frequently provide insights into personal experiences that may have influenced an individual's theoretical perspective. *The Making of Mind: A Personal Account of Soviet Psychology* (1979), edited by Michael and Sheila Cole, was Luria's autobiography. However, the text contains little biographical information and no anecdotes about events in his personal life, because it was, according to Cole, "written in accord with Alexander Romanovich's philosophy that people are transitory, that only their ideas and actions are of enduring interest" (Cole, 1979, p. 189). The book that results is primarily an informal presentation of the theories and research of Soviet psychology, but it still provides the reader with some awareness of personal experiences. Thus, it constitutes the major source of the following brief review of factors in Luria's background that may have influenced his theory.

Alexander Romanovich Luria was born July 16, 1902, in Kazan, USSR, which was a large commercial city located on the Volga River, southeast of Moscow. His father, Roman Albertovich Luria, was a Jewish physician who had received his medical training at the University of Kazan, where (as in other universities) Jewish students were not permitted to constitute more than 5% of the student body. It was a matter of family pride that he had qualified for such training, rather than being forced to study in Germany, which was the alternative for Jewish "intelligentsia" families with sufficient resources. However, Roman Albertovich did study medicine in Germany for several summers after receiving his degree; and eventually became well-known for his studies in psychosomatic medicine.

Luria's intellectual life was heavily influenced by the German writings he read during his youth. German was the family's second language, and Alexander Romanovich learned it at an early age. Consequently, he read Freud and Jung long before they were available in Russian translation.

The Bolshevik Revolution of 1917 occurred when Luria was only 15 years old. His family was sympathetic with the Revolution although they were not directly involved in it. It did, however, have direct consequences with respect to Alexander Romanovich's formal eduction. Instead of following the rigid format of classical education that had previously existed at the University of Kazan, Luria was essentially able to design his own educational curriculum because the abrupt change in the political climate had left the faculty and the curriculum in a state of disarray. Typically, Luria was in a hurry, and completed the formal degree requirements in 3 years, graduating in 1921 with an undergraduate degree that emphasized the biological and social sciences. Then, from 1921 to 1923, Luria continued his formal schooling simultaneously at both the Kazan Medical and Pedagogical Institutes.

The Revolution also affected A. R. Luria's academic and professional career following his graduation. Michael Cole gives us a vivid picture of the impact of this influence as well as some insight into Luria's personality:

In the chaos that immediately followed the Revolution Alexander Romanovich simultaneously held down a research position in one institution, did graduate work in another, attended medical school part-time, and ran tests of therapy on mentally ill patients. He also started a journal, organized a commune for wayward adolescents, directed a psychoanalytic discussion group, and published his own study of psychoanalysis. The contrast between these diverse activities and the limited possibilities for professional fulfillment that existed before the Revolution reveals the fundamental source of Alexander Romanovich's strong identification with the Revolution and the party which organized it. An activist down to his toes, he was set free by the Revolution. It gave him life. In return, he applied all of his energy to realizing the hopes and ideals that had been liberated in October 1917. (Cole, 1979, pp. 200—201.)

The changes that the Revolution precipitated in the previously rigid social structure also permitted Luria's father to achieve prominence. Among other projects, he assisted with the reorganization of medical education throughout the USSR. Because Roman Albertovich Luria had always wanted his son to become a physician, he did not approve of Alexander Romanovich's decision to focus on an area of study that would now be termed *psychology*. In part, his father's influence may explain why Luria continued to maintain a connection with medical school and medical psychology until finally, he and Vygotsky decided in the late 1920s to actively seek medical degrees. At that time, Luria had already completed approximately 2 years of medical school through intermittent attendance, and Alexander Romanovich Luria eventually received his M.D. from the First Moscow Medical School in 1937.

Luria's formal educational experience was not totally limited to medical training during this time, since he also received a Doctor of Education from the University of Moscow in 1936. A.R. Luria's formal education ended in 1943 when he received his second medical degree, a Doctor of Medicine. His work on sensory aphasia for this degree would provide the nucleus for *Traumatic Aphasia: Its Syndromes, Psychology and Treatment* (1970b).

Soon after his graduation from the University of Kazan, Luria was employed by a laboratory that was attempting to increase the efficiency of industrial workers. During his work there, he developed a laboratory technique to be utilized in conjunction with free-association, which he called the "combined motor method." It attempted to trace the influence of emotions on voluntary behavior. The publication of his findings in the journal he had founded brought his work to the attention of K. N. Kornilov, who had just become head of the Institute of Experimental Psychology in Moscow. Kornilov was seeking young scholars for the institute who might be able to reconstruct the field of psychology in keeping with his particular behaviorist views and, he hoped, the new philosophic outlook of the country. Luria's research on worker fatigue using a reaction-time methodology made him appear quite suited to such a task. Kornilov appointed Luria to the institute in 1923 as a "scientific worker of the first degree and a scientific secretary of the institute" (Radzikhovskii & Khomskaya, 1981, p. 9).

Luria and Vygotsky first met at the Second All-Russian Congress in Psychoneurology held in Leningrad in January 1924. A. R. Luria was quite impressed with Vygotsky's paper, and Vygotsky was invited to join the institute in Moscow as a research fellow. Thus, Vygotsky and Luria together with Alexei N. Leont'ev formed the "troika," which began to reconstruct Soviet psychology as they attempted a comprehensive approach to higher psychological functions. They based their approach, however, not on the behaviorism of Kornilov or the combined motor method of Luria, but on the philosophic theories developed by Vygotsky, who continued to be the acknowledged leader of the group until his death in 1934.

A logical question is why did the leadership role go to Vygotsky rather than to Luria, who was his superior in rank both at the Institute of Experimental Psychology and at the Krupskaya Academy of Communist Education? In addition, Luria had an established reputation for innovative research while Vygotsky had done no real psychological investigations. Radzikhovskii and Khomskaya (1981) grant that personal factors and the social situation of the time may have had some influence, but

> From Luria's standpoint, the basis for their collaboration and Luria's recognition of Vygotsky as his teacher was very simple: Vygotsky's ideas were vitally necessary for Luria . . . .
> First, the style of thought and scientific work of Vygotsky complemented Luria's style very nicely . . . . Luria, with his clarity and economy of thought can be compared with representatives of the classical science of the 19th century. Vygotsky's style of thought was completely different. Vygotsky was much less concrete and unambiguous. It is no accident that his works are sometimes interpreted differently even today . . . . Vygotsky represented the typical style of humanist thinking, with a tendency toward sweeping generalizations (not necessarily firmly founded on adequate experimentation), the use of metaphor in his statements, and an extremely wide range of cultural-historical side associations. Luria's thought and Vygotsky's thought embodied two facets of psychological science, different but both equally necessary. (Radzikhovskii & Khomskaya, 1981, pp. 11–12)

A. R. Luria's affiliation with the institute continued from 1923 to 1936. But his career during this period included other professional affiliations such as the "troika's" association with the psychology laboratory at the Academy of Communist Education.

Following Vygotsky's death in 1934, Luria also worked at the Medico-Genetic Institute until the cessation of research there in 1936. Upon completion of his initial medical training, Luria worked in Bourdenko's neurological clinic; and following the outbreak of war with Germany, he organized a rehabilitation hospital for neurosurgical patients. Modern explosives had rendered commonplace new and terrible brain injuries. As a result, Luria and his colleagues were required to develop new methods of diagnosis of local brain lesions and their subsequent complications as well as new therapeutic techniques to restore lost psychological functions.

From 1936 to 1943 and from 1945 to 1950, Luria was affiliated with the Institute of Neurology and the Institute of Neurosurgery at the USSR Academy of Medical Science in Moscow. From 1945 until his death in 1977, Luria was a Professor of Psychology at the University of Moscow (becoming head of the Section of Neuropsychology). In addition, he was assigned to the Institute of Defectology in 1948, which was the institute that Vygotsky had founded some 20 years previously. During the latter part of his career, he maintained an association with the Institute of Psychology and the Institute of Neurosurgery.

If this picture of Luria's professional career appears quite varied and there is no clear differentiation between occupational niches, it is because the energetic Luria was typically engaged on several fronts simultaneously and thus often occupied several jobs at once. A vivid example of Luria's typical working environment was given to us by MacDonald Critchley:

> To work as a visitor in his Bordenko [Bourdenko] Institute was a heady but exasperating experience. Oblivious of all sense of time, Luria seemed immune to such frailties as hunger and fatigue. He would move on from patient to patient, coping with one brash interruption after another. Disciplined orderliness and regimentation were not there. His working conditions, let us face it, were astounding. Among the plethora of patients with brain trauma, Luria's researches were carried out in an office which was more like a busy airport than the sanctum of a reflective scholar. Doors to the right and to the left of him opened and shut. Bells rang. All and sundry—nurses, technicians, porters, assistants—seemed to use his study like a public highway. Privacy there was none. Luria's careful case studies were impervious to noise and distraction. (Critchley, 1978, p. v)

Always addressing him as Alexander Romanovich, Luria's friends and colleagues described Luria the person as being a warm and friendly man, generous and hospitable, receptive to the ideas of others, and never exhibiting professional jealousy or hostility. A. R. Luria firmly believed that understanding the human mind was an international enterprise. Acting on that belief, he strongly supported international cooperation in research and despite his many commitments, gave of his time and effort to international journals and professional societies. Luria personally trained a number of young psychologists from all over the world as another contribution to international scholarship. It was as a new Ph.D. arriving for such training that Michael Cole first met Luria:

My overwhelming impression of Alexander Romanovich during that year [1962] was of a man in a hurry. His appetite for work exhausted me. Even his lunch breaks were more than I could keep up with. On occasions when we lunched together, he would walk rapidly from his laboratory to a small coffee-shop near the institute. Although he was sixty years old at the time and I was only twenty-four, I found it difficult to keep in step. At the coffee-shop he would then order two rolls and two scorchingly hot cups of coffee, which we ate standing at the corner. At least I drank and ate. Alexander Romanovich seemed to inhale the scorching coffee while I blew timidly on the glass to cool it. Leaving me to deal with my tender palate, he loped back to the laboratory, where I could catch up with him when I was ready. (Cole, 1979, p. 193)

A. R. Luria's prodigious energy and enormous capacity for work explains, in part, the large volume and complexity of the Lurian corpus. All previous studies of Luria in English have dealt with his work in isolated fragments, so I found that any attempt at an integrated understanding of Luria's theory had to come from a direct consideration of his own writings.

THEORETICAL UNITS

Higher Mental Processes

Alexander Romanovich Luria devoted his entire professional life to the study of human mentality. It is no coincidence that his autobiography is entitled *The Making of Mind* (1979), because his constant goal was always a satisfactory theory of higher mental processes, no matter how diverse his studies might have appeared to the casual observor. Because of this unwaivering goal, clear comprehension of how he conceptualized "higher mental processes" is essential to an understanding of his work.

A simplistic explanation would be that higher mental processes equate with what many scholars have labeled *mind*. Such a label, however, has too great a melange of connotations to be useful in closely reasoned theory, and was rarely used by Luria, no doubt for similar reasons.

A. R. Luria was philosophically a deductive rationalist and held that all research should be guided by some sort of theoretical paradigm. Accordingly, he built his own work on a base of Vygotskian theory. Obviously Vygotsky's ideas were not the only ones that impacted on the explanation of mind that evolved over Luria's lifetime. Throughout the text, the reader will note two other major influences: linguistic and semiotic theory as well as the physiological research of scholars such as Pavlov and

Bernshtein who searched for a physical base for human psychological activity (Wertsch, 1982, p. 2). Yet these influences remained subordinate to that of Vygotsky, and constituted only embellishments upon a theoretical core that resulted from Luria's association with Vygotsky.

Despite his frequent insistence that Vygotsky was a genius, Luria brought an expertise to his own research on higher mental processes that Vygotsky did not possess. Specializing in neurology upon receipt of his M.D. in 1937, Luria pursued advanced training in that area. This training made him capable of linking Vygotsky's theoretical constructs about "mind" with concrete evidence manifested in anatomical or neuronal characteristics of the human organism. However, this work in the physical realm never converted Luria to an inductive, empirical approach to theory-building.

Because A. R. Luria's concept of higher mental processes evolved from a base of Vygotskian theories, it is appropriate to begin with an examination of the concept's origins. Attempting to facilitate a more precise understanding of mental processing, Vygotsky (1978) distinguished between elementary processes, which were biologically determined, and "higher psychological functions," which had socio-cultural origins. The elementary processes produce the most general and fundamental activity of the cerebral hemispheres in higher animals including man—signalization:

> Contingent signalization is the basis for the formation of temporary, conditioned, special relations between the organism and its environment; it underlies and is a mandatory biological prerequisite for the higher activity we conventionally refer to as signalization. But this system of connections formed in the animal's brain is a copy, or the reflection, of the natural ties among "all kinds of natural agents" that signal the appearance of immediately beneficial or destructive events. (Vygotsky, 1977, p. 62)

The two levels of reflexive activity that comprise signalization (contingent signalization and signalization) are inadequate to explain human behavior according to Vygotsky because signalization only requires that an organism passively reflect naturally created connections among naturally occurring stimuli. This is not sufficient as an explanation of human mental functioning in his view, because humans are active organisms rather than merely passive ones. In fact, humans can not only actively alter nature, but are capable of creating new stimuli or

> artificial connections among environmental stimuli that *signify* behavior and create new connections in the brain. This concept of human activity introduced a new regulatory principle of behavior: the *signification principle,* which holds that the connections created among external stimuli then form connections inside the brain, and external connections are thus incorporated into internal ones. (Vygotsky, 1977, p. 63)

Thus, according to Vygotsky, humans are the only animals that can actively alter both nature and themselves. This alteration of the physical is accomplished, he theorized, via two means: the tool and the sign.

> The tool's function is to serve as the conductor of man's influence on the object of his activity; it is *externally* oriented; it must lead to changes in objects. It is a means of man's external activity aimed at mastering, of triumphing over nature. The sign, on the other hand, changes nothing in the object of a psychological operation. It is a means of internal activity aimed at mastering man himself; the sign is *internally* oriented. These activities are so different from each other that the nature of the means they use cannot be the same in both cases. (Vygotsky, 1977, p. 72)

Yet, despite their incongruity of activity and orientation, the usage of tool and sign are, according to Vygotsky, intertwined in humans because both are mediated activities engendered by human society. And it is the combination of the two that precipitates the higher psychological functions for Vygotsky:

> We use the term *higher* psychological function, or *higher behavior* (i.e., more complex), to refer to the combination of tool and sign in psychological activity. (Vygotsky, 1977, p. 73)

The preceding discussion delineates what constituted higher psychological functions for Vygotsky, but it was primarily the source of these functions, the sociocultural origins, that would shape future research by Vygotsky, Luria, and much of Soviet psychology.

Given such origins, Vygotsky held that higher psychological functions are gradually assimilated into the child through a long series of developmental events resulting from social interaction. Thus,

> Every function in the child's cultural development appears twice: first, on the social level, and later, on the individual level; first, *between* people (*interpsychological*), and then *inside* the child (*intrapsychological*). This applies equally to voluntary attention, to logical memory, and to the formation of concepts. All higher functions originate as actual relations between human individuals. (Vygotsky, 1978, p. 57)

Such an acquisitional paradigm, together with the sociocultural origins, supported Vygotsky's conviction that all the higher psychological functions of humans were voluntary in nature rather than merely reflexive, which he considered a limitation of the mental functioning of other higher animals. In fact, he noted that

There is reason to believe that voluntary activity, more than highly developed intellect, distinguishes humans from the animals which stand closest to them. (Vygotsky, 1978, p. 37)

From these explanations of higher psychological functions, Vygotsky proposed a new approach to psychology. The approach would focus on three features of the social relations with the external world through which society and social history had molded the higher functioning that distinguishes man from all other animals. These three features caused him, at various times, to call his new approach *cultural* psychology, *historical* psychology, or *instrumental* psychology.

Explicating these labels in retrospect, A. R. Luria stated that they also actually denoted the different elements of the active interaction molding the higher psychological functions in more detail than the phrase "sociocultural origins":

"Instrumental" referred to the basically mediated nature of all complex psychological functions. Unlike basic reflexes, which can be characterized by a stimulus-response process, higher functions incorporate auxiliary stimuli, which are typically produced by the person himself. The adult not only responds to the stimuli presented by an experimenter or by his natural environment, but also actively modifies those stimuli and uses his modifications as an instrument of his behavior . . . . examples of this principal were uncovered in studies of changes in the structure of children's thinking as they grow from the age of three to ten years.

The "cultural" aspect of Vygotsky's theory involved the socially structured ways in which society organizes the kind of tasks that the growing child faces and the kinds of tools, both mental and physical, that the young child is provided to master those tasks. One of the key tools invented by mankind is language, and Vygotsky placed special emphasis on the role of language in the organization and development of thought processes.

The "historical" element merged into the cultural one. The tools that man uses to master his environment and his own behavior did not spring fully developed from the head of god. [*sic*]. They were invented and perfected in the long course of man's social history. Language carries within it the generalized concepts that are the storehouse of human knowledge. Special cultural instruments like writing and arithmetic enormously expanded man's powers, making the wisdom of the past analyzable in the present and perfectible in the future. This line of reasoning implied that if we could study the way the various thought operations are structured among people whose cultural history has not supplied them with a tool such as writing, we would find a different organization of higher cognitive processes but a similar structuring of elementary processes. (Luria, 1979, pp. 44–45)

Always maintaining his moorings to these theories of Vygotsky about the origins of higher psychological functions, A. R. Luria expanded his definition of such functioning to include the physiological and neurological realms, thereby providing, or at least attempting to provide, physical verification of Vygotsky's theories:

> If the higher mental functions are complex, organized functional systems that are social in origin, any attempt to localize them in special, circumscribed areas ("centers") of the cerebral cortex is even less justifiable than the attempt to seek narrow, circumscribed "centers" for biological functional systems. The modern view regarding the possible localization of the higher mental functions is that they have a wide, dynamic representation throughout the cerebral cortex, based on constellations of territorially scattered groups of "synchronously working ganglion cells, mutually exciting one another" (Ukhtomskii, 1945). Hence, the higher mental functions are accommodated in the brain in systems of "functional combination centers," as Pavlov called them (*Complete Collected Works*, Vol. 3, p. 288) .... We therefore suggest that the *material basis of the higher nervous processes is the brain as a whole* but that *the brain is a highly differentiated system whose parts are responsible for different aspects of the unified whole.* (Luria, 1966b, p. 35)

Just as the social origins of higher psychological functions together with their physiological complexity preclude any isomorphic relationship between a function and a particular cortical locus, so too would such origins and physiological evidence suggest that higher psychological functions are acquired in a developmental manner:

> the complex functional system of conjointly working cortical zones ... are not found ready-made in the child at birth (as in the case of respiratory and other systems) and do not mature independently, but are formed in the process of social contact and objective activity by the child .... These intercentral systems, or functional brain organs, arise under the influence of the child's practical activity and are extremely stable .... Naturally, these functional systems can exist only in the presence of an apparatus allowing for the formation of new, dynamically variable, yet enduring intercentral connections .... the upper associative layers of the cerebral cortex, the vertical connections arising in the secondary associative nuclei of the thalamus, and the overlapping zones uniting different boundaries of cortical analyzers evidently constitute the apparatus that performs this highly complex task. It is in man that this apparatus of the brain has attained its highest development, sharply distinguishing the human brain from that of animals. We, therefore, agree with the view that evolution, under the influence of social conditions, accomplishes the task of conversion of the cortex into an

organ capable of forming functional organs (Leont'ev, 1961, p. 38) and that the latter property is one of the more important features of the human brain. (Luria, 1966b, p. 35)

The actual physical apparatus underlying the functional brain systems also changes as the systems themselves go through regular stages during development:

The structural variation of the higher mental functions at different stages of ontogenetic (and, in some cases, functional) development means that their cortical organization likewise does not remain unchanged and that at different stages of development they are carried out by different constellations of cortical zones . . . . The essential thing to remember . . . is that this change in the character of localization (or, more accurately, cortical organization) of the higher mental functions is strictly regular, conforming to a pattern ascertained by Vygotsky (1960, pp. 390–391) . . . .

Observations have shown that the relationships between the individual components of the higher mental functions do not remain the same during successive stages of development. In the early stages, relatively simple sensory processes, which are the foundation for the higher mental functions play a decisive role; during subsequent stages, when the higher mental functions are being formed, this leading role passes to more complex systems of connections that develop on the basis of speech, and these systems begin to determine the whole structure of the higher mental processes. For this reason, disturbance of the relatively elementary processes of sensory analysis and integration, necessary, for example, for the further development of speech, will be decisively important in early childhood, for it will cause underdevelopment of all the functional formations for which it serves as a foundation. Conversely, the disturbance of these forms of direct sensory analysis and integration in the adult, in whom the higher functional systems have been formed, may have a more limited effect, compensated for by other differentiated systems of connections. This concept implies *that the character of the cortical intercentral relationships does not remain the same at different stages of development of a function and that the effect of a lesion of a particular part of the brain will differ at different stages of functional development.* (Luria, 1966b, pp. 36–37)

It was Luria's contention that both ratiocination and an examination of the physical evidence would reveal three fundamental, characteristic features of higher mental processes, which is the phrase he generally used rather than higher psychological functions. The first feature, as has already been discussed in some detail, is the sociocultural origin of such processes. The process of social genesis produces the second fundamental feature of higher mental processes, their mediate structure, which results from the combined usage of tool and sign:

As examples of the mediate structure of higher mental functions, we may use any performance of a practical task by means of tools or solution of an internal, psychological problem by means of an auxiliary sign in order to organize the mental processes. When a person ties a knot in his handkerchief [the Russian equivalent of a string around one's finger] or makes a note in order to remember something, he carries out an operation apparently quite unrelated to the task in hand. In this way, however, the person masters his faculty of memory; by changing the structure of the memorizing process and giving it a mediate character, he thereby broadens its natural capacity. Mediate memorizing illustrates the structural principles of the higher mental functions. A closer analysis shows that this mediate structure is a characteristic feature of all higher mental processes. (Luria, 1966b, p. 33)

The third and, according to Luria, the most important feature of higher mental processes is that the speech system is a factor in their formation. This basic feature of higher mental processes incorporates the other two fundamental features:

Speech plays a decisive role in the mediation of mental processes. By being given a name, an object or its property is distinguished from its surroundings and is related to other objects or signs. The fact that "every word is a generalization" (Lenin) is vitally important to the systematic reflection of the outside world, to the transition from sensation to thinking, and to the creation of new functional systems. Speech not only gives names to the objects of the outside world; it also distinguishes among their essential properties and includes them in a system of relationships to other objects. As a result of language, man can evoke an image of a particular object and use it in the absence of the original. At the same time, speech, differentiating among the essential signs and generalizing on the objects or phenomena denoted, facilitates deeper penetration of the environment. Human mental processes are thereby elevated to a new level and are given new powers of organization, and man is enabled to direct his mental processes.

The reorganization of mental activity by means of speech and the incorporation of the system of speech connections into a large number of processes, hitherto direct in character, are among the more important factors in the formation of the higher mental functions, whereby man, as distinct from animals, acquires consciousness and volition.

The fact that the speech system is a factor in the formation of the higher mental functions is their most important feature. Because of this, Pavlov was justified in considering the "second signal system," which is based on speech, not only "an extraordinary addition, introducing a new principle of nervous activity," but also "the highest regulator of human behavior" (*Complete Collected Works,* Vol. 3, pp. 476, 490, 568–569, 577). (Luria, 1966b, pp. 33–34)

All of the preceding discussion was condensed by A. R. Luria into a very succinct definition of higher mental processes: ". . . the higher human mental functions are complex reflex processes, social in origin, mediate in structure, and conscious and voluntary in mode of function" (Luria, 1966b, p. 32).

The following is a summary of the general characteristics of higher mental processes embodied in the theory of A. R. Luria and corroborated by his research.

General Characteristics—Higher Mental Processes

1. Higher mental processes have sociocultural origins. Consequently, such processes transcend the individual's experience and reflect the cultural level of the social environment of the individual.

2. Higher mental processes are complex functional systems built on a functional base of the more elementary sensory systems of the brain, and capable of controlling such systems.

3. Higher mental processes arise from a material base that is a "complex functional system of conjointly working cortical zones . . ." (Luria, 1966b, p. 35).

4. Higher mental processes evolve through a pattern of developmental stages rather than existing as static, innate qualities of the brain.

5. Higher mental processes have a mediated structure in that they incorporate auxiliary stimuli ("*stimuli artificially introduced into the situation*" (Vygotsky, 1966, p. 24), which are usually produced by the individual himself.

6. Higher mental processes are distinguished by the fact that the speech system is always a factor in their formation.

7. Higher mental processes are originally both conscious and voluntary in nature rather than being passive and merely reflexive.

In the interest of clarity, it should be noted that Luria utilizes the phrase "complex functional system" to refer to physiological/neurological phenomena as well as to mental or phychic phenomena, and defines a function as a

complex adaptive activity (biological at some stages of development and social-historical at others), satisfying a particular demand and playing a particular role in the vital activity of the animal. A complex adaptive "function" such as this will usually be executed by a group of structural units and . . . these will be integrated into a "functional system." The parts of this system may be scattered over a wide area of the body and united only in the execution of their common task . . . . Between these parts there is a pliable yet strong temporary connexion, uniting them into one system and synchroniz-

ing their activity. This "functional system" works as a complete entity . . . .
(Luria, 1963b, p. 36)

Thus, it is illustrative of the enormous complexity of the organization of higher mental processes rather than contradiction in terms to state that their structure includes complex functional systems simultaneously existing on two levels—a psychic or mental level complex functional system that arises from a cortical level complex functional system.

Spoken Language

The speech system that reorganizes mental activity to permit the conscious voluntary functioning of higher mental processes is very complex and includes both speech and language. These components are often studied in isolation from each other; yet, as Luria indicates, the origins of speech and language are intertwined:

> Under the conditions of primitive society language began to develop as a means of communication; there, in accordance with laws not yet known to us, *verbal speech* appeared. In the development of verbal speech words gradually became separated from work activities and from signalling gestures; words began to abstract and at the same time to generalize various characteristics of objects. They thus achieved designating and at the same time generalizing-systematizing functions.
> In later social history language attained its complex, phonetic, lexical, and grammatical structure and gradually became the *objective system of codes* which is well known to contemporary linguistics. (Luria, 1970b, pp. 20–21)

This complexity, which developed gradually, necessitates the separation of "verbal speech" into its speech and language components before one can hope for a clear understanding of the phenomenon:

> It was de Saussure who was responsible for the clear differentiation between the concept of language (langue), as an objective system of sounds formed in the course of history, and the concept of speech (parole), by which he understood the process of transmission of information with the aid of the language system . . . . (Luria, 1976a, p. 10)

The term *language* is used throughout the book to refer to an "objective system of codes" as Luria defined it; or more precisely to "The culturally determined syntactic systematization of signs and/or symbols" (Dance, 1979, p. 2). This conceptual definition will assist in understanding the theoretical unit of spoken language although it is not sufficient to delineate the same.

Consideration of Luria's "speech" or "the process of transmission of information" must, for the sake of clarity, first become a concern with modality—spoken versus written. When Luria uses the term "speech" rather than "speech system," it is not an instance of careless phrasing nor an assumed inclusion of both modes. He studied linguistics and language theory too carefully to be guilty of such errors. Rather, it results from his conviction that oral speech differs from written speech in origin, structure, and function. Consequently, Luria utilizes "speech" without modifiers to refer to oral speech *only*. When he occasionally refers to "written speech," such phrasing is a reflection of what he considered to be the different and derived nature of that modality.

A careful delineation of how the two modes of speech differ is provided by Luria:

> Careful analysis by Vygotskii (1956) and El'konin (1954) indicated that written speech represents an entirely new psychological phenomenon, different from oral speech.
>
> Oral speech forms during immediately practical intercourse and its component elements long remain insufficiently conscious, unseparated by the child from general speech activity (Morozova, 1948; Karpova, 1955). Written speech follows exactly the opposite course. It is always the product of special training, which presupposes the separation of individual words from the flow of living speech and individual sounds from the living word. It also involves abstraction from individual phonations of sounds and the conversion of sounds into stable phonemes. This process of analysis, described in the Soviet literature by Luria (1950), Nazarova (1952), and others is a necessary technical premise for the act of writing, which from the very beginning requires conscious effort.
>
> Oral speech always originates in close connection with immediate experience, as, for example, in sympractical and situational activity. It relies on intonation and gesture and usually becomes intelligible only if the general setting of the conversation is considered. It permits extensive abbreviation. For a prolonged period it continues to bear traces of the period when the subject was contained in speech and the predicate in a gesture, a tone, or in the immediate situation. Written speech . . . is deprived of this sympractical context, and therefore it must be more detailed, contextual, or, to use Buhler's term, synsemantic. Written speech like a work of art, to paraphrase Leonardo da Vinci, should contain within itself all means of expressiveness and in no way depend on the concrete environment. (Luria, 1969c, pp. 141–142)

One point of contrast between the spoken and written modes of speech mentioned above may require further clarification, namely that oral speech is characterized by sympractical activity and that written speech is synsemantic. Essentially, this means that oral speech can include the nonlinguistic as a means of conveying information while the written mode is constrained to expression by linguistic means alone. Oral speech is

> supported by extralinguistic (sympractic) aids—knowledge of the situation, facial expression, gestures . . . information can be transmitted by extralinguistic aids, and incomplete expansion, ellipsis, the participation of intonation, and so on, can exist. (Luria, 1976a, pp. 36–37)

Although this difference may be observed in the successive developmental states of childhood language acquisition, it originates in the historical development of language:

> It is an important fact that in the early period of history language did not include all the constructions necessary to express a complex communication. Language itself was an inseparable part of practical activity, it had a relatively simple structure, and the adequate understanding of these relatively simple constructions requires the participation of a "sympractic context"; for this reason, primitive languages could remain unknown without knowledge of the concrete situation in which a particular communication was used, of the gestures that accompanied it, of the intonation with which it was uttered, and so on. That is why, as the famous ethnologist Malinowski (1930) pointed out, the expressions used by many peoples standing at a primitive level of social development can be understood only if the concrete situation is known and if their gestures are observed . . . .
> Only in the course of its long historical development has language gradually developed its own "synsemantic" forms of expression of relations, and so, as Buhler (1934) stated, it has become "a system that includes in itself all the means of expressiveness." Thus the whole evolution of language can with full justification be represented as the path of liberation from dependence on the sympractic context and of gradual formulation of methods increasing the role of the linguistic (grammatically constructed) synsemantic context proper. (Luria, 1976a, p. 156)

To say that Luria's usage of the Russian term *rech* (speech) refers to the spoken modality is not to limit it to a simple notion of phonation. Rather, the concept also includes all of the stages that comprise "the conversion of an initial subjective sense into an expanded objective system of meanings . . . ." (Luria, 1982, p. 152), as well as the reverse process of "decoding . . . on the basis of the language codes involved, . . . isolating the general thought . . . and finally, . . . identifying the sense . . . ." (Luria, 1982, p. 233). Thus, it includes the encoding/decoding process and parallels the meaning of "speech" as it is used in naming the academic discipline of speech communication. Such scholars occasionally utilize "spoken language" in an attempt to avoid the ambiguity of "speech." and define it as:

"Uniquely human. The process, or the product of the process of the fusion of genetically determined speech with culturally determined language" (Dance & Larson, 1972, p. 11). Consequently, in the theoretical unit of spoken language the psychological activities of encoding/decoding and the culturally created objective system of codes are united. This union first occurs at that ontological stage when preintellectual speech and prelinguistic thought join and thought becomes verbal (Vygotsky, 1962).

"Written speech" sounds awkward to our ears, but it reflects Luria's attempt to clarify that such a phenomenon includes the psychological activities of encoding/decoding rather than merely referring to the objective system of codes denoted by "language." Despite the fact that Luria's speech system includes both the spoken and written modes of language, his theory deals primarily with the oral mode. Consequently, this text deals with the written mode only when that mode serves to increase an understanding of higher mental processes, spoken language, or the relationship between them.

Originally Alexander Romanovich Luria was concerned with spoken language only as a means of revealing or giving form to the mental processes that resulted from the hidden workings of the human mind. However, as his investigations progressed, Luria became more and more involved with spoken language as a phenomenon worthy of study in its own right. Consequently, the following is a summary of the general characteristics of spoken language delineated in the writings of Luria.

General Characteristics—Spoken Language

1. Spoken language is a higher mental process, and embodies all the characteristics of such processes:
   a. It has sociocultural origins.
   b. It is a complex functional system built on a functional base of the more elementary sensory systems of the brain, and is capable of controlling such systems.
   c. It arises from a material base that is a "complex functional system of conjointly working cortical zones . . ." (Luria, 1966b, p. 35).
   d. It evolves through a pattern of developmental stages rather than existing as a static, innate quality of the brain.
   e. It has a mediated structure in that it incorporates auxiliary stimuli (*"stimuli artificially introduced into the situation"*) (Vygotsky, 1966, p. 24), which are usually produced by the individual himself.
   f. It is distinguished by the fact that the speech system is always a factor in its formation.
   g. It is originally both conscious and voluntary in nature rather than being passive and merely reflexive.

2. Spoken language is the most readily influenced of all the higher mental processes.

3. Spoken language can be either excitatory or inhibitory as a stimulus. Developmentally, the excitatory or impulsive aspect precedes the inhibitory or semantic aspect of spoken language.

4. Functionally, spoken language has three dimensions:
   a. It is a form of social communication.
   b. It is a tool for intellectual activity.
   c. It is a method of organizing or regulating mental processes.

5. Spoken language's process can be subdivided into two processes: impressive speech or decoding, and expressive speech or encoding.

6. Spoken language has both a paradigmatic (vertical) and a syntagmatic (horizontal) structure.

7. Spoken language's semantic component includes both "sense" and "meaning."

8. Spoken language is sympractic in nature.

As previously noted, the term *spoken language* is synonymous with Luria's term *speech,* and is used to reflect the inclusion of psychological activities as well as the code of language in this theoretical unit. Other terminology used above in outlining the general characteristics of spoken language is clarified during discussions of these characteristics in the ensuing chapters concerning various topical areas of Luria's work.

METHODOLOGICAL APPROACHES

With an understanding of the major theoretical units of spoken language and higher mental processes, we can proceed to an identification of the strategies that guided Luria in his study of these phenomena.

A. R. Luria's ultimate goal was always the development an adequate theory of higher mental processes regardless of the focus his research efforts might appear to have had at the various stages of his career. Thus, it is not surprising that Vygotsky and Luria both argued that one cannot arbitrarily refuse to consider or study higher mental processes, à la the behaviorists, simply because they are not readily available for examination or are so complex as to seem impossible to isolate for study. Their position was that because the sphere of influence of higher mental processes permeates all human functioning, its mere existence mandates its study regardless of inaccessibility, complexity, or lack of clear comprehension of what it is one is purposing to examine.

To accomplish this study, Vygotsky and Luria developed two complementary strategies. One was to trace the development of higher mental processes out of the elementary processes that preceded them. The second was to study the dissolution after brain trauma of higher mental functioning that had achieved mature development before the individual adult had undergone the injury. Throughout his lifetime, Luria's study of higher mental processes was guided by these approaches, which had been developed in conjunction with Vygotsky—the developmental and the pathological.

In addition to these strategies, two methodological mandates guided A.R. Luria in his consideration of human mental functioning. First, the method of examination had to be objective in contrast to the subjective reports emanating from exponents of the purely psychic explanation of human mental functioning. Secondly, the analysis of mental functioning had to be made in as natural a setting as was possible to avoid the fallacious findings that could result from contrived situations. Otherwise, Luria was methodologically free to utilize whatever means or approaches might be available and seem the most logical to him in any given situation. Although some of his methods may appear simplistic at first glance, his research provides substantive evidence for his theories.

ORGANIZATION OF TEXT

A. R. Luria's long career included so many apparent shifts in interest to accommodate changing circumstances that it is impossible to present his theory in a strictly chronological format. Consequently, the chapters that follow cover six topical areas that were foci of Luria's investigations and were approximately chronological in their order of development: (a) verbal regulation of behavior—Chapter 2, (b) consciousness—Chapter 3, (c) memory—Chapter 4, (d) cognitive development—Chapter 5, (e) functional organization of brain/brain lesions—Chapter 6, and (f) neurolinguistics—Chapter 7.

Each chapter commences with a literature review of Luria's work in that particular topical area, and then presents the findings of research in that area relevant to first, an understanding of his theory with respect to higher mental processes, and second, with respect to spoken language. The eighth chapter—functional relationships between higher mental processes and spoken language—presents postulated relationships resulting from an analysis of all of Luria's writings available in English. These relationships, in my opinion, constitute the laws of interaction comprising Lurian theory on the mind/speech relationship.

2 Verbal Regulation of Behavior

LITERATURE

The first book length work to be available in English translation was *The Nature of Human Conflicts* (1932a), which presented Luria's work in the topical area of the verbal regulation of behavior. Utilizing the "combined motor method," which measured the motor reaction of the hand in conjunction with free association that had brought him to the attention of Kornilov in 1923, Luria had attempted to trace the influence of emotions on the disorganization of behavior.

Already, Luria's real interest was the functioning of the human mind, and this analysis of motor reactions was seen as one way of examining the inaccessible recesses of the "black box" of the mind:

> Taking upon ourselves the problem of the study of the structure and dynamics of the processes of the disorganisation of human behaviour, we should stand firmly upon the ground of the psychological experimenters; we should on the one hand, produce the central process of the disorganisation of behaviour; on the other hand, we should try to reflect this process in some system accessible and suitable for examination. The motor function is such a systematic, objectively reflected structure of the neuro-dynamic processes concealed from immediate examination. And there lies before us the use of the motor function as a system of reflected structure of hidden psychological processes. Thus we proceed along the path which we call the combined motor method. (Luria, 1932a, p. 18)

These early research studies were innovative and unique, including such subjects as university students standing in line awaiting their decisive examination during the purging of 1924; murderers who had been arrested only hours or days before the experiment; clinically verified neurotic patients; and individuals with artificially created conflicts, such as those set during hypnosis.

The concept is presented (which reflects Luria's reading of Western sources such as Head, Jackson, and Lewin) that the cortex and the older, sub-cortical systems are in conflict, although the cortex is the usually dominant and controlling system. If the cortical control is weakened by factors such as extreme fatigue or stress, then the sub-cortical processes (emotions) will seize power over the motor reactions, which will then directly reflect the diffuse, irregular excitation patterns of the emotions. However, Luria was emphatic that human behavior cannot be explained merely by the interaction of simple neurophysiological processes. Rather, he postulated a "functional barrier," which is cultural and not organic in its origins, and which keeps the emotions from being transferred directly to the motor system. Small children have not yet developed such a "functional barrier," which is the reason for their diffuse motor responses.

The "functional barrier," which delays impulses enroute to the motor system, is also an intervening link that organizes the excitation prior to its execution in the motor system. Consequently, reaction is changed into a two-step process rather than being merely a S-R type response to sub-cortical processes. The primary mechanism in this organization of excitation is speech, but Luria speculated that all symbolic systems might be a means of organizing affect.

Such an organizing intervention between emotion and motor response also permits the existence of human will or voluntary action. The latter is defined as "*the ability to create stimuli and to subordinate them; . . .* to bring into being stimuli of a special order, directed to the organization of behaviour" (Luria, 1932a, p. 401). The process of the organization of behavior is vague. However, it does not result from a direct exercise of "will power," but rather from a complex, concealed system of speech mechanisms. These mechanisms serve as internal stimuli that somehow, in turn, indirectly control the motor system.

During the approximately 20 years before his next English publication on the verbal regulation of behavior, Luria expanded and refined his concept of speech being the mechanism whereby behavior is directed. A two-part article appeared in *Word* (1959) entitled "The Directive Function of Speech in Development and Dissolution." As might be anticipated, the two parts reflect his two fundamental strategies: Part I presents the developmental view, and Part II is concerned with the pathological view.

In "Part I: Development of the Directive Function of Speech in Early Childhood" (1959a), Luria outlines the stages by which verbal signals gradually supplant the directive influence of the immediate visual signal for the child. Speech has both an excitatory and an inhibitory function; and developmentally, the excitatory precedes the inhibitory. Due to the insufficient mobility of the 3–3½ year-old child's neurodynamics, the excitatory is still strongest so that if one alternates excitatory and inhibitory stimuli to a child of that age, the excitatory will come to dominate and motor perseveration will result.

The impulsive or excitatory aspect of speech continues to dominate until approximately 4–4½ years. Then,

> as soon as the directive role passes to the semantic aspect of speech and that aspect becomes dominant, external speech becomes superfluous. The directive role is taken over by those inner connections which lie behind the word, and they now begin to display their selective effect in directing the further motor responses of the child. (Luria, 1959a, p. 351)

In "Part II: Dissolution of the Regulative Function of Speech in Pathological States of the Brain" (1959b), Luria maintains that for external speech to influence behavior, the subject must not only hear the verbal instruction but also:

> A number of further conditions must be fulfilled; important among them is the maintenance of the strength, the equilibrium, and the mobility of the neural processes which determine the flow of higher neural activity. (Luria, 1959b, p. 453)

If any one of these conditions of the neural processes is disturbed, then the directive function of speech with suffer, perhaps substantially.

Evidence is then presented on how the directive function of speech is affected in three types of neural disorders: Parkinson's disease, cerebroasthenic syndrome, and oligophrenic children.

The sub-cortical area is damaged in Parkinson's disease, but the cortical motor centers are fully intact. The sub-cortical motor centers' damage causes muscles to exhibit a pathological perseverating tension soon after any initial movement, and thus involuntary action becomes impossible. However, movement can be tied to cortical control by requesting the patient to tap his finger once each time the interviewer says, "Now," and thereby controlled for longer periods. In addition, linking the movement more closely with the patient's speech system by imbuing it with a symbolic function also resulted in the patient demonstrating no difficulty in controlling his execution of movement (finger taps) in response to "How many wheels on a car?" or similar questions.

In cases of cerebroasthenic syndrome, the cortex exhibits a stimulational weakness because neural strength is weakened and equilibrium of the neural processes is impaired. In other words, the cortex itself is in a pathological state, rather than just the sub-cortical processes, as in Parkinson's disease. However, Luria found that the verbal response of a child with this syndrome suffered less than his motor processes. Khomskaya's experiments are presented as evidence that it is the inhibitory or semantic aspect of speech that is still capable of directing the child's behavior because nonsense syllables or irrelevant utterances had no influence on the child's motor reactions.

The speech system is more drastically affected in cases of oligophrenia. This is a form of deep mental retardation that results from intrauterine or very early childhood damage to the brain, and:

> It is particularly characteristic of these children that the dynamics of neural processes underlying speech activity are in their case impaired not less, but more than the dynamics of neural processes which are materialized in simpler sensorimotor reactions. (Luria, 1959b, p. 458)

Consequently, Soviet researchers found that this profound impairment of the mobility of the neural processes in particular resulted in speech losing its significative or semantic control over motor reactions as well as its impulsive or excitatory control.

"Experimental Analysis of the Development of Voluntary Action in Children" (1960a) constitutes one chapter in *Perspectives in Personality Research,* but had already been translated by the U.S. Dept. of Health, Education, and Welfare in 1959 in *The Central Nervous System and Behavior: Selected Translations from the Russian Medical Literature.*

The chapter/article provides a succinct review of the philosophy and experimental evidence underlying the prevalent Soviet view of the formation of voluntary action. In his introduction, Luria states that Soviet psychology views an examination of the development of such action "as its fundamental task" (Luria, 1960a, p. 139).

Luria then goes on to summarize Soviet theories and findings under the headings of: "Voluntary Action and External Signals," "Voluntary Action and Internal Signals," "The Regulatory Influence of Internal Signals," and "External Signals as a Compensating Factor in Abnormal Motor Development." The latter section is a review of how speech can compensate for the disturbed motor reactions of children with cerebroasthenic syndrome.

"Verbal Regulation of Behavior" (1960b) is the transcript of Luria's presentation to the Josiah Macy, Jr. Foundation's Third Conference on The Central Nervous System and Behavior, which was held February 21, 22, 23, and 24, 1960, in Princeton, New Jersey. There were only six other presentations, which explains why the transcript is 64 pages in length. Participants in the conference included Karl H. Pribram, Erik H. Erikson, Eugene N. Sokolov, John C. Lilly, Frank Fremont-Smith, and Harry F. Harlow.

A. R. Luria's presentation was basically in two parts: one was a summary of his theories on the development of the regulatory function of speech in the child, and the other summarized how various pathological states of the brain influence the regulatory function.

Developmentally, he outlines three stages: First, the child's verbal activity plays no significant role in organizing the child's behavior. Verbal instruction may initiate behavior, but has no inhibitory function, and is still subordinate in influence to an orienting reflex. The second state is characterized by the influence of the excitatory or impulsive aspect of speech that can regulate the child's motor behavior. At this stage, if there is a conflict between the semantic aspect and the impulsive aspect of speech, the impulsive aspect will dominate. Only in the third stage does the semantic aspect of speech assume its pre-eminence. When this occurs, the child no longer requires externally vocalized speech to regulate his behavior.

Luria categorizes pathological states into two types: Type A, when lower cortical levels are disturbed, but the higher levels are intact; and Type B, when the lower cortical levels are relatively adequate, but the higher levels are disturbed. He classifies Parkinson's disease as an example of Type A, and also cerebral asthenia cases, which are, in contrast, usually curable because the pathology typically results from temporary impairment rather than permanent damage. For these pathologies, he presents case studies supporting his claim that the possibility exists of compensating for the pathological states of lower cortical levels through speech.

Type B pathologies are exemplified by oligophrenic children, and patients with frontal lobe lesions. Those suffering from pre-frontal lobe lesions display especially severe decrements in the regulative functioning of speech:

> It is interesting that these patients cannot even obey a verbal instruction. Not only the motor component of the behavior is disturbed, but even the semantic, the attitudes, the content of behavior. When the patient is told to write his name, he signs. But when this is followed by a request to write the letter "A", he again signs his name. He is then asked to draw a circle, but he signs his name once again. He cannot shift from one type of activity to the other. (Luria, 1960b, pp. 402–403)

The Role of Speech in the Regulation of Normal and Abnormal Behavior (1961a) is a book-length work providing the text of three lectures that Luria gave at University College, London, in 1958. The first lecture was entitled, "The Role of Speech in the Formation of Mental Processes"; the second, "The Development of the Regulatory Role of Speech"; and the third, "Modifications in the Regulatory Role of Speech Resulting from Pathological States of the Brain."

The first lecture was essentially an introduction for the other two. In it, Luria explains that higher mental processes are not innate mental properties, but rather follow a developmental course that for most mental activities correlates with the developmental progression to internalized speech. He reviews how this capacity of speech mediated mental functioning influences various human behaviors, and is the characteristic that distinguishes human activity from that of other animals.

In the second lecture, Luria reviews theories and experiments that lead to his belief, at this state of his theory, that there are basically four developmental stages of the regulatory role of speech in the child: (1) Speech has no influence on the child's behavior; (2) External speech has an impellant, initiating effect on action; (3) External speech has an inhibitory effect on action due to the development of significative connections in the child; and (4) Control of behavior shifts to the inner speech of the child with the attendant formation of verbal principals to guide behavior.

Noting that almost any pathological state of the brain is accompanied by a disturbance of higher mental processes, Luria utilizes the third lecture to review such manifestations in patients with Parkinson's disease, children with cerebroasthenic syndrome, and oligophrenic children. His anlaysis focuses on the changed correlation between speech and action, or in Pavlovian terms almost mandatory at the time, *"the changed correlation between the activity of the two signalling systems . . ."* (Luria, 1961a, p. 102).

"The Genesis of Voluntary Movements" (1961b) is the translation of a 1957 *Voprosy Psikhologii* article that constitutes a chapter in *Recent Soviet Psychology.* In the article/chapter, Luria focuses on the differences between the impulsive and inhibitory aspects of speech in regulating the child's behavior, and the developmental progression that has as its main feature the fact

> that *regulation shifts over more and more from the mediation by the nervous impulses associated with speech to that system of separate selective thought associations which are stimulated by the word;* what is more interesting, is that at the same time control becomes transferred *from the child's spoken word to its own internal speech.* (Luria, 1961b, p. 182)

"The Role of Speech in the Formation of Temporary Connections and the Regulation of Behaviour in the Normal and Oligophrenic Child" (1963c) is a chapter in *Educational Psychology in the USSR.* The chapter discusses the differences in mental functioning between the normal and oligophrenic school-age child, and originally appeared in a brief book written for Russian educators, or anyone involved in the diagnosis, care, or education of retarded children.

As a preface to his discussion of the differences in mental functioning between normal and abnormal children, A. R. Luria briefly explains the generalizing function of speech:

> The function of generalisation is the main function of human speech, without which mastery of the experience of preceding generations would be impossible. But it would be wrong to think that this is the only basic function of speech. Language is not only a means of generalisation; it is at the same time the source of thought.
>
> When the child masters language he gains the potentiality to organise anew his perception, his memory; he masters more complex forms of reflection of objects in the external world; he gains the capacity to draw conclusions from his observations, to make deductions, the potentiality of thinking.
>
> When the child names something, pronouncing, for example, "that is a steam engine," he is at the same time analysing with the aid of means developed through many generations . . . . Saying the word "steam engine" (*paravoz*) he begins to understand that in the movement of the machine named steam (*par*) plays a role and that it moves other objects. In mastering words and using them the child analyses and synthesises the phenomena of the external world, using not only his personal experience but the experience of mankind. He classifies objects, he begins to perceive them differently and with this to remember them differently.
>
> But the speech mastered by the child does not consist of single words; it consists of complex grammatical combinations, of whole expressions. These expressions allow not only for the analysis and synthesis of perception, but also the connection of things with actions, and still more the posing of things in certain relations with each other. Acquiring forms of developed, connected, speech the child acquires the potentiality not only to form concepts but also to draw conclusions from accepted assumptions, to master logical connections, to cognise laws, far surpassing the boundaries of direct, personal experience; in sum, he masters science, gains the potentiality to foresee and foretell phenomena, which he could not do by merely witnessing them.
>
> What has been said up to now does not fully cover the role of language, the role of speech, in the formation of man's mental processes. Speech activity besides being a means of generalising and the source of thought is also a means of *regulating behaviour.* (Luria, 1963c, pp. 85–86)

As might be anticipated, Luria considers the essential difference between normal and oligophrenic school-age children to be the fact that the latter's mental connections are not formulated via the speech system. In contrast to the normal child, the oligophrenic's mental connections are created mechanically by means of time-consuming conditioning, remain unstable, and are never cognitively understood by the child. These difficulties with mental connections are also reflected in the child's attempts to control his behavior. This leads Luria to the conclusion that:

Disturbance of the participation of speech in the formation of complex mental processes and defects in its generalising and regulatory function are the traits which differentiate the intellectually backward child. (Luria, 1963c, p. 97)

"The Regulative Function of Speech in Its Development and Dissolution" (1967d) is a chapter in *Research in Verbal Behavior and Some Neurophysiological Implications,* which reviews the theories and research of Luria and other Soviets on the developmental stages of the regulative function of speech together with its disturbance in cases of Parkinson's disease, cerebroasthenic syndrome, and oligophrenia. The discussion is more neurologically oriented than previously discussed works from his corpus concerned with the verbal regulation of behavior. For example, Luria explains that the complexity of a child's self-directed negative verbal instruction derives from the fact that such an utterance is physiologically excitatory and thus connected to the positive phase of an innervation, yet simultaneously the semantic aspect requires a physiologically inhibitory effect. When the semantic aspect of speech becomes dominant, then external speech becomes superfluous and the excitatory/inhibitory conflict no long prevails.

Noting again that pathologies of the brain are reflected in a changed interaction between the two levels of neural processing indicated by Pavlov's two signal systems, Luria goes on to note for the first time in this topical area a link between the directive function of speech and the frontal lobes of the brain:

the directive (regulative) function of speech, disturbed when the frontal lobes are involved, can function only when the closest participation of the frontal area of the cortex. This is due to the part that the frontal lobes play in stabilizing the impulses arriving from the reticular formation and in the selection of the impulses which they receive, thus enabling the healthy cortex to produce stable action.

Furthermore, the fact that the final formation of the directive function of speech is observed at the age of 4–5 years, when the frontal lobes mature sufficiently and begin to function, confirms this hypothesis with new data. (Luria, 1967d, p. 421)

This connection between the frontal lobes and the directive function of speech is addressed in more detail in Luria's final work, *Language and Cognition* (1982). The text was based on lectures through which Luria introduced university students to current issues in Soviet psychology, and contains two chapters relevant to the verbal regulation of behavior. The first, "The Development of the Role of Speech in Mental Processes: The

Regulative Function of Speech and its Development," reiterates the developmental stages of a child's acquisition of voluntary behavior that have been identified previously, and notes that further research is needed to identify the mechanisms that make the directive function of speech possible.

It is the second chapter, "Inner Speech and the Cerebral Organization of the Regulative Function Speech," that attempts to delineate current knowledge about such mechanisms. Luria notes that a voluntary act is one that is mediated by speech, which includes not just the communicative dimension of external speech characterizing initial stages, but more typically the child's own regulative forms of speech. The usual form of the latter is inner speech that originates as external speech but then develops into a complex psychological formation. It is in this state that inner speech becomes the chief mechanism for volitional acts in normal adults. In attempting to identify the cerebral regions that underlie inner speech, Luria cites his own research, and concludes that the frontal lobes are intimately involved in inner speech and consequently, voluntary acts. The role of inner speech in voluntary acts is discussed in more detail in the Spoken Language and Voluntary Behavior section of this chapter.

HIGHER MENTAL PROCESSES AND VOLUNTARY BEHAVIOR

Given Vygotsky's tenet that volitional activity is the primary feature distinguishing humans from other animals, it seems appropriate that the first topical area of Luria's theory focuses on the higher mental process of voluntary behavior. Initially, A. R. Luria had conceived of behavioral control as being a point of conflict between reason and emotion (1932a). Emotions were portrayed as continually attempting to seize control from reason, and being able to do so only when the organism was in a state of general debility, such as during extreme stress or fatigue. Thus, the characteristic that higher mental systems normally dominate or control lower mental systems is established early in Luria's work, but continued to be refined as his theory evolved.

His concern with reason versus emotion changed to a consideration of higher mental processes versus lower mental processes as Luria's understanding of the neurological bases and development of mental functioning expanded. Such knowledge made it evident that in addition to being more complex, higher mental processes are "higher" for physical reasons as well. They are located spatially above the lower processes—neocortex versus sub-cortical—and they develop on a foundation of the more elementary systems.

The dominance of the cortical level over the sub-cortical level is adduced by Luria's research with Parkinson's disease patients (1959b, 1960b, 1961a, 1967d), which demonstrated that it is possible to transfer the control of defective involuntary (sub-cortical) motor behaviors to the voluntary (cortical) motor areas so that the subject can still perform the desired action because the pathology has left the cortical areas intact.

In Parkinson's disease patients:

> The injured subcortical apparatus excites repeated tonic responses, and the pathologically perseverating tension of all muscles is an obstacle to the execution of the instruction. It is easy to imagine such a difficulty in carrying out a voluntary movement if one briefly tenses all the muscles of one hand and then tries to move it without relaxing the tension. (Luria, 1959b, p. 455)

However, if the origin of the motor act is shifted from the automatic movement realm governed by the sub-cortical motor apparatus to the conscious movement domain of the cortical motor areas, the patient is able to carry out the required movements. This may be accomplished by

> attaching a symbolic function to his movements. He is asked to reply to the experimenter's questions by beating out the necessary numbers with his finger. If we then ask him, "How many wheels on a car?" or "How many points on a compass?" we see that the same patient who had failed in the previous experiment and could not automatically strike the table with his fingers even two or three times, easily begins to do so, switching his movements into his speech system and subordinating them to the complex dynamic constellation of cortical connections. (Luria, 1959b, p. 455)

Similarly, the Parkinson's disease patient who is unable to walk more than one or two steps will find that his difficulties

> in successive automatic movements may be compensated for temporarily if they are transferred to the cortical level, and if the continuous movement is superseded by a cycle of isolated responses to individual stimuli. Such a patient cannot take several steps on a smooth floor but can easily cross several lines marked on the floor or several objects placed on the floor. (Luria, 1967d, p. 417)

Such mechanisms force the control of the normally automatic components of walking to the conscious, voluntary control of the cortical level by separating them into individual responses to individual stimuli, thus requiring cortical level processing.

Even when both cortical levels have been physiologically weakened, as in the case of cerebroasthenic children, the cortical level will dominate the sub-cortical and can be used to assist in the latter's defective functioning. The pathology of cerebroasthenia (general physiological weakness of the cortex) is usually reversible (Luria, 1960b, p. 387), but in the interim the basic physiological properties of the nervous processes—their strength, equilibrium, and mobility—are impaired. The pathology originates from various sources; some children so afflicted

> have suffered from an infectious disease, others from brain traumata and others from prolonged dystrophia. All these children have normal brains and learn successfully, but are considerably hindered by their pronounced susceptibility to exhaustion. Usually they can assimilate material well over a short period, but they cannot maintain the tempo of the class and after ten or fifteen minutes are so exhausted that they cease to absorb what they are given to do and become incapable of carrying out any complex intellectual activity. In some children the exhaustion manifests itself as listlessness or sleepiness and in others as distractability. From no point of view can they be accounted as mentally retarded . . . . (Luria, 1963a, p. 20)

The impact of the pathology on the basic physiological properties of neural processes is also manifested in the children's motor behaviors. They respond easily to a given signal with the appropriate motor reaction if they are given sufficient time. However, when the allotted response time as well as the duration of the signal is shortened, they are no longer able to respond accurately

> and they either omit the response to positive signals or begin responding with impulsive movements to inhibitory signals. The number of erroneous responses frequently reaches 40–60%. Such children do, however, remember the instructions and are conscious of their mistakes. The equilibrium and mobility of the excitatory and inhibitory processes are so disturbed in these children that an adequate execution of the corresponding instructions becomes impossible. (Luria, 1967d, p. 415)

Using the experiments of Khomskaya as his evidence, Luria indicates that the regulative capacity of the impulsive aspect of spoken language is lost for such children, but that by utilizing the semantic aspect of speech and thus moving control to the cortical level, such children can compensate for their defective motor reactions (Luria, 1967d, pp. 415–416).

The self-control necessary for voluntary behavior is made possible by the mediated structure that typifies higher mental processes. A process with such structure incorporates artificial stimuli or auxiliary stimuli into its nature, and that incorporation is a focus of Luria's work in this topical area.

In *The Nature of Human Conflicts* (1932a), Luria defined voluntary behavior as "the ability to create stimuli and to subordinate them; or in other words, to bring into being stimuli of a special order, directed to the organization of behavior" (Luria, 1932a, p. 401). Consequently, there is a perceived relationship between auxiliary stimuli that have been created by the individual and volitional control of the individual's actions even in his early work. The implication throughout his writing is that volition cannot exist without the existence of auxiliary stimuli.

Physiologically, any motor act, even a reflex, has a beginning and a conclusion. The latter is based on the fact that:

> Many outstanding neurophysiologists have repeatedly pointed out that the regulation of action requires a system of "feedback" afferentations which give a signal for the discontinuance of the action after its accomplishment; and they have also stated that without such a system of signals, arising from the effect of the action, movement cannot become controllable. (Luria, 1961a, p. 63)

Given this need for afferent feedback to end action, Luria and his colleagues hypothesized that it might be possible to utilize a contravening movement by the young child in response to verbal instructions as the afferent signal to end diffuse motor impulses:

> Experiments on these lines performed by S. V. Yakovleva yielded very interesting results: in 50 percent of all children tested at eighteen months to two years, and in 75 percent of children at the age of two to three years, this change in the instructions resulted in the complete disappearance of accidental intersignal pressures of the bulb and produced clear cut reactions coordinated with the conditioned signal . . . . on the other hand the removal of the sanctioning afferentation led, in the overwhelming majority of children, to the recovery of the original diffusiveness of the motor reactions. (Luria, 1961a, p. 66)

In these examples, the auxiliary stimuli were introduced into the situation by the experimenters, and Luria calls the outcome "*the first and simplest model of a voluntary movement in a very young child*" (Luria, 1961a, p. 66). Gradually, through developmental stages, the initiation of afferent feedback to end action will change in locus from the external source of the adult to the child himself. The final developmental stage will then be voluntary action or behavior that is a higher mental process since it has sociocultural origins, evolves through developmental stages, is conscious as well as voluntary in nature, and the speech system has played a part in its development:

> voluntary action arises in the process of the child's relationships with the adult, and passes through a number of successive stages in its development.

Originally taking the form of the fulfillment by the child of the adult's verbal instruction, it is gradually—with the development of the child's own speech—transformed into a system of self-regulating acts in which the decisive role is played first by external and subsequently by internal speech, the chief mechanism of voluntary action. (Luria, 1960a, p. 139)

SPOKEN LANGUAGE AND VOLUNTARY BEHAVIOR

Originally, Luria had intended to use the "combined motor method" measuring motor reactions of the hand to trace the influences of human emotions on behavior. However, Vygotsky saw in Luria's research method a way of examining how speech serves as a means of organizing behavior. The resultant shift in emphasis is reflected in the later chapters of *The Nature of Human Conflicts* (1932a); and the role of speech in regulating behavior became an important focus of A. R. Luria's work in the late 1940s and early 1950s. Unfortunately, this facet of his work is viewed by some spoken language scholars in the U.S. as comprising the total domain of Lurian theory, rather than being just one aspect of his continuing study of the human mind.

In his early thought (1932a), the mechanism maintaining reason's control of behavior was referred to somewhat euphemistically as a "functional barrier." This functional barrier was described as not a natural or organic mechanism, but as having cultural origins and serving to delay and reorganize excitations en route to the motor system. Thus, an individual's reaction to a stimulus was made into a two-step process rather than being a direct, reflexive one. Luria identified speech as the primary means by which impulses were reorganized, but speculated that all symbolic systems might have such effects. The particular process by which speech accomplished this was left quite vague, but in this early analysis are the beginnings of Luria's conceptualization of speech as the auxiliary stimulus organizing mental processes.

Luria's later work in this area indicates that spoken language as a stimulus, however, follows the rule of emergent specificity with respect to development, so that initially the excitatory or impulsive aspect of speech dominates, and produces a nonspecific, diffuse effect. Gradually, the inhibitory or significative aspect of spoken language gains supremacy, and its specific, elective effect becomes dominant over the excitatory aspects as speech evolves to the complex functioning typical of higher mental processes.

In the early stages of development, therefore, verbal instruction can only initiate action on the part of the child and is incapable of either inhibiting action or of changing it.

From a number of experiments of this kind, it can be concluded that in this early stage of the child's life, about 1 year and 2 months and even up to 1–1/2 years, verbal instruction can only *initiate* behavior. It cannot yet either *stop* or *reverse* behaviors. It fails when it comes into conflict with an orienting reflex or the factor of *inertia* working in a different direction. (Luria, 1960b, p. 360)

An example of such conflict was demonstrated in the following experiment:

We place before a child of 1;0 to 1;2 two toys: a fish and a horse, this time placing them at the same distance and giving them dimensions and colors that are equally attractive. We ask the child to give us the *fish:* he does this easily. We repeat this experiment three or four times, and the effect remains the same. In exactly the same tone of voice, we now utter a different instruction and ask the child to hand us the *horse.* Despite the fact that the meaning of the word is well known to the child, the inertia of the connections evoked by the first word is so great that in many cases the child again offers the experimenter the fish. The directive function of the changed verbal instruction is here vitiated by the inertia of the connection that has been established . . . .

The directive role of the word at an early age is maintained only if the word does not conflict with the inert connections which arose at an earlier instruction or which began with the child's own activity. (Luria, 1959a, p. 343)

This diffuse effect of spoken language as a stimulus eventually subsides and

will disappear at a later stage of development, at ages 5 to 6, when the child's motor reactions become regulated by the system of elective connections which by that time assume decisive significance. (Luria, 1960a, p. 146)

One reason for the later development of the inhibitory aspect of spoken language is that it is neurologically more complex in its execution than the excitatory aspect. For example, a negative verbal instruction is physiologically excitatory while, at the same time, it is semantically inhibitory:

The verbal responses "Press" and "Don't press!" turn out to have a complex structure. Physiologically they are, first of all, motor responses of the speech apparatus and thus always connected with the positive phase of an innervation. But with regard to their meanings they are systems of connections which, in the former case, have a positive, and in the latter case, an inhibitory signal value. (Luria, 1967d, p. 412)

This apparent contradiction in terms that the spoken instruction is simultaneously excitatory and inhibitory is explained by the fact that the semantic aspect of speech neurologically initiates an excitatory impulse which then conflicts with, and hence inhibits, the excitatory impulse of the action. This capability on the neurological level means that:

> Verbal instruction, previously ineffective, could now produce the required effect, thanks to the inhibitory influences prepared by the preliminary conflict between the two successive excitations. (Luria, 1961a, p. 60)

To move from the neurological level to a concern with the behavioral outcomes of such neurological functioning, the stages are generally referred to as the motor and semantic stages of spoken language. A. R. Luria postulates that one stage in the development of spoken language is when the motor component of speech can organize the child's behavior and the semantic side is not yet able to do so. The following example is taken from an experiment with a 3-year-old child, and illustrates that the child may repeat the instruction but lack the neurodynamic ability to carry it out:

> In the next part of the experiment, I say to the child, "On every signal, don't say 'Toot, toot,' but say 'I press twice.'" He says, "I press twice, I press twice," but he presses only once. Why? Because the dominating influence is not the semantic meaning, but the motor component of the speech reaction. (Luria, 1960b, p. 377)

The motor stage of spoken language, as mentioned previously, can initiate behavior and consequently, in a sense, has some control over action. However, any true guidance or organization of behavior must await the development of the semantic stage of speech:

> It is very important that such a regulatory influence of speech occurs only when the speech is semantically meaningful. If the child is instructed, "Press every time, and just say, 'I see, I see, I see,'" in positive and negative cases, there is no normalizing effect . . . . If instead the child says, "Yes," for positive and "No" for negative, the result is all right, for the speech has semantic sense. (Luria, 1960b, p. 391)

In verification of this idea that organization of behavior can be derived from spoken language only in its semantic stage, Luria (1960b) found that the spoken word could compensate for defects in motor control in cerebroasthenic children only via the cortically based semantic aspect of speech. The reason, of course, being that the motor aspect of spoken language usually arises from the same sub-cortical areas as those producing the motor defects, and even in the generally weakened state of the brain that typifies cerebroasthenia, the cortical dominates the sub-cortical.

That the semantic stage of speech depends on a cortical base is substantiated by the fact that the control of behavior possible at that stage requires the close participation of the frontal lobes, and parallels their functional maturation.

It should be noted that since spoken language arises on a physical base like all higher mental processes, any pathology of the physical disrupts the normal functioning and developmental progression of the stages of speech. Consequently, the normal dominance of the semantic stage in the regulatory function of speech is upset by early pathologies such as those experienced by oligophrenic children:

> The specific feature characterizing the derangement of the functional systems in oligophrenics consists precisely in the fact that this predominance of elective (abstracting and generalizing) verbal connection is here not sufficiently strong. Consequently, the primitive, non-specific functions of speech easily begin to take the upper hand. (Luria, 1961a, pp. 140–141)

This dependence on the physiological base by spoken language is also evidenced by the fact that motor defects in cerebroasthenic children *can* be compensated for because the higher neurological base of the semantic aspect of speech is still intact, but that is not a possibility for the oligophrenic child because

> the child's own speech can regulate his motor processes only if the nervous processes underlying it are themselves more concentrated and more mobile than the nervous processes underlying motor reactions . . . . the speech connections of the oligophrenic child are not more, but even less, mobile than his motor reactions and are easily converted into a stereotyped form. (Luria, 1963c, p. 96)

The dependency of spoken language on underlying cortical systems descends even to the most elementary level, as it does for all higher mental processes, and includes a reliance also on the strength, equilibrium, and mobility of neural activity in its physiological base.

This dependency of spoken language on its material base also provides Luria with evidence for his claim that spoken language's developmental stage of inner speech is the primary mechanism for voluntary behavior (Luria, 1982). He cites the research of Sokolov and others which found that problem-solving children have weak electromyographic responses in their speech organs, thus indicating that the egocentric speech that had directed their behavior had changed to an unobservable, unaudible internal speech. Complementing these findings is the physiological evidence from

Luria's own research that individuals with sensory or motor aphasia (impairments in the processing of sound/meaning necessary for communicative speech) continue to be capable of directing their own behavior. Thus, the mediation necessary for voluntary acts cannot be provided by external or egocentric speech, and must be a product of internal speech.

The dependence of internal speech and volition upon the frontal lobes is adduced by studies that reveal that damage to the prefrontal areas of the brain precipitate severe disturbances in voluntary, programmed acts. Often, the external speech of such patients has also lost its directive role. Consequently, it appears that the frontal lobes are vital for the regulative function of speech, whether external or internal (Luria, 1982).

Thus, in this topical area, spoken language is presented as a higher mental process incorporating many of the characteristics of such processes. Apart from those features, we also find that as a stimulus, speech can be either excitatory or inhibitory, although the developmental progression of its regulatory function moves from the impulsive (excitatory) aspects to the significative (inhibitory) aspects. The developmental stages of spoken language in organizing the child's behavior are: (1) Speech has no effect; and action is separated only by the child's own movements; (2) External speech has an impellant, initiating action of the child's movements; (3) External speech elicits significative connections, and organizes the child's movements; and (4) Control shifts to the child's internal speech and there is an attendant formation of verbal principles that guide the child's movement (Luria, 1961a, pp. 94–96).

Simultaneous with the development of voluntary control, there is a developmental progression from external speech to internal speech as the tool making such control possible. Luria viewed internal speech as the "chief mechanism of voluntary action" (Luria, 1960a, p. 139) because of its capacity for formulating new mental connections, or to use Luria's phrasing, "temporary connections" in the brain.

Spoken language in this topical area is viewed primarily in terms of its functional dimension as a method of organizing or regulating mental processes. However, the increasing importance of spoken language to Lurian theory is reflected in A. R. Luria's statement that

> There is every reason to believe that the speech system, which is formed in the process of the child's social intercourse with the adult, is a powerful means of systemic organization of our mental processes, and that the precise study of this will help us to solve the highly important task of modifying and perfecting the higher nervous activity of man; consequently, it can help us to approach the solution of the basic task of psychology—to make known the scientific foundations of the organization of human behavior. (Luria, 1961a, p. 144)

3 Consciousness

" 'Brain and Conscious Experience' ": A Critical Notice from the U.S.S.R. of the Symposium Edited by J. C. Eccles (1966)" (1967a) is Luria's review for the *British Journal of Psychology* of the transcript of an international symposium on brain/consciousness called by the Vatican Academy of Sciences and organized by its President, Sir John Eccles.

Luria chides the majority of the prominent participants for their archaic philosophical orientations to the brain/consciousness question, and notes that

> In spite of the fact that the definitions of consciousness given by the participants were varied, not one of them understood consciousness as the reflexion of objective reality, as "conscious being" or as complex activity which has a semantic and systematic structure. (Luria, 1967a, p. 469)

Rather, according to Luria, the participants were roughly divided into two groups: one group, exemplified by Penfield, sought the material basis for consciousness inside the brain and anticipated discovery of the formations in neuronal structure that give rise to this phenomenon; the other group, typified by MacKay, rejected any study of neuronal structure and called for the study of logical systems concerned with the processing of information, which are somehow the basis for conscious experience.

After reviewing the new directions in brain research represented at the symposium, Luria goes on to note that the central problem of the conference was "the question of the role played by the non-specific system of the brain stem in providing an active and waking state for the cerebral hemispheres . . . ." (Luria, 1967a, p. 471). This problem arises from the knowledge that the non-specific reticular system of the brain stem interacts with the specific or cortical formations of the brain—stimulating and receiving stimulation.

However, one view posits that the essential function of the nervous apparatus is not the transmission of excitation but rather the limitation of excitation. This has lead to the discovery that the brain systems are selective in their reception of information, selecting only essential stimuli and inhibiting extraneous stimuli. One study is reviewed by Luria which demonstrates that separate neurons exist which "can be activated only in the presence of conditions corresponding to a specific 'aim' . . ." (Luria, 1967a, p. 472). To Luria, this is additional evidence that motor processes are influenced by broad systems of cortical control extending beyond the limits of the "motor" cortex.

After reviewing the work of Phillips on "optimal points" of excitation, which indicates that the musculature of areas with the greatest mobility and directability such as lips and tongue, also have the densest population of motor neurons in the cortex and thus the greatest accessibility to direction from other areas of the cortex, Luria concludes

> This symposium is one of the most significant that has been devoted to the problem of the relation of brain to conscious experience. Physiological science, having rid itself of its one-sidedness, has begun to arrive at a synthesized understanding of nervous processes underlying psychological activity and has brought out facts concerning the wholeness of the relations between the non-specific and specific systems of the brain, and the selective operation of the brain in reflecting reality; it is now approaching an objective analysis of the workings of functional systems. All these scientific achievements will receive new directions of development when the problem of the relation of the brain to consciousness is posed on a correct theoretical basis.
>
> Physiology now has the task of uncovering the mechanism of consciousness. Consciousness is intelligible, not as an insubstantial subjective state, but as achieving the most complex form of the reflexion of reality by means of its equipment of semantic and schematic structure. (Luria, 1967a, p. 475)

In "The Quantitative Assessment of Levels of Wakefulness" (1973b), A. R. Luria points out that physiologists have made the most significant contributions in objective techniques to the study of disorders of wakefulness, and cites Pavlov's research as evidence that the transition from wakefulness to sleep is accompanied by changes in neural processes. These physiological changes, of course, also change the mental processes dependent upon the physiology:

> In the normal (optimal) state of the cortex, important (significant) stimuli easily become dominant, and weak (insignificant) stimuli are forced into the background; and the course of conscious processes assumes an organized character. However, as the cortex passes into the "phasic" state and cortical tone is reduced, this selective functioning of mental processes is inevitably disturbed. Important (significant) stimuli are reduced to the same level of importance as weak (insignificant) stimuli, and they lose their domi-

nantaracter; they cease to act as determinant factors, and the train of
thought no longer gives the appearance of organization; well-ordered associations directed toward a particular goal give way to incidental, uncontrolled
associations; haphazard images begin to rise to the surface of consciousness,
and the organized flow of consciousness is disrupted. (Luria, 1973b, p. 76)

Using the writings of James Joyce, Marcel Proust, and Leo Tolstoy as
vivid examples of how random images and phonetic associations begin to
dominate as the mind moves toward sleep, Luria suggests that such changes in associations manifested in the train of thought might serve as a starting point for assessing levels of reduced cortical tone, or even, eventually,
as a means of quantitatively assessing wakefulness in a clinical setting.

Language and Cognition (1982) contains some five chapters relative to
the topic of human consciousness. In the first chapter, entitled "The Problem of Language and Consciousness," Luria clarifies his view of human
consciousness and how it comes into existence. For him, consciousness is
the reflection of objective reality (Vygotsky's signalization); and the most
crucial problem to be investigated is how people are able to form a subjective image of the objective world. This human reflection of reality is
unique in that humans are not limited to immediate sensory perception,
but can transcend that to form abstract concepts and draw conclusions
based on reason without any concrete experience. Hence, humans are capable of both rational and sensory cognition. This capability gives rise to
the mind/body problem discussed briefly in the initial chapter of our text
under "Theoretical Foundations."

As one might anticipate because of his roots in Vygotskian theory,
Luria criticizes both the psychic and the physical extremists. The
Würzburg School is condemned for it's belief that thought is the "primary
property of the spiritual world which distinguishes humans from animals
and distinguishes the rational from the sensory" (Luria, 1982, p. 22).
Sherrington and Eccles are cited as examples that such idealism has even
impacted on physiologists. Equally erroneous, in Luria's opinion, are the
associationist psychologists and the American behaviorists who state that
thinking is just an aggregate of sensory representations. These two extreme views practically split psychology into two disciplines according to
Luria—one "descriptive," which denied the possibility of explaining the
higher forms of psychological life, the other "explanatory," but which
could only explain elementary psychological processes.

Luria sees the logical resolution of this dichotomy as being available in
the theoretical premise of Vygotsky that to explain human consciousness,
one must go outside of the individual human organism to the external
processes of social life, i.e., the sociocultural origins of higher psychological functions which were reviewed earlier in our text. Humans participate

not only in a physiological assimilation, but also in a psychic assimilation accomplished "through sense activity and with the help of language" (Luria, 1982, p. 26).

Two decisive factors permit the transition from animal consciousness (sensory) to human consciousness (sensory and rational)—a transition that Luria equates in importance to the transition from inorganic to living matter. The first is social labor and the division of labor, the second is language. Luria cites Engel's idea that it was the process of social labor that precipitated a need for people to convey information to each other, yet he deals only minimally with the activity of labor and states that his "central concern is with the role of language in the formation of human consciousness" (Luria, 1982, p. 31). However, his articulation of the basic position of Marxist psychology on consciousness reflects this tie of language to social labor and the sociocultural environment central to Marxist theory:

> Language, in the course of social history, became the decisive instrument which helped humans transcend the boundaries of sensory experience, to assign symbols, and to formulate certain generalizations or categories. Thus, if humans had not possessed the capacity for labor and had not had language, they would not have developed abstract, "categorical" thinking. That is why we should not seek the origins of abstract thinking and categorical behavior, which mark a sharp change from the sensory to the rational, within human consciousness or within the human brain. Rather, we should seek these origins in the social forms of human historical existence. Only in this way (which differs radically from all the teachings of traditional psychology) can we explain the appearance of complex forms of conscious behavior that are uniquely human. (Luria, 1982, p. 27)

In the other chapters on consciousness in *Language and Cognition* (1982), Luria concentrates exclusively on the role of language in forming human consciousness. Consequently, discussion of those chapters is reserved for the section on "Spoken Language and Consciousness."

HIGHER MENTAL PROCESSES AND CONSCIOUSNESS

Given Vygotsky's emphasis on consciousness as an appropriate area of study (even in 1924, when such an advocacy was not in vogue), and Luria's definition of higher mental processes as both conscious and voluntary in nature, one would naturally anticipate that consciousness would be a major focus of Lurian theory—and it is. However, it is generally treated as an attribute of higher mental processes, and addressed only in conjunction with a particular process such as memory, or cognition.

Yet, the term *consciousness* does not always refer to higher mental functioning in Luria's writings, nor does "human consciousness" exist as an innate quality of the human brain. Rather, two developmental stages occur in humans: Initially, animal consciousness exists which is mere wakefulness or the passive "reflexion of objective reality . . ." (Luria, 1967a, p. 469). Secondly, consciousness may develop into a "complex activity which has a semantic and systemic structure" (Luria, 1967a, p. 469). The latter stage constitutes uniquely human consciousness and is an attributional aspect of higher mental processes. It includes the active alteration of connections in both external and internal reality as well as volitional self-awareness. The differentiation of the two stages has obvious ties to Vygotsky's thought on the differences between animal and human mental functioning.

The dependence of higher mental processes on the brain's elementary sensory systems which create the first stage of consciousness is demonstrated by the physiological discovery that the upper brain stem area plays a significant role in maintaining a state of wakefulness, and by Luria's experiments (1973b), which indicate that any lessening of that basic state of wakefulness disrupts the functioning of the higher mental processes.

Similarly, Luria notes that higher mental processes are affected by the operational level of the physiological law that Pavlov termed "the law of strength" (Luria, 1973a, p. 5). This law holds that strong or significant stimuli elicit strong responses, and that weak or insignificant stimuli call forth weak responses regardless of whether the responses elicited are inhibitory or excitatory in nature. The operational level of this law, however, can be affected by a general physiological decrement in the central nervous system such as the reduction in cortical tone that occurs when there is a lessening of the state of wakefulness of the organism:

> The laws governing these phasic states have been thoroughly studied by the Pavlovian school. Their manifestations can readily be observed in a human when he is asleep or half awake. Such observations suggest that no organized thought is possible in these states and that selective connections are replaced by nonselective associations deprived of their purposeful character. It is possible that much of the peculiar logic of dreams can be explained by these physiological facts. (Luria, 1973a, p. 5)

SPOKEN LANGUAGE AND CONSCIOUSNESS

It is in this topical area that Luria announces that

> Humans differ from animals because of the existence of human language —a system of codes that designates external objects and their relationships, and helps to arrange these objects into certain systems of categories. This

system of codes leads to the formation of abstract thinking, to the formation of "categorical" consciousness. (Luria, 1982, p. 30)

Natural animal languages are not languages according to Luria but only quasi-languages because they lack the above characteristics with the concomitant ability to abstract, analyze, and place an object or quality into a system of relationships and associations. Luria maintains that natural animal languages can only express "*condition* or *what the animal is going through.*" (Luria, 1982, p. 29) As a result, rather than conveying information, the "language" merely serves to infect others of its kind with the same feelings that the animal expressing the sign is experiencing. This is in keeping with Luria's idea that animal consciousness is constrained to the sensory level.

The experiments of American psychologists who teach visual or gestural language to apes are dismissed by Luria "as a case of complex forms of the artificial development of conditioned responses which resemble human language in its external characteristics" (Luria, 1982, p. 30). This dismissal becomes theoretically sound when we understand Luria's view of how human language is tied to human consciousness, or the active reflection of reality.

The word is the basic unit of language, and has two functions in the reflection of objective reality. First and most basic is the word's "referential" function, which means that it can substitute for an object, an act, a property, or a relationship. This enables humans to expand their world and deal with things that are not present. The ability to elicit these images apart from the thing permits humans to regulate their perception and memory. Other advantages resulting from this function of the word include the ability to act internally, and to transmit knowledge from one person to another so that the experience of previous generations can be acquired.

The meaning of the word is not limited to its referential function since a single word may have several possible meanings. In other words, the meaning of a word is not just the designation of a specific object, which may vary according to context, it also includes all the associative meanings that are included in the word's semantic field. These associations include phonetic, situational, and conceptual associations. In a normal cortex, the meaning associations (situational and conceptual) dominate while the phonetic ones are inhibited.

Luria further classifies word meaning associations into two systems originally introduced by Vygotsky in *Thought and Language* (1962)—meaning and sense. "Meaning" is a stable system of associations that is the same for all speakers of a particular language and parallels our usage of denotative meaning, while "sense" refers to the unique system of relations and associations that may be pertinent to a particular speaker in a particular situation. Hence, the latter is basically the same as connotative meaning. Knowing that the word's system of meanings includes both objective and subjective systems of situational and conceptual associations serves to illustrate that the second function of the word is much more complex than the referential function.

This second function of the word in reflecting reality is its conceptual or what Luria calls its "categorical" meaning. This designates the word's abstracting and generalizing function which results from the word's capacity to analyze objects. This is accomplished by "*introducing it* [a thing] *into a system of complex associations and relations*" (Luria, 1982, p. 37). Luria uses word roots and affixes to delineate how a word serves to single out essential properties of things, and at the same time to generalize that thing by relating it to other objects in a category. This function means that

> a word is a *unit of thought.* It is a unit of thought because the powers of abstraction and generalization are the most important functions of thinking. (Luria, 1982, p. 38)

Consequently, it is as a result of the word's second function that humans are able to achieve "that *leap from the sensory to the rational world,* which is essential for human consciousness" (Luria, 1982, p. 41).

Luria maintains that the meaning of a word continues to develop through ontogenesis although it may retain the same particular referent. As the word meaning changes, it is accompanied by psychological changes so that the evolution of word meaning is also the evolution of the capacity of consciousness to reflect reality. Initially, the chief characteristic of word meaning is affect, then concrete image, and then the system of logical connections that stand behind the word. It is in the latter stage that the word enters into a system of categories and acquires what Luria refers to as its "paradigmatic" character, meaning that its "meaning is situated in an hierarchial system of abstract oppositions" (Luria, 1982, p. 52). It is Luria's contention that the structure of consciousness also evolves and parallels the evolution of word meaning so that

> During the earliest stage of ontogenesis, consciousness has an affective character. During the next stage, it begins to assume a concrete character. Words, through which the world is reflected, evoke a system of practically actuated connections. It is only at the final stage that consciousness acquires an abstract verbal-logical character, which differs from the earlier stages both in its meaning structure and in psychological processes, although even at this stage the connections that characterize the previous stages are covertly preserved. (Luria, 1982, p. 53)

Noting that psychologists have known for a long time that differentiation precedes generalization in development, Luria suggests that the proper explanation for this "is that differentiation is characterized by *concretely based thinking . . .*" (Luria, 1982, p. 59). That such thinking is tied to sociocultural conditions is supported by his studies in the 1930s which revealed that people in relatively elementary socioeconomic conditions and who were nonliterate tended to classify objects according to a concrete situation (Luria, 1976b). They could understand the categorical form of classification but did not use it and considered it unimportant. It is only with the acquisition of literacy and more complex, socially organized forms of production that the categorical form of generalization becomes the natural one (Luria, 1982, p. 63). Hence, cultures as well as individuals appear to pass through stages of consciousness that parallel the evolution of word meaning.

It is also in this topical area that Luria reports his discovery of a correlation between levels of consciousness and levels of word association inherent in the paradigmatic structure of spoken language. As noted previously, the latter refers to the vertical dimension of language or its schema for storage, and can include any vertical association such as "the sets that are tied together by some grammatical rule, such as pronouns with their cases, or verbs with their inflections for number, tense, and person" (Bolinger, 1975, p. 27). However, Luria uses the term to mean the hierarchy of mental associations/connections evoked by the word apart from any consideration of syntax. Thus, phonetic, morphological, and semantic (situational and conceptual) associations are the only possible ones given his definition of paradigmatic structure, and his early writings on consciousness consider only the phonetic and the semantic.

Using the hypothesis that

> Waking consciousness is characterized by the predominance of the system of semantic associations evoked by a word, while phonetic associations, which play no significant role whatever, remain incidental and are inhibited. (Luria, 1973b, p. 77)

Luria presented research that he had done in conjunction with Vinogradova which measured orienting responses to verbal stimuli by normal children and those with either mild or severe forms of oligophrenia via changes in the temporal artery and arteries in the hand.

Their findings were that normal, awake subjects had an orienting response only to words with semantically similar meanings. The mildly retarded children responded equally to semantically similar, phonetically similar, or neutral words with none of the three possible responses being dominant. In contrast, the severely retarded children produced orienting reflexes only in response to those words which were phonetically similar to the original word stimulus. Also, it was found that the dominant system of association could be changed by fatigue, stress, or the degree of wakefulness of the subject. Luria, therefore, concluded that the techniques used by Vinogradova and himself could aid in detecting not only pathological cortical states, but also varying cortical tone in a healthy cortex.

As a result of these studies, Luria suggested that similar research using associations evoked by the word should be done in cases of severe lesions of the reticular formation that may affect tone, and should be used to assess the effectiveness of drugs that attempt to increase cortical tone and thereby normalize mental functioning. Thus, the associations inherent in spoken language are seen as accurate indicators of neurological states.

4 Memory

LITERATURE

"Towards a Neurodynamic Analysis of Memory Disturbances with Lesions of the Left Temporal Lobe" (1967) was written in conjunction with E. N. Sokolov and M. Klimkowski and reported on experiments done with two patients with left temporoparietal lesions.

The authors dismiss the tendency by some to equate memory with the creation and reproduction of conditioned reflexes, and note that even Pavlov insisted on distinguishing between "the external rules of conditioning and the inner mechanisms of retention of traces in the nervous system" (Luria, Sokolov, & Klimkowski, 1967, p. 1).

Based on their research, the authors concluded that the patients' disturbances of audio-verbal memory traces had the following probable causes:

> Two basic nervous mechanisms could be supposed as taking part in the genesis of both syndromes: the effect of pathological *accumulation of inhibitory influences* which blocked the traces and which masked traces already fixed and the effect of pathological *equalization of excitations,* which made dominant and subdominant, present and former traces equal in strength. (Luria, Sokolov, & Klimkowski, 1967, p. 9)

"Disturbances of Auditory-Speech Memory in Focal Lesions of the Deep Regions of the Left Temporal Lobe" (1968) was co-authored with T. A. Karasseva and presents one case of an "especially clear syndrome of auditory-speech memory loss without any disturbances of acoustic analysis of speech sounds" (Luria & Karasseva, 1968, p. 97).

The case was of particular interest because the lesion was in only the white matter of the left temporal lobe. The gray matter of Wernicke's area together with that of nearby lower parietal and occipital regions was intact. The latter areas are commonly involved in dysfunctions of auditory-speech memory.

Their experiments found a

pathologically heightened inhibition of auditory-speech traces. This defect
appeared especially clearly in auditory-speech memory and at a significantly lower level in visual and motor (kinaesthetic) memory.

There was no loss of any firm traces established during former experience. Intellectual operations (to the extent that they did not depend on operational auditory-speech memory) remained unimpaired. Phonetic hearing,
writing, reading and speech comprehension were conserved in the patient as
well. (Luria & Karasseva, 1968, p. 103)

The Mind of the Mnemonist: A Little Book About a Vast Memory (1968)
is an account of Luria's study of S. which began in the 1920s and continued for almost 30 years. At the outset, Luria intended to measure S.'s prodigious memory capacity, but realizing that there were no practical limits
to the man's memory, he decided instead to attempt a qualitative study of
the *"psychological aspects of its structure"* (Luria, 1968, p. 12).

Luria's narrative of how S.'s memory affected the pattern of his life includes a unique combination of empathy for the patient's many frustra-
tions together with an objective analysis of tests and interviews. This hu-
manized presentation of S. provides the book with a poignant appeal that
surpasses a concern with the function of memory per se.

S.'s memory retained material via visual images and synesthesia. Thus,
the modes were combined for him, and the multiple sensations aroused
by any stimulus ensured multiple checks for accurate recall later. S. explained it thusly:

I recognize a word not only by the images it evokes but by a whole complex
of feelings that image arouses. It's hard to express . . . . it's not a matter of vision or hearing but some over-all sense I get. Usually I experience a word's
taste and weight, and I don't have to make an effort to remember it—the
word seems to recall itself. But it's difficult to describe. What I sense is
something oily slipping through my hand . . . . or I'm aware of a slight tick-
ling in my left hand caused by a mass of tiny, light-weight points. When that
happens I simply remember, without having to make the attempt . . . .
(Luria, 1968, p. 28)

From this account, it should be evident that memory was an involuntary process for S. He had memories of infancy that most of us lose because his memory never evolved to an active mechanism for recoding
memories into words. Consequently, his vivid, amazing memory had
ramifications with respect to his higher mental processes that are more
significant for our purposes than the memory itself:

Given such a tendency, cognitive functions can hardly proceed normally. The very thought which occasions an image is soon replaced by another—to which the image itself has led; a point is thus reached at which images begin to guide one's thinking, rather than thought itself being the dominant element. (Luria, 1968, p. 116)

In other words, because each stimulus aroused multiple sensations, S. was always in a passive-receptive attitude and not able to generalize nor set goals for his thought normally. Consequently, his highly developed memory constrained him to highly concrete thinking, relying almost exclusively on images. This, Luria points out, is the type of thinking typical of young children, which is usually replaced in adolescence by a shift to dealing with abstractions and

Once we have made the transition to another level of thought, the problem of abstractions is just a memory of a painful experience we had in the past. S., though, could not make the transition . . . . (Luria, 1968, p. 133)

"On the Organization of Short-Term Memory by Modality" (1970) is an article co-authored with M. Klimovskiy that reviews experiments with patients having lesions of the left temporal region to ascertain how mode interacts with the retention and reproduction of a presented series. Various combinations were utilized of oral or written presentation and reproduction. It was their conclusion that

mere written reproduction of an orally presented series causes an appreciable rearrangement of memory mechanisms through the elimination of the abnormally strong retroactive inhibition that had completely dominated oral reproduction of a verbally presented series. (Luria & Klimovskiy, 1970, p. 261)

In "Memory Disturbances in Local Brain Lesions" (1971a) Luria delineates his organizational schema for considering memory disturbances. He notes that two explanations have been advanced for defects in memory: One attributes the defects to trace decay, or impaired storage, while the other attributes the defects to the blocking of traces by interfering stimuli, or defective retrieval. Luria's work with brain lesions causes him to give support to the second position, and he indicates that memory defects seldom occur from simple trace decay.

Luria categorizes memory disorders into general disorders which are specific with respect to modality and those which are modality nonspecific; and he presents the characteristics of each type. In addition to these general classifications, he ends the article with a review of memory disturbances resulting from frontal lobe lesions, and a consideration of those disturbances which are system-specific memory disorders:

> A special kind of memory disturbance is seen in patients with lesions in the cortical "speech area", in particular the tertiary (temporo-parietal-occipital) zones of the left hemisphere. This is concerned essentially with verbal retrieval in the ordinary course of speech. It is well-known that incoming input has to be coded, and that coding by means of language plays an essential role in memory. It is accepted, too, that a *word* is by no means a simple association of a sound complex with an image; rather is it a multidimensional matrix having its phonetic, morphological and semantic structure . . . . Only a correct word choice within such a matrix can provide a selectively organized language-system. (Luria, 1971a, p. 372)

He goes on to explain that such disturbances may not be system-based, but may have physiological bases so that, for example, any disruption of Pavlov's "rule of force" will prevent an appropriate selection in the language system from taking place.

The Neuropsychology of Memory (1976c) is a compendium of all of the work to that date done by Luria and his colleagues with respect to memory. The introduction by Karl Pribram notes that Luria's division of memory defects into the categories of modality-nonspecific and modality-specific is remarkably similar to the classifications of modality-specific and contextual that Pribram had evolved based on his primate laboratory experiments.

Luria's classification schema is the basic organizational format for the book. Part One presents case studies and experiments dealing with modality-specific disorders, while Part Two presents a detailed analysis of case studies and experiments dealing with modality-nonspecific disturbances. Because these often involve the upper brain stem area, they are frequently accompanied by disturbances of consciousness as well.

The neurological details and case studies are quite interesting, but for this book the primary interest is in Luria's presentation at the outset of Part One of current theories of the basic memory processes— remembering and forgetting. It is obvious from this discussion that human memory for Luria is an active, conscious process rather than merely the passive reception and retention of stimuli. Initially, he sees the process of memory as being an extension of perception. It operates on simple sensory cues, combining them into more complex forms. The next step is a coding or an

> incorporation into a system of conceptual connections. It is through this coding that the transition takes place from rapid, short-term memory with its restricted possibilities into long-term memory, with a wider scope, that must be understood psychologically as a complex cognitive process performed at a high level and comprising a series of logical operations.

The existence of this complex process of coding of material, which many workers regard as the basic characteristic of human memory, is particularly apparent during the investigation of the remembering of nonsense syllables or words. Remembering can be regarded as a gradual process resting on a multidimensional system of connections incorporating elementary (sensory) and more complex (perceptual) and, finally, the most complex (cognitive) components. (Luria, 1976c, p. 4)

A. R. Luria goes on to explain that because a word incorporates this multidimensional system within itself, the imprinting of a word always includes "a process of selection of the dominant system of connections and inhibition of the rest" (Luria, 1976c, p. 4). Consequently,

the word potentially conceals many connections evokable on different bases, and that only under normal conditions can the semantic system of codes, in which the word is incorporated, dispel all the other, more elementary connections. If this fact of the multidimensional connections inherent in the word is of decisive importance for its imprinting, or "coding," it remains just as important for its recalling. (Luria, 1976c, p. 7)

Having reviewed the previously cited explanations for forgetting, Luria reiterates his position that forgetting normally occurs because of defective retrieval due to the blocking of traces by interfering stimuli. In support of this, he cites the common finding that learning a similar series of words can block remembrance of the first series of words one learned, while learning a series from a different system, i.e., a numerical series, will have no effect on recall of the originally learned series of words.

Memory is conceived by Luria to be an active, complex process that involves different portions of the brain working together while each makes unique contributions to the whole process of memory.

"Interhemispheric Relations and the Functions of the Minor Hemisphere" (1977) was co-authored with E. G. Simernitskaya and reports the results of experiments with three matched groups: normal adults, patients with left hemisphere lesions of the temporoparietal region, and patients with comparable lesions of the right hemisphere.

The authors conclude from their experiments that both hemispheres are involved in the memorization of verbal materials, but that perhaps they are responsible for different levels of the psychological process of memory. More specifically, they state that "Active or intentional memorizing is more affected by left and passive or incidental memorizing by right hemisphere lesions" (Luria & Simernitskaya, 1977, p. 177).

"Syndromes of Mnemonic Disorders Accompanying Diencephalic Tumors" (1978) was written in conjunction with N. K. Kiyashchenko, L. I. Moskovichyute, To. O. Faller, and N. A. Fillippycheva and was originally published in Russian in 1973, so its content predates *The Neuro-psychology of Memory* (1976c). The article reports on studies of forty-eight patients with focal lesions of the diencephalic region or upper part of the brain stem, and notes that the resultant memory disturbances are not specific with respect to any modality. In addition, they appear in conjunction with general disturbances of the level of consciousness as a result of neurophysiological depression of the activating system of the brain stem.

HIGHER MENTAL PROCESSES AND MEMORY

Throughout his writing, Luria (1976c) argues that memory is not merely a reflex, but can also achieve existence as a higher mental process. Consequently, for Luria, there are two levels of memory functioning: memory that consists of active, intentional memorization and recall is a higher mental process, while memory that is comprised of incidental, involuntary memorization and recall is a lower, more elementary process.

Similar to the development of voluntary behavior, auxiliary stimuli have a role in the transformation of memory from a passive, elementary process to a volitional, higher mental process. How auxiliary stimuli alter the functioning of memory is clearly delineated in Luria's studies of children given memory tasks (Luria, 1928a, pp. 503–504). Asked to recall a list of words that had been read to them, children relying on natural, passive memory could remember only five or six words at most. Those using nonisomorphic pictures that they mentally associated in some way with each word could reproduce 25 to 30 or more words after listening to one reading. Making use of such an active mediation by auxiliary stimuli, Luria found a 60% increase in memory production in children of 10 to 12 years of age.

Based on these studies of memory in children of various ages, Luria postulates three developmental stages with respect to the usage of auxiliary stimuli: (1) The pre-instrumental phase in which the child is incapable of associating the task with an auxiliary means such as cards or pictures; (2) The pseudo-instrumental phase in which the child attempts to use the auxiliary stimuli, but assumes they have some inherent magic rather than viewing them as an aid in his/her own mental association of aid and referent; and (3) The real instrumental phase in which the child is able to solve memory tasks by the active use of auxiliary stimuli to form conscious, selected mental associations between aid and referent. With the attainment of stage three, the child's memory has been transformed from passive, sensory imprinting to a conscious, voluntary process.

Intentional memory constitutes higher functioning because it must be understood as an active process. This is manifested in the fact that man actively processes incoming information and does not simply imprint traces of stimuli received by him, but codes this information, chooses its essential features and incorporates it into a definite system, into a certain "subjective organization" (Feigenbaum, 1970; Reitman, 1970; Shiffrin, 1970). In some cases, moreover, man makes a special task of remembering or recalling the corresponding material, which converts the process of unpremeditated passive imprinting into an active form (Leont'ev, 1959; Smirnov, 1948, 1966; and others) and it confers on memory its selective and specifically human character. (Luria, 1976c, p. 14)

This active reorganization of both external and internal stimuli typifies the voluntary nature of higher mental processes.

This type of active reorganization of stimuli was impossible for S. with his visual and synesthetic memory (Luria, 1968). It was S.'s tragedy that his prodigious memory was in a sense a case of arrested development. He was never capable of inhibiting the dominant sensory and perceptual associations in his mind so that he could make selective connections on the conceptual level, and thus gain control of his own memory.

Throughout his theory, Luria holds that one higher mental process can be a component in the complex functional system constituting another higher mental process thereby augmenting the complexity of the latter. In the case of S., however, the interdependency of systems became a negative factor because the limitations of one system (memory) constrained the capacities of another system (logical thought) so that he

was unable to grasp an idea unless he could actually see it, and so he tried to visualize the idea of "nothing," to find an image with which to depict "infinity." And he persisted in these agonizing attempts all his life, forever coping with a basically adolescent conflict that made it impossible for him to cross that "accursed" threshold to a higher level of thought. (Luria, 1968, p. 133)

Intentional memory arises from a material base as do other higher mental processes. This base consists of

a complex system of different parts of the brain, working together and each making its own contribution to the activity as a whole.

Those facts [research evidence from physiology and neuropsychology] suggest that the hippocampal structures are responsible for the elementary comparison of actual stimuli with traces of previous experience. The gnostic and speech areas of the cortex are concerned with the analysis and coding of incoming information and establishing the essential conditions for the organization of the material to be memorized. The anterior (frontal) areas of the cortex perform completely different roles in this system, since they provide

for maintenance of the plan, the programming of behavior, and the performance of active, selective mnestic activity. (Luria, 1976c, p. 15)

That higher mental processes must build on a functional base of the
more elementary sensory systems of the brain is supported by the physiologically verified fact that gross memory disorders produced by tumors in
the diencephalon are highly correlated with neurophysiological depression of the activating system of the brain stem (Luria, Kiyaschenko,
Moskovichyute, Faller, & Fillippycheva, 1978). In other words, the level
of wakefulness or alertness in the patient maintained via the brain stem
affected the level of memory dysfunction.

Further evidence that different cortical systems underlie different
mental processes is provided by the experiments of Luria and
Simernitskaya (1977), which indicated that although both hemispheres of
the brain participate in the processes of memory, it appears that voluntary
memory results primarily from activities of the left hemisphere, while
involuntary memory is associated with the activities of the right
hemisphere.

SPOKEN LANGUAGE AND MEMORY

The selective recoding of stimuli that characterizes memory as a higher
mental process is accomplished primarily by means of language. As noted
earlier, mental associations engendered by the word constitute a multidimensional matrix including phonetic, morphological, and semantic connections with the latter dominating in normal, healthy individuals. Thus,
the word is the means by which the coding aspect of memory can shift
from the combination of simple sensory cues to the incorporation of such
cues into a system of conceptual connections. This change in coding
makes possible the move from rapid, short-term memory to the wider
scope of long-term memory. Organization into a definite semantic system
limits the inhibiting effect of irrelevant stimuli, and explains why recall is
impaired more by the learning of homogeneous material than by the
learning of heterogeneous material.

Similarly, recall or decoding is not a passive process, and should be
understood

as a complex process of active searching. It is thus seen as a special form of
cognitive activity. A person who has to recall a series of words read out to
him must first choose the necessary connection or necessary component
from among a large number of possible alternatives, inhibit the outpouring
of random, irrelevant components, and pick out the essential ones.
This process of active selection of the required trace is similar in its struc-

ture to the process of "decoding" of a complex text and it consists of a conflict between different (sensory, figurative, and conceptual) connections
and cues incorporated into the multidimensional system, from which only
the one essential connection must be chosen. (Luria, 1976c, p. 5)

It was, no doubt, because of the hierarchy of connections made possible
by the word that Luria thought that breakdowns in mnemonic processes
could most easily be examined by looking at verbal memory and the disturbances of the same that resulted from different brain lesions.

The significant role of the speech system in the functioning of active
memory as well as the dependence of such functioning on the cortical base
of speech is clarified in Luria's discussion of memory and lesions of the
cortical speech areas:

> The numerous observations published in the world literature, commencing
> with the classical work of Goldstein and his collaborators, Head, Isserlin,
> and others, and including my own investigations . . . suggest that the process
> of coding incoming information into certain logical-grammatical and se-
> mantic systems, without which it would be difficult to imagine how traces of
> short-term memory can be converted into long-term, requires the participa-
> tion of the parietal-temporal (speech) areas of the cortex in memory pro-
> cesses. Naturally, their role in the organization of mnemonic processes is
> quite different from the role of the hippocampus and the modality-specific,
> gnostic zones of the cortex.
>   The cortical speech areas, through which speech participates in the pro-
> cessing of information, make an important contribution to the organization
> of individual special impressions into whole, differentiated systems or, in
> other words, they participate directly in the conversion of isolated, fraction-
> al actions into enlarged, organized structure. A lesion of the cortical speech
> zones is bound to be reflected on [sic] the ability to retain discrete material.
> For that reason . . . a lesion of the speech zones and a disturbance of the or-
> ganization of incoming information with the aid of the semantic system of
> language must inevitably lead to substantial disturbances of memory . . . .
> the disturbances are system-specific and not modality-specific in character
> . . . . (Luria, 1976c, p. 13)

The semantic component of spoken language that aids memory includes both "sense," which is the subjective meaning or connotation, and
"meaning," which is the culturally engendered meaning or denotation.
The case study of S. in this topical area provides an example of the sense
of confusion that results when "sense" and "meaning" are not compatible.
S. explains:

> Take for example, the word *ekipazh* . . . . This definitely has to be a cab. So
> how am I to understand right off that it can also mean the crew of a ship? I

have to perform quite an operation in my head, to block details that come to mind, if I'm to understand this. What I have to do is to picture to myself not just a driver or a footman in the cab but an entire staff manning it. That's the only way I can make sense of it. (Luria, 1968, pp. 118–119)

The word, of course, is a Russian word meaning both "cab" and a "ship's crew." That was the "meaning" of the word, however, S. with his visually dominated memory could not make his "sense" of the word fit without great difficulty. Less severe discrepancies between "sense" and "meaning" give rise to those misunderstandings that are frequently labeled communication breakdowns.

5 Cognitive Development

"The Problem of the Cultural Behavior of the Child" (1928a) takes the position that the maturation of natural inborn processes is an inadequate explanation of mental development, since it does not take the influence of the environment into consideration. This stance continued to prevail throughout the decades of Luria's work on cognitive development in the child.

Based both on observations of children and his reading of Kohler's experiments with apes, Luria concludes that children have

> the same dependence of primary intellectual operations on the outer form of the object, and we can suppose that it is precisely the conception of form which predetermines the success of the intellectual activity at the primary stages of development. (Luria, 1928a, p. 496)

Yet, his real interest was the point at which this natural law of form yielded to culturally engendered forms, because he announces that the task of modern psychology is "to consider the *psycho-genesis of the cultural forms of the child's behavior*" (Luria, 1928a, p. 494).

Luria reports the design and outcomes of experiments with preschool and school-age children on memory tasks, and indicates that

> the difference between the intellectual operations of a preschool child and a schoolboy is not of a purely quantitative kind, that the schoolboy is armed differently from a preschool child in point of quality, that the structure of his processes is essentially different. (Luria, 1928a, p. 501)

As noted in our discussion of "Higher Mental Processes and Memory," this qualitative difference in intellectual operations is achieved in three

59

stages: The first is the "pre-instrumental" stage during which the child is incapable of utilizing auxiliary means to aid his memory. During the second or "pseudo-instrumental" stage, he expects the auxiliary aid to assist through a magic inherent in it; and finally, in the "real instrumental" stage of development, the child is able to establish a rational connection between the task and the auxiliary aid and thereby augments his memory.

Ten representatives from the USSR attended the Ninth International Congress of Psychology that convened at Yale University, September 1–7, 1929. Included in that number was Luria, who gave a presentation of the paper he co-authored with Vygotsky entitled "The Function and Fate of Egocentric Speech" (1930). They indicated that the stage of childhood speech that Piaget termed "egocentric" does not merely accompany behavior but rather has an organizing function. In addition, rather than simply disappearing as it is replaced by more socialized verbal behavior, Luria and Vygotsky stated that

> On the strength of our experiments we consider it possible to change the traditional schema of the verbal evolution of explicit speech, viz., external speech—internal speech, into external speech—egocentric speech—internal speech. We thus consider egocentric speech as one of the most important processes having a specific function in the evolution of the cultural behavior of the child. (Vygotsky & Luria, 1930, p. 465)

In 1931, Luria organized and directed an expedition to Uzbekistan to study

> the variations in thought and other psychological processes of people living in a very primitive economic and social environment, and to record those changes which develop as a result of the introduction of higher and more complex forms of economic life and the raising of the general cultural level. (Luria, 1931, p. 383)

The names of participants in the expedition and a brief outline of their various studies were reported in the "Scientific Notes and News" section of *Science* under the title "Psychological Expedition to Central Asia" (1931), and ended with an invitation to foreign psychologists to participate in the next expedition the following year.

The second expedition was reported in *Science* in a format similar to the first under the title "The Second Psychological Expedition to Central Asia" (1933). The studies were expanded to include youths as well as adults; and having accepted Luria's invitation, one of the participants was Kurt Koffka of Smith College.

Luria noted that the first expedition's research had

shown that in the primitive community life one finds a specific system of thinking which is characterized by its own structure and by a different role which speech takes in it. A fact was noted that the main function of this thinking is not the formation of abstract connection and relationship between symbols, but reproduction of whole situations, whole complexes closely connected with specific life experiences; ... (Luria, 1933, p. 192)

After outlining which official institutes and/or academic departments were to be involved in the planned future research, Luria indicated that detailed accounts of the studies of both expeditions were being prepared for publication and should be published the following year. Political considerations intervened, however, because the participation of such traditional peasants in the nationwide collectivized agricultural campaign was tenuous. Luria had stressed the benefits of this campaign to the people, but critics of his preliminary findings were quick to point out that his results could be construed as an insult to the uneducated peasants and might impact on their participation. Consequently, Luria's account of these studies was not published until some 40 years after they were done.

Attempting to isolate the roles of heredity and environment in the mental development of children, Luria and Vygotsky together with their colleagues undertook a series of experiments with identical and fraternal twins on some types of memory. The studies are reported in "The Development of Mental Functions in Twins" (1936–1937), which appeared in *Character and Personality.*

Also in this article, Luria delineates the role of speech in the development of higher mental processes more clearly than he had in the earlier writings:

The higher psychological functions are developed by social contact, and in the first place by the intercourse of the child with adults. The first function developed in this process is speech, which is the main factor rendering these relations indirect; through speech the relations between mental functions are changed, and new forms of activity of the human mind are thus created. A good example is the development of discursive, verbal thinking, in which speech activity, formerly a process of intercourse between human beings, becomes an inner dialogue, and, in fact, a form of organization of thought processes. (Luria, 1936–1937, p. 36)

However, the central focus of the article is on the question of whether the ratio of heredity to environmental influence on mental functioning is a stable one or if it changes throughout developmental stages. Based on the intra-pair differences revealed by their various experiments, Luria concludes that the ratio changes during development and that those complex psychological processes which form the basis of higher mental functions are largely determined by non-genetic factors . . . . there is a group of psychological functions which in the course of development undergo changes in their relation to the genotype. Their development sets in when the elementary mental processes (geno-typically conditioned to a high degree) are transformed into complex, socially conditioned functions.

We have grounds for assuming that these functions include not only memory functions, but that all higher mental functions are of a similar origin. We believe that we have described a special process of development which enables us to understand the growth of the complex forms of psychological activity. (Luria, 1936–1937, pp. 46–47)

"The Role of Language in the Formation of Temporary Connections" (1957b) was published in Russian in 1955 and reflects the Pavlovian terminology that was almost mandatory in Soviet psychological articles of that period.

Noting that the word can replace either conditioned stimuli or unconditioned reinforcement, Luria calls on the field of psychology to investigate the role of language in the formation of human temporary cortical connections—the links or associations made mentally between objects, events, or actions. Then, following his own mandate, A. R. Luria begins his discussion by stating that speech is

one of the essential means whereby the child finds his bearings in the external world; it activizes the generalized connections formed in past experience, which play a substantial part in the mediated, specifically human, form of regulation of action. (Luria, 1957b, p. 116)

Reviewing the progression of external speech to egocentric speech to inner speech, Luria suggests that there are similar developmental stages in the formulation of temporary connections. Initially, speech plays no role and the child utilizes practical action to form new connections directly; then action is followed by external speech; and finally, changing positions, inner speech leads action and becomes the main mechanism for the formation of new mental connections. This now permits "consciousness" in the Lurian sense, and he states that "It is this regulation by the verbal system of direct actions that comprises the real basis of conscious behaviour" (Luria, 1957b, p. 118).

Having presented the integral role of speech in the formation of new connections in humans, Luria then contrasts the formation of connections in animals with the same process in humans. In animals, it is a very gradual, difficult process and the results are inflexible and unstable, requiring frequent reinforcement. In contrast, connections formed in humans via the verbal system are immediate, yet they are stable, easily altered, and serve as their own reinforcement.

Luria concludes by stating that

> All these data show that the introduction of speech—which analyses and synthesizes the given signals, and transforms the process of developing new connections into a process, mediated through words, of forming generalized systems of connections—changes certain important rules governing the development, preservation and remoulding of connections; it gives to this process the character of conscious activity. (Luria, 1957b, p. 123)

Prefacing a section on the effects of brain pathologies on the formation of temporary connections, Luria presents the hypothesis that a disturbance of the role of language's abstracting and generalizing functions with the resultant decrement in its role in the formulation of temporary connections "is one of the principal features of pathological changes in man's higher nervous activity" (Luria, 1957b, p. 124).

The "Dynamic Approach to the Mental Development of the Abnormal Child" (1958a) is a vigorous indictment of child psychiatry's past tendency to attribute anomalous development to a deficiency of inborn mental abilities. He notes that

> Such assertions would hardly differ much from the judgments of Molierè's physician who regarded the soporific action of opium as a result of its inherent "soporific force" and explained derangements in speech by the fact that the patient's tongue does not move properly. (Luria, 1958a, p. 40)

Instead, Luria calls for a causal-dynamic approach to diagnosing and treating the abnormal child:

> *The effect produced by an early disturbance of a certain function depends primarily on the role played by this function in the general mental development of the child,* as well as on *the period of development during which the given disturbance occurred.* Therefore, as stated by L. S. Vygotsky, one and the same localization of a lesion may evoke quite different consequences, depending on whether the lesion occurred in early childhood or at a mature age. (Luria, 1958a, p. 41)

Following this assertion, various case studies are presented in support of his approach and as an illustration of its application.

Such an approach, Luria argues, leads to a more accurate diagnosis than any mere listing of symptoms. In evidence, he cites Kurt Goldstein's postulate of some thirty years prior, that in analyzing any syndrome one must first of all attempt to discover the basic, causal disturbance that gives rise to the secondary symptoms rather than confining oneself to describing the secondary symptoms only. Additionally, Luria notes that his approach will also result in more practical outcomes:

> the causal-dynamic analysis of the abnormal child aimed at disclosing its primary defect and deducing from it the secondary systemic consequences, simultaneously enables us to find adequate means of compensating this defect, and in the case of adults also adequate ways of corrective training. (Luria, 1958a, p. 51)

"Experimental Study of the Higher Nervous Activity of the Abnormal Child" (1959d) is a follow-up article also published in the *Journal of Mental Deficiency Research*. In it, Luria notes that an analysis of the basic physiological properties of the nervous processes—their strength, equilibrium, and mobility—is sufficient to explain peculiarities in mental functioning in animals, but is inadequate to explain similar malfunctions in humans.

> The behaviour of man . . . . is at the same time a *conscious* and *voluntary* nature. This, first of all, means that a human being responds with this or other action to the *verbal instructions* of the people with whom he is associated; he orients himself in the surrounding reality with the help of language through which he systematizes his impressions, realizes his own actions, and, what is particularly important, subordinates his behaviour to verbally formulated intentions. Along with the system of direct signals of reality, man is constantly influenced by language and speech. (Luria, 1959d, p. 4)

For these reasons, in addition to the physiological characteristics of the higher mental processes of humans, one must

> also specially ascertain the specific features which characterize the dynamics of his speech processes (or processes developing at the level of the second signalling system) and, above all, establish *to what extent these speech processes organize the course of his more elementary reaction,* and to what degree the *connections of his second signalling system are able to regulate the acts of his behaviour.*
> Precisely this *physiological characteristic of the processes of regulation of behaviour,* or, in a broader sense, the interaction of the two signalling systems, will serve us as a fundamental indicator in the study of the normal and pathologically modified behaviour of the child. Therein we expect to find the basic "units" which will allow us to make a proper step towards a more precise qualification of various forms of abnormal development. (Luria, 1959d, p. 4)

Using the recording of motor reactions to verbal instructions while si-

lent and when accompanied by the child's own speech, Luria then proceeds to report on experiments with cerebroasthenic children and oligophrenic children. He concludes that the research is valuable because it delineates features of higher mental processes in such children that are not
available by other means, and also because "it enabled us to facilitate the
differential diagnosis between oligophrenics and the cerebroasthenic syndrome, which in children often present considerable difficulties" (Luria,
1959d, p. 22).

Speech and the Development of Mental Processes in the Child (1959) is a
book-length work co-authored with F. Ia. Yudovich relating the authors'
work during the 1930s with identical twin boys, Lura and Liosha, who
combined a complex phonetic impairment with the idiosyncratic speech
of the "twin situation."

The book is comprised of eight chapters: the first four present the
twin's performance levels prior to the experiment, and the underlying rationale for the experimental design; the remaining four delineate the
treatment, the outcomes, and the authors' conclusions.

The treatment was basically special language training, and the authors
found that the acquisition of spoken language transformed all the twin's
activities. Prior to the experiment, their play activities had been similar to
those of any young animal—constrained by the immediate stimuli of vision and direct action. Occasionally, conditional meanings might be at-
tached to objects, but these were never integrated into a system, nor maintained throughout an episode of play activity, and any extraneous
stimulus could change such a meaning abruptly. Consequently, the twins
were generally excluded from the play of other children in their age group
(5 years) because organized, objective-oriented play was as impossible for
them as abstraction and generalization. This changed attendant with
their acquisition of spoken language.

A. R. Luria considered their most important finding to be the fact that
the development of spoken language totally reorganized the children's behavior. Given the short time span of the experiment (approximately one
year), he also thought that their results disproved the theory that higher
mental activity results from simply a process of physical maturation
alone.

"An Objective Approach to the Study of the Abnormal Child" (1961c)
is the text of a speech Luria gave to the 38th Annual Meeting of the American Orthopsychiatric Association in New York in March, 1961. The
speech is an indictment of psychometric tests which, according to Luria,
should be used for primary orientation only. He notes that there are four
groups of children who fail in school: (1) the educationally backward, (2)
the feebleminded, (3) the asthenic children, and (4) children with partial
defects. Yet, all may test as having an IQ of 70, which is of no value in

differentiating between the children nor in an analysis of their potential development.

Introducing Vygotsky's concept of the "zone of proximal development," which in this article Luria refers to as the "zone of potential development," Luria indicates how this approach of comparing results of tests when the child is working independently, when he is receiving assistance, and again when he works independently after having received assistance gives the psychologist a much more dynamic picture of the mental functioning and capabilities of the anomalous child.

Luria then goes on to outline current physiological evaluative techniques that measure the orienting reflexes—"depression of alpha—rhythm in the EEG, galvanic skin response, constriction of blood vessels, etc." (Luria, 1961c, p. 8); and that are then utilized to determine if the child's problem is one of hearing, active attention, or understanding.

The speech ends with a call for international cooperation in order to provide the abnormal child with every opportunity for reaching his maximum level of development.

"Speech Development and the Formation of Mental Processes" (1961d) in *Psychological Science in the USSR, Volume I* was published by the U.S. Joint Publications Research Service and is the only translated article that seems to be a product of careless editing. Phrases are repeated needlessly, and the syntax is often awkward. Even so, this is a valuable article because in it Luria selectively reviews the results of all Soviet psychology from the Revolution to the date of the article.

Reviewing the major guidelines of Soviet psychology, Luria notes that consciousness is considered the highest form of mental activity; consequently, it is the principal subject for research while the unconscious occupies a very subordinate role in the Soviet schema.

Two methodological mandates exist for the study of conscious higher mental processes: objective methods must be utilized, and the research must occur in "natural" conditions. In addition, the unity of theory and practice is a cardinal principle, so the correctness of research outcomes are evaluated in practice. This explains why pedagogical psychology is one of the most important areas of study for the Soviets.

It was during the second decade of Soviet psychology that

the speech problem was introduced in a considerably wider channel of thinking and the study of speech, its development and its roles in the formation of mental processes turned into the principal chapter of Soviet psychology, which has decisive significance for the study of the formation of all human cognitive activity. (Luria, 1961d, p. 710)

Because the two central concerns with respect to speech are the stages of its development as a complex activity in itself, and how speech functions in the formation of higher mental processes, Luria then discusses the stages of each in detail.

The discussion is too lengthy to repeat totally, but one aspect of interest for our purposes concerns the developmental stages of the generalization function of the semantic content of the word. Initially, the word has no major role and generalizations are the product of immediate impressions. This is situational generalization, and it is

> accomplished by the leading role of visual connections of a previous experience and in essence is the operation of reproduction of these actual relations with which the child has dealt with previously; the effective memory fills with concrete content the semantic structure of speech and determines the nature of the operations accessible to the child. Finally, this higher form of generalization, which thinking represents in ideas, proves to be a psychological process accomplished with the leading role of complex and specific connections for the word which abstract the necessary aspect and unite the objects of the external world on the basis of this complex mediated operation. In L. S. Vygotsky's account the development of thinking ceases to be considered as the mastery of well-known logical operations; it acquires its own complex psychological content. The semantic development of speech becomes, at the same time, a *system development*. The study of the change of forms of thinking, which in each stage reflects objective activity with varying depth and in different, deeper connections and relations, is converted into the study *of semantic and systemic structure and consciousness*. (Luria, 1961d, pp. 725–726)

Because each word preserves in itself all the systems of connections that were gradually incorporated into its current complexity, one can examine the dynamics of semantic connections in the same subject during conditions of fatigue, stress, etc. As evidence of this, Luria cites studies done by colleagues in which, under conditions of pharmacological intervention, they found more elementary sound connections emerged, rather than the semantic connections that dominated in the normal, healthy adult subject.

Despite the importance of the word, Luria states that the basic unit of speech is the connected utterance, a subject-predicate association, rather than one of the object and name, or nominative association, which is a later development. This dependence on the situation for the predicate, or some aspect of the meaning of the utterance, is what was referred to in Chapter 1 as the "sympractic" aspect of oral speech, and Luria suggests that spoken language continues to retain some sympractic aspects, even after the individual has acquired written speech, which requires the total elimination of such aspects in its effective production.

The organizing role of the verbal system makes it possible to use it to compensate for some defects in nervous activity, and Luria recounts such cases in concluding the article.

The Mentally Retarded Child: Essays Based on a Study of the Peculiarities of the Higher Nervous Functioning of Child-Oligophrenics (1963a) is a book-length work edited by Luria. He is sole author of three chapters, and co-author of two of the book's remaining five chapters. The book was written to assist those who are involved in the problem of training, educating or treating mentally retarded children.

The chapter of most interest relative to the focus of this book is entitled "The Role of Speech in the Formation of Temporary Connections in the Regulation of the Behaviour of Child-Oligophrenics," written by Luria. In it he notes that

> The inability to make use of knowledge obtained in the course of speech communication, the inability to assimilate speech instructions in a generalized form, and the inability to use speech as a means of independent thinking, are characteristic of mentally retarded feeble-minded children. Evidently these features constitute one of their basic characteristics. (Luria, 1963a, p. 159)

In the chapter entitled "Peculiarities of Verbal Association in Child-Oligophrenics," which Luria co-authored with A. I. Meshcheryakov, they suggest that since the abstract level of thinking engendered by the speech system is usually beyond the abilities of the anomalous child, one should attempt to use the spatial relationships of the stage of concrete thinking to assist the retarded child, since it is closer to his level of development.

In the concluding chapter, Luria notes that the semantic associations of the retarded child are more primitive and less stable than those of the normal child and that

> speech processes play a much smaller role in the organization of the activity of the mentally retarded child than that of his normal peer; his actions more easily cease to be mediated by verbal connections, escape from verbal control, and assume a spontaneous impulsive character. (Luria, 1963a, p. 196)

"The Variability of Mental Functions as the Child Develops (Based on a Comparative Study of Twins)" (Luria, 1963d) is a presentation of data collected by Luria when he was at the Institute of Medical Genetics about 25 years before. The studies were done with fraternal and identical twins and led to the conclusion that the relationship of various types of memory to genotypic characteristics changes during development.

Luria uses this data to conclude that psychometric tests do not measure naive intelligence, but rather psychological characteristics that change with the child's social and mental development:

> *It has now become generally accepted that a profound qualitative reorganiza-*
> *tion of the psychological activity of man occurs in the process of mental devel-*
> *opment,* and that the principal feature of this reorganization resolves itself
> to the fact that *elementary direct forms of activity are replaced by complexly*
> *organized functional systems* shaped on the basis of association of the child
> with adults in the course of the child's education. These functional systems
> are complex in structure and are implemented with the direct participation
> of language. As language is, to begin with, the major means of human inter-
> course, it has at the same time become one of the principal tools for shaping
> man's mental activity and regulation of his behavior. It is specifically as a
> consequence of this that complex forms of psychological activity, which are
> gradually implemented with the participation of the second signal system,
> acquire new characteristics and begin to function in accordance with new
> laws that replace many of the rules followed in the elaboration of the ele-
> mentary conditioned reflexes of animals . . . . (Luria, 1963d, p. 18)

The quote also clarifies the role of language in mental development for
Luria, and this is examined in more detail in the section of this chapter on
"Spoken Language and Cognitive Development."

"Speech Development and the Formation of Mental Processes" (Luria,
1969c) appears in *A Handbook of Contemporary Soviet Psychology,* edited
by Michael Cole and Irving Maltzman. The article, as its title suggests, focuses more directly on the role of speech than any of the articles or books
previously reviewed, and progresses from a consideration of "The Earliest
Forms of Speech" through "Complex Functional Systems Mediated by
Speech: Voluntary Attention."

In the section "Concept Formation and Semantic Systems," Luria provides a clear portrayal of the interaction between speech and concept formation:

> In the earliest states of development, grouping geometric figures into one
> whole designated by a single word is very difficult. In response to this task
> the child simply selects all figures which fall within his gaze, uniting into one
> conglomerate set all those blocks which he sees. The word still does not play
> the role of a unifying sign, and grouping does not continue beyond the limit
> of this random, syncretic approach to objects . . . . Such syncretism without
> preliminary orientation to attributes and without preliminary analysis con-
> stitutes the earliest stage of thinking, in which the word does not play a
> substantial role but is subordinated to the influence of immediate impres-
> sions . . . .
>   . . . there follows a second stage which has a distinct and internally regu-
> lar structure. Attempting to select all objects which are designated by one ar-
> tificial word, the child makes a preliminary analysis of the group of objects

placed before him and singles out certain attributes. However, this signal attribute is far from obligatory and may change for trial to trial . . . . The conditional designation in no way resembles the original concept at this stage;
rather it resembles a family name.

Only in the next stage, which is formed under the influence of systematic
training, is there substantial change. The word, changing its structure, is
given a new, important meaning in the execution of the task. In this stage
which, according to Vygotskii, is attained only during adolescence, the word
becomes freed from the influence of direct impressions. It abstracts now
one, now another attribute and synthesizes them into a complex of attributes. The process of classification acquires a complex character mediated
by the word. The selection of each figure is determined not by direct impression, but by a stable preserved system of attributes abstracted with the aid of
the word and shared by the objects selected in the required group. Generalizations underlying the word lose their concrete character. A system of abstract meanings becomes the guiding criterion for further intellectual operations. The word becomes the basic instrument of thinking, and thinking
acquires a mediated character. (Luria, 1969c, pp. 134–135)

A similar developmental stage delineation is presented for voluntary
attention, perception, and regulation of behavior as they interact with
speech. In addition, in this article Luria explains that the speech system
that shapes higher mental processes has two components that differ in origin, structure, and function. Those components are speech or spoken language and what Luria terms *written speech*. A consideration of the differences in these components was presented in Chapter 1.

"A Child's Speech Responses and the Social Environment" (Luria,
1974b) is based on research that Luria had done in the 1930s on the role of
the social environment in shaping the intellect of rural, urban, and homeless children. Luria states that social conditions have a very significant
role in forming the child's speech, and because speech in turn is involved
in all of the child's intellectual experience one can thus by examining the
speech also examine the influence of the social environment on the
intellect.

Noting that "Speech may fulfill its communicative functions quite adequately, yet be poorly suited for complex intellectual activity" (Luria,
1974b, p. 47), Luria goes on to indicate that the streetchild is not more
stupid than the schoolchild, but merely different because he or she has not
yet learned to reason formally.

Maintaining that speech is the most readily influenced of the psychological processes, Luria indicates that the pedagogical implications of his
research are that one must vary one's teaching according to the different
levels of socialization engendered by different social environments.

"Speech and Intellect Among Rural, Urban, and Homeless Children.

An Empirical Study Edited by A. R. Luria: Foreword" (1974c) is, just as
the title indicates, a brief foreword introducing the previously reviewed
article and giving some background on the studies before they were published in *Soviet Psychology.*"

Cognitive Development: Its Cultural and Social Foundations (Luria,
1976b) is a presentation of the data that had been collected in 1931 and
1932 during the expeditions to central Asia. In the "Foreword," Michael
Cole notes that Luria's

> general purpose was to show the sociohistorical roots of all basic cognitive
> processes; the structure of thought depends upon the structure of the domi-
> nant types of activity in different cultures. From this set of assumptions, it
> follows that practical thinking will predominate in societies that are charac-
> terized by practical manipulations of objects, and more "abstract" forms of
> "theoretical" activity in technological societies will induce more abstract,
> theoretical thinking. (From the Foreword, by Cole, in Luria, 1976b, pp. xiv–
> xv)

A. R. Luria's ingenious data-gathering interviews result in chapters on
"Perception," "Generalization and Abstraction," "Deduction and Infer-
ence," "Reasoning and Problem-Solving," "Imagination," and "Self-
Analysis and Self-Awareness." In the "Conclusion" chapter, Luria presents a succinct summary of the results that were obtained. Essentially,
they were that illiterate people are characterized by concrete, situational
thinking. Such thinking is necessitated by the fact that the speech system
of an oral culture is constrained to always include the sympractic dimension of spoken language in its mental connections.

"The Development of Writing in the Child" (Luria, 1978b) was originally published by the Academy of Communist Education in Russia in
1929. In it, Luria presents the developmental stages of writing based on
his observations of children learning to write:

> in the first state, writing is for him not a means of recording some specific
> content, but a self-contained process involving imitation of an adult activity
> but having no functional significance in itself. This phase is characterized
> by undifferentiated scribblings; the child records any idea with exactly the
> same scrawls. Later ... differentiation begins: the symbols acquire a func-
> tional significance and begin graphically to reflect the content the child is to
> write down.
>   At this stage, the child begins to learn how to read: he knows individual
> letters, and he knows that these letters record some content; finally, he
> learns their outward forms and how to make particular marks. But does this
> mean that he now understands the full mechanics of their use? ... we are
> convinced that an understanding of the mechanisms of writing takes place

much later than the outward mastery of writing, and that in the first stages of acquiring this mastery the child's relation to writing is purely external. . . . Believing completely in this new technique, in the first stage of development of symbolic alphabetic writing the child begins with a stage of undifferentiated writing he had already passed through long before. (Luria, 1978b, pp. 186–187)

"Paths of Development of Thought in the Child" (Luria, 1978e) is an article that originally appeared in Russian in 1929, but was not translated until it appeared in Michael Cole's *The Selected Writings of A. R. Luria.* The article is early Luria, but still valuable for the insight it provides into the origins of later, more sophisticated Lurian theory.

Having examined the parallels between the instinctive, rigid behavior of animals and that of the young child, Luria progresses to an examination of primitive thought and presents a interesting concept—transductive logic, which Luria notes originated as a term with Stern, and was then applied to the concept by Piaget and Claparede, who were Luria's sources.

In transductive logic, the child draws conclusions directly from a perceived event without an awareness of his reactions. The conclusions require no verification because the child is totally oblivious to any contradictions to his conclusions. It will not, according to Luria, truly become logical thought until the child is socialized.

"Experimental Psychology and Child Development" (Luria, 1978c) originally appeared in Russian in 1930, and is based on research Luria did at the Krupskaya Academy of Communist Upbringing. The article reports on the results of cleverly designed experiments undertaken to determine when the child first perceives form or structure; and the author then proceeds to an examination of how this elementary skill underlies the development of the cultural abilities of counting and writing.

"The Development of Constructive Activity in the Preschool Child" (1978a) appeared originally in Russian in 1948, and deals with whether or not play activity can be utilized to augment cognitive development. The subjects utilized were monozygotic twins so that the factor of heredity would not be an issue, and Luria found that the training in constructive activity "did indeed held to develop . . . ability to discriminate voluntarily a figure in a uniform field . . . " (Luria, 1978a, p. 218), as well as result in an improvement in the ability to perceive geometric relationships.

HIGHER MENTAL PROCESSES AND COGNITIVE DEVELOPMENT

In this topical area, Luria takes care to clarify that the fact that higher mental processes arise from and are dependent upon the elementary physiological functioning of their cortical base does not also mean that a physical explanation alone is sufficient to understand their function-ing:

> The characteristic properties of the basic nervous processes—their strength, equilibrium and mobility—as well as changes which take place under pathological states, are quite sufficient to qualify the peculiarities of the higher nervous activity in animals, but they are by no means sufficient to qualify the peculiarities of the higher nervous activity in man. The behav-iour of man, which always bears a reflex character, in the broad sense of these words (each action being invariably a response to certain conditions arising in his interrelation with the outer world), is at the same time a *con-scious* and *voluntary* nature. (Luria, 1959d, p. 4)

Thus, psychic or mental activity may arise from physical activity, but this fact does not preclude a qualitative difference in their nature.

A vivid example of a qualitative difference engendered by the social or-igins of higher mental processes is provided by Luria in the following de-scription of the evolution of voluntary attention which, in turn, becomes a component in the higher mental process of active perception:

> If the mother shows the child an object at the same time saying "this is a cup," this object is distinguished from the remaining objects and as a signal becomes a strong component of the complex of stimuli acting on the child. The cup begins to attract the child's attention, which at this time remains "involuntary" in its form but social in its content.
>
> However, when the growing child, forming his behavior in intimate inter-action with the adult, himself begins to *point* to the proper object, to change its position in space, to note its additional signal sign or simply to call it by a specific word, the child produces in the environment those changes which in the future begin to act on him as a type of "feedback" and which, thereby, begin to attract his attention. In this case we have a new structure in organi-zation of attention, which, remaining reflex in its nature, acquires, however, the quality of a mediated act and becomes in the original scientific sense of this word *voluntary attention.*
>
> Under "voluntary attention" (as, however, even under any complex "vol-untary" function) we should, consequently, understand such a reflex act as social according to its genesis and mediated according to its structure and with which the subject *begins to submit to changes themselves produced by him in the environment and in this way to master his own behavior.* (Luria, 1961d, p. 748).

In addition to the social origins characteristic, the preceding example of voluntary attention also demonstrates how the speech system com-ponent, in this instance spoken language, can act as a mediating fac-tor between the individual and the environment; and there is again the implication that volition cannot exist without the prior existence of auxiliary stimuli.

A similar link between developmental stages of higher mental processes and auxiliary stimuli is provided by Luria in this topical area when he considers the child's acquisition of the ability to use and control such stimuli.

The progression of the developmental stages of the higher mental process of written speech is very clearly delineated by Luria (1978b), but a more generally applicable portrayal of the ties between development and auxiliary stimuli is provided in the stages of mental development that Luria extrapolates from his observations of children given memory tasks, and various materials such as chips, strings, playing blocks, hailshot, and pictures to assist them:

> (1) The child is not in a state to perform the task by the complicated auxiliary means. He is incapable of connoting the objects offered as the auxiliary means and fails to remember a series of words "with the aid" of cards; such is the *pre-instrumental* stage of development.
>
> (2) The child begins to attempt to use the objects offered as the means for attaining the object, but does it clumsily, without attempting to establish a rational connection between the task and the auxiliary means, looking at the latter as a sort of magic . . . . This phase is characterized by a purely formal attitude to the method adopted, a blind faith in its efficacy though it is thoroughly inadequate. This phase (which we have observed in children of five to seven though it may appear in later years) we can call the magical or the *pseudo-instrumental* phase.
>
> (3) Finally, much later we observe the *real instrumental* stage in the development of the child, the main features of which are the complicated structure of acts of behavior, the ability to adapt one's self to difficult tasks by using adequate means and the outer auxiliary stimuli. It is precisely this part of behavior which develops most in a schoolboy and the modern civilized man, and is of utmost significance. (Luria, 1928a, pp. 503–504)

Not only is it necessary for higher mental processes to evolve via a number of developmental stages, but the completion of each link or sequential step in the developmental progression is mandatory for the full realization of the higher mental process and to ensure the avoidance of anomalous development:

> Indeed, the formation of complex mental activity always requires strict consistency and succession of individual operations; sometimes, if only a single link of training is missed, if a certain stage in the development of the necessary operation is not properly worked up, the entire process of further development becomes retarded, and the formation of higher mental functions assumes an abnormal character. (Luria, 1958a, p. 40)

The importance of each sequential step in the developmental growth of a higher mental process is emphasized further by the fact that brain pathologies in the very young have more far-reaching ramifications (i.e., oligophrenic children) than a similar pathology in an older child. Oligophrenic children ("from the Greek words "oligo"—small, "phrenos"— mind) (Luria, 1963a, p. 10), refers to a type of mental retardation that

> develops as a rule after inflammation, intoxication, or trauma affecting the child's brain even at the fetal stage, at the time of birth, or in very early childhood.
>
> The profound retardation of such children is manifested in the entire organization of their complex neural activity, but as was shown in special investigations (Lubovskij, 1956; Muscerjakow [Meshcheryakov], 1956, 1958; Pevzner, 1956; and others), the damage is greatest in those forms of neural organization which are the basis of speech activity or which are achieved by means of speech.
>
> These children form complex temporary connections with difficulty, and find it especially hard to carry out those operations of abstraction and generalization which are accomplished by means of speech. Consequently, the information which reaches them is greatly reduced, and its organization is simplified. A newly established connection is easily destroyed under the influence of external agents (or "noise"). However, if a system of connections does become consolidated, it becomes pathologically inert and almost incapable of being restructured (Luria, 1956, 1958a [1958b]; Pevzner, 1956). It is particularly characteristic of these children that the dynamics of neural processes underlying speech activity are in their case impaired not less, but more than the dynamics of neural processes which are materialized in simpler sensori-motor reactions. (Luria, 1959b, p. 458)

Similarly, the importance of a single link to the entire structure of higher mental processes is evidenced by the fact that

> Thorough observations carried out by a number of Soviet psychologists, physicians and teachers (R. M. Boskis, T. A. Vlasova, L. V. Neiman, and others) have shown that derangements of speech and retardation of intellectual development in children suffering from defects of hearing since early childhood are *inevitable systemic consequences of the auditory* defect, and need not be explained by any other additional causes. (Luria, 1958a, p. 43)

Another, perhaps obvious, consequence of the evolution of a higher mental process through developmental stages is that each stage is progressively more complex than its predecessor until it makes a qualitative shift to the psychic or mental level of functioning, and it then proceeds to developmentally increase its complexity in that realm:

> Soviet researchers have demonstrated convincingly that the most signifi-
> cant forms of psychological activity and, especially, the higher psychological
> functions, come into being as the product of the association of the child with
> adults, and undergo profound qualitative changes in the course of develop-
> ment. Arising on the basis of natural gifts, they are reorganized in the proc-
> ess of psychological development. The structure of developed perception
> mediated by memory or voluntary attention becomes considerably more
> complex than the structure of elementary perception, immediate memory
> or simple involuntary attention. (Luria, 1963d, p. 17)

The studies of the 1931 and 1932 expeditions to central Asia portray
the developmental stages of higher mental processes once they have made
the qualitative shift to the psychic or mental level of conscious, voluntary
activity. At this level, there *can* be two developmental stages: first, concrete situational thought which may or may not, depending upon the cultural development of the individual's social environment, progress to the
second stage of complex, abstract, and theoretical thought. In contrast
with abstract, theoretical thought, the main function of concrete, situational thought is

> not the formation of abstract connection and relationship between symbols,
> but reproduction of whole situations, whole complexes closely connected
> with specific life experiences; . . . separate psychological operations, such as
> memory, comparison, generalization and abstraction, are formed in this
> type of thinking quite differently, and . . . with the change of economic con-
> ditions this situational, or complicated thinking very quickly becomes
> changed, giving place to other more complex forms of thought. (Luria,
> 1933, p. 192)

It should be noted that in his detailed reports of these studies, which
were published some 40 years later (Luria, 1976b), Luria indicates that
the cultural developments that engendered abstract, theoretical thought
were much more involved than a simple "change of economic conditions," and included a radical reorganization of social structures together
with the introductions of literacy, and theoretical knowledge.

Once the stage of abstract, theoretical thought has been reached

> It becomes possible to take assumptions as they are formulated in language
> and use them to make logical inference, regardless of whether or not the con-
> tent of the premise forms a part of personal experience. The relationship to
> logical reasoning that goes beyond immediate experience is radically re-
> structured; we see the creation of the rudiments of discursive thinking,
> whose inferences become as compelling as those from direct, personal
> experience.

All these transformations result in changes in the basic structure of cognitive processes and result in an enormous expansion of experience and in the construction of a vastly broader world in which human beings begin to live. In addition to the sphere of personal experience, we see the appearance of the sphere of abstract general human experience as established in language and in the operations of discursive thinking. Human thought begins to rest on broad logical reasoning; the sphere of creative imagination takes shape, and this in turn vastly expands man's subjective world. (Luria, 1976b, p. 163)

Thus, as noted in the chapter on "Consciousness," we are presented with evidence that cultures may also proceed through developmental stages in their reflection of reality, stages that parallel the evolution of word meaning—moving from a focus on the concrete to a concern with verbal-logical connections.

SPOKEN LANGUAGE AND COGNITIVE DEVELOPMENT

It is in his work on cognitive development that A. R. Luria announces the primacy of spoken language as a higher mental process as well as reiterating its social origins:

The higher psychological functions are developed by social contact, and in the first place by the intercourse of the child with adults. The first function developed in this process is speech . . . . (Luria, 1936–1937, p. 36)

Not only is spoken language or speech the first of the higher mental processes to develop, it is also the most readily influenced of all the higher mental processes. When talking about the formation of mental connections, Luria (1957b, p. 118) declared that "the participation of a verbal system in the formation of new connections can be significantly accelerated by training." As was noted earlier, it is this participation of the verbal system in the formation of new connections that gives human mental connections their unique characteristics. Consequently, it seems logical that any expedition of such participation in the formation of mental connections should also hasten the cognitive development of the child.

Evidence of the transformation of cognitive functioning as a result of speech training is provided by the case study of identical twin boys who combined a complex phonetic impairment with the idiosyncratic speech of the "twin situation." Luria and Yudovich created an objective necessity for the development of spoken language by separating the twins; and in addition, they provided the physically weaker twin with special spoken language training designed to make speech an object of conscious perception. The results indicated that the acquisition of spoken language transformed all the activities of the twins, and that the twin who had received special training achieved higher levels of development than his brother. Consequently, even though he was physically the weaker of the two, following the training he assumed the dominant position in their relationship. Because the experiment was only approximately 1 year in duration, Luria thought the short time span effectively demonstrated that the results obtained could not have been caused by simply physical maturation alone (Luria & Yudovich, 1959).

Although we are not concerned specifically with the mode of written speech, the susceptibility of spoken language's developmental stage of internal speech to the influence of the higher mental process of written speech is further evidence of spoken language's characteristic of being easily influenced:

> the functional and structural features of written speech . . . have . . . one important aspect; they inevitably lead to a considerable development of *inner speech*. Delaying the direct revelation of speech connections, inhibiting them and showing increased requirements for the preliminary speech act not being revealed at once by training, written speech produces such a rich development of inner speech as could not have a place in the earlier phases of development. Therefore, neuropathologists are not working at random when, desiring to investigate the possibilities of inner speech, they turn to the nature of the written speech of their patients. (Luria, 1961d, p. 738)

Despite the unique qualities of being the first of the higher mental processes to develop and the one most readily influenced, spoken language is typical of the other higher mental processes in that it must evolve through a series of developmental stages rather than being an innate quality of the brain. The most general of these developmental stages are: (1) external speech, (2) egocentric speech, and (3) internal speech. These stages were first identified by Vygotsky and Luria in their paper for the Ninth International Congress of Psychology, which met at Yale University in 1929.

External speech includes the spoken language first of others in the child's social environment and thus is the stage that includes the initial sociocultural origins of spoken language. The child's external speech is initially imitative and then evolves into egocentric speech, which, according to Luria, serves a special function in aiding the child in organizing his behavior, and is characterized by its "coding for self" nature. Such speech is gradually internalized, and becomes internal or inner speech. However, in the process of internalization, it is modified somewhat so that its most distinctive feature becomes its predicative nature and it becomes characterized by its ellipsis, synthesis of meaning, and silence. A. R. Luria presumes a familiarity by his reader with these basic developmental stages, and consequently does not discuss them in great detail. However, reflecting his philosophical ties to Vygotsky, periodically he refers his reader to Vygotsky's writings for a more explicit explanation of the general developmental stages of spoken language.

The fact that these developmental stages of spoken language parallel the general physical maturation of the child often leads to a confusion about the effects of the two processes according to Luria (Luria, 1969c, p. 144). Such confusion can obscure the roles of the sociocultural origins of speech and simple physical maturity in cognitive development. However, the significance of social origins is supported by the fact than an absence of communication with others produces widespread ramifications in the child's mental development despite a normal physical development:

> a lack of oral communication with others cannot avoid producing a natural retardation in intellectual development, and whilst, with respect to their capabilities, such children remain normal, they begin to lag in the development of verbal thought and do not succeed in school. (Luria, 1963a, p. 19)

Social conditions are important in the development of spoken language not only at the point of origin, but continue to have a role in shaping it throughout its development, so that

> the social circumstances in which a child grows up will inevitably leave their mark on the mechanisms underlying complex psychological processes, not just on the content of those processes. This is especially true of associative processes, which in both their genesis and their function are the most directly exposed to the influence of environmental factors acting on them. (Luria, 1974b, pp. 49–50)

Thus, spoken language, an associative higher mental process, will reflect an individual's social circumstances. This conclusion arose from Luria's studies of mental functioning in three groups of children: urban children, rural children, and homeless children, and from his early research with the illiterate people of Uzbekistan.

In addition to the social environment, speech is influenced by and incorporates aspects of the concrete environment that give rise to its sympractic nature. This characteristic refers to the fact that spoken language is

> supported by extralinguistic (sympractic) aids—knowledge of the situation, facial expression, gestures ... information can be transmitted by extralinguistic aids, and incomplete expansion, ellipsis, the participation of intonation, and so on, can exist. (Luria, 1976a, pp. 36–37)

In fact, the beginnings of spoken language are always closely linked to concrete reality, and, as Luria indicates, with concrete experience:

> Oral speech always originates in close connection with immediate experience, as, for example, in sympractical and situational activity. It relies on intonation and gesture and usually becomes intelligible only if the general setting of the conversation is considered. It permits extensive abbreviation. For a prolonged period it continues to bear traces of the period when the subject was contained in speech and the predicate in a gesture, a tone, or in the immediate situation. (Luria, 1969c, pp. 141–142)

This dependency of spoken language on the sympractic for completion of its meaning persists ontogenetically for a long time, and although its influence lessens, it is never totally eliminated. Developmentally, its influence does not really begin to diminish until school age:

> Only during the preschool age (4–7) does this situational, sympractic comprehension of connected speech begin to recede into the background. Gradual separation of the child's speech from practical action becomes the essential factor in the formation of the *child's speech structure.* If the word is learned only in the practical situations in which it is used, there are no objective conditions created in the child to force the word (or the entire expression) to acquire a differentiated character. *Tpru!* can designate either "horse," or "they're off," or "stop;" the meaning is determined by the situation, gesture, intonation of the utterance, and so forth. The objective necessity for *morphological differentiation* of the word occurs only when the word is separated from the sympractic context. This differentiation, marking the end of the period of autonomous speech, is first manifested in the appearance of suffixes. When a suffix is joined to the word *tpru,* the new word *tprun'ka,* has a narrower meaning and it begins to designate a "horse." For the designation of the action, "stop," it becomes necessary to form new, special words. The formation of grammatical structure powerfully stimulates the separation of speech from its immediate, practical context . . . . (Luria, 1969c, p. 140)

The sympractic nature of spoken language at any level of development is mandated by the need for comprehension of meaning that underlies the semantic aspect of speech. This semantic component, too, evolves through developmental stages, and the first step is

> a process of *gradual delineation of verbal signals from all the remaining components of the situation acting on the child* . . . . the earliest stages of "understanding the word" in the child could not be considered as the original grasping of clear meaning of the word similar to that which takes place in the child of pre-school and even later nursery age, and that the word of the adult

does not immediately become for the child that "signal of signals" which it is in the later stages of development.

[Rather, the earliest understanding of the word arises in] . . . that direct emotional-active association with adults which is reflected in a fixation of the eyes on the face of an adult, in a responsive smile to the smile of the adult, in attempts of the child to reach the adult, the child in the first six months of life increases its reaction to the words of the adult. Certain words beginning at the fifth and sixth month produce an orienting reaction in the form of turning of the head and the eyes, a smile, and later even the execution of very simple actions (turning the attention to the object, reproduction of well-known movements, etc.) in response to word addressed to the child [*sic*]. (Luria, 1961d, p. 715)

The next step in the initial stage of comprehension of meaning is a total dependence on the sympractic aspects of the utterance to such an extent that it reminds one of an exercise in conditioning. The intonation, the gestures, and the circumstance must remain the same for the child to respond with an appropriate reaction. As discussed previously, these will continue to play an important part in augmenting the child's comprehension of the word, but gradually the child is able to isolate or perceive the word as more salient than other stimuli in a situation.

The second stage in the comprehension of meaning is also a complex one comprised of several steps and results in "the formation of a clear system of generalized relations which are concealed by the word" (Luria, 1961d, p. 716). This system of generalized relations includes both the generalizing or associative aspect and the designating or nominative aspect of meaning.

And, just as there are two semantic functions (nominative and associational) to spoken language, so too are there two structural dimensions to speech. Luria takes his terminology from R. Jacobson and designates them as the paradigmatic and the syntagmatic dimensions. Luria utilizes the term *paradigmatic* to refer to the vertical dimension of language or the structural organization of the word, and it reflects the fact that

the word preserves in itself all systems of connections inherent in it, beginning with the very elementary and visual and ending with the very complex and abstract; and . . . depending on the different tasks, dominating connections can be established either by this or other systems of connections. Without this, any plastic thinking could not be possible and the person using the system of most abstract relations for the solution of more concrete everyday problems, always risked finding himself in the position in which a schizophrenic patient in whom the second signaling system is severed from the first and behavior loses its sensible and expedient character [*sic*]. (Luria, 1961d, p. 728)

Syntagmatic for Luria refers to the horizontal dimension of language or the subject-predicate association inherent in the connected utterance that groups individual words into a meaningful sentence. This level of structure is more complex even than the paragidmatic, in part because it incorporates the paradigmatic in its structure. Luria underscores its importance by stating that

> the unit of speech is not so much the individual word as the *connected utterance.* The sentence and a significant part of that which is conveyed to us by speech is based on the possibility of connecting individual elements into a word combination, or a *syntagma.* There is every reason to believe that, if the first stage of the origin of language should be considered the appearance of the first word, then the second, very important stage is connected with the formation of the first syntagma, which reflects the connection between the object and the action or between two objects and two events. (Luria, 1969c, p. 138)

The neurological bases for these dimensions are discussed in Chapter 6, "Functional Organization of the Brain/Brain Lesions."

6

Functional Organization of Brain/Brain Lesions

LITERATURE

"Disorders of 'Simultaneous Perception' in a Case of Bilateral Occipito-Parietal Brain Injury" (Luria, 1959c) reports on experiments with a Polish Army officer who suffered a bilateral occipito-parietal bullet wound that resulted in the restriction of his visual perception to one element or a single configuration. The condition could be improved temporarily by injections of caffeine, and it is Luria's conclusion that the syndrome results from a general reduction in cortical tone in the affected area.

"An Objective Study of Ocular Movements and Their Control" (1962) was co-authored with E. D. Khomskaya, and reports on photoelectric registration of ocular movements while following an oscillating luminous spot, in response to verbal instruction, and a repetition of ocular movements from memory. Smooth ocular movements were possible only when following the luminous spot and if the speed of the same stayed below a certain critical point. Ocular movements from memory and in response to verbal instructions were always saccadic, which leads the authors to the conclusion that there are two cortical "oculomotor centers." They suggest that the movements following a moving object are essentially visual reflexes, while those engendered by verbal instructions or memory are closer to being "voluntary" movements.

Restoration of Function After Brain Injury (Luria, 1963b) was originally published by the Academy of Medical Sciences of the USSR in 1948, and discusses two explanations for functional restoration—deinhibition and reorganization. Deinhibition presumes no cellular damage, but rather that the function is simply in a state of inactivity as a result of the trauma to the brain. Reactivation of the function may be accomplished spontaneously without apparent cause, may be accomplished by drugs that chemically counter the inhibition, or may require changes in the patient's mental orientation in cases of "hysterical" inhibition.

The book concentrates six of its seven chapters on the reorganization explanation, which Luria indicates is the only practical approach in those cases that involve destruction of neuronal structures in the cortex. But before proceeding further with a review of this approach to the restoration of mental functions, it is appropriate to again clarify what constitutes a "function" according to Luria.

Functions are not inflexible, inevitable processes of activity; rather the term refers to a

> complex adaptive activity (biological at some stages of development and social-historical at others), satisfying a particular demand and playing a particular role in the vital activity of the animal. A complex adaptive "function" such as this will usually be executed by a group of structural units and ... these will be integrated into a "functional system." The parts of this system may be scattered over a wide area of the body and united only in the execution of their common task (for example, respiration or locomotion). Between these parts there is a pliable yet strong temporary connexion, uniting them into one system and synchronizing their activity. This "functional system" works as a complete entity, organizing the flow of excitation and coordinating the activity of the individual organs. (Luria, 1963b, p. 36)

Moving from somatic physiological functions to mental functions, Luria postulates that higher mental processes also are, in fact, complex functional systems. Consequently, a reorganization of the same to restore one's mental functioning is feasible because

> in the course of development complex inter-systematic relationships are created on the basis of deliberate objective action and speech, which permit completely new relationships between the higher centres. This modified task may thus lead to the creation of new functional systems, and almost any area of the cerebral cortex may be included in a particular functional system in order to reintegrate the disturbed activity of the brain. (Luria, 1963b, p. 55)

In addition, he notes that mental reorganization does occur naturally and unconsciously, as when visual fields are reorganized without effort by the individual, or during the individual's normal ontogenesis when

> the originally diffuse and inarticulate hearing was organized with the aid of such a system of generalization inherent in the spoken language. When a young infant ... starts to learn to speak sensibly, it in fact reorganizes its hearing on the basis of the permanent phonematic system of the spoken language. (Luria, 1963b, pp. 62–63)

Following the introductory rationale, the remainder of the book consists of presentation of the experience of Luria and others attempting to reorganize the complex functional systems of praxis, perception, speech, and active thinking in brain-damaged patients.

"An Experimental Analysis of the Behavioral Disturbance Produced by a Left Frontal Arachnoidal Endothelioma (Meningioma)" (1964) reports on collaborative studies by Luria, K. H. Pribram, and E. D. Khomskaya, which were made possible through cooperation of the Soviet Ministry of Health and the U.S. Department of Health.

An extensive battery of tests was run on a patient at the Bourdenko Institute of Neurosurgery who had an arachnoidal endothelioma pressing on the anterior left frontal lobe. The large tumor extended deep into the frontal regions of the brain, and the accompanying edema had spread through the whole left hemisphere as far as the occipital lobe. The patient died following surgery approximately one month after her admittance, and the details of the histological examination are reported.

Cautioning that conclusions should be qualified by the extensive degree of brain damage, the authors report that their observations and tests led them to the opinion that, among other symptoms, frontal lobe lesions produce a "general deficiency in the execution of any type of complex and symbolic instructions and intentions (internalized versions of such instructions)" (Luria, Pribram & Khomskaya, 1964, p. 278).

"Factors and Forms of Aphasia" (Luria, 1964a) was a paper presented at the Ciba Foundation Symposium. Dr. Luria was unable to attend the meeting and his paper was read for him by Dr. Macdonald Critchley.

During the introduction, Luria gives his rationale for the importance of studying the speech processes:

> Man's speech activity, which is based on the interaction of separate analysers, not only participates in the creation of an abstract and generalized picture of the world, but also creates new conditions for the regulation of human behaviour. Speech allows us to single out the essential aspects of the stimulation which impinges on us, to analyse the conditions of the tasks which are posed, to formulate an intention, to plan for their solution and to collate the results obtained with the initial plans. In all of these ways, speech provides for flexible self-regulation of man's psychological activity. (Luria, 1964a, p. 143)

These are the things that the speech processes do, but what is speech? Prior to providing such a definition, Luria explains that the cerebral cortex is morphologically a complex hierarchical system comprised of primary, secondary, and tertiary zones. The primary or "extrinsic" zones receive afferent fibers that, via the nuclei of the thalamus, have a direct connection to outside stimuli. Similar in organization are the secondary or "projectional-associative" zones that overlay the primary zones.

However, they are characterized by more complexly developed cellular formation in the second and third layers of the cortex, which provides them with the capacity for more systemic and complex operation of the analyzer in question.

The tertiary or "intrinsic" zones are referred to by Luria as "overlapping zones" since they are less modally specific and serve to integrate several analyzers for the performance of complex functions. They receive stimuli from both the nuclei of the thalamus and from other primary areas of the cerebral cortex.

Keeping in mind that all these zones or systems are subject to the tonic influence of the reticular formation, and that they not only receive stimuli but also produce multilevel excitation in the central nervous system, it becomes more clear why Luria defines speech as follows:

> Speech, then, is a complex functional system which is supported by the combined work of a whole series of zones in the cerebral cortex, each of which makes a specific contribution to the development of speech. (Luria, 1964a, p. 146)

Having lain the foundation for his approach to aphasias, Luria then proceeds to delineate what he considers the various forms of aphasia. Basically, he groups them into four categories: phonemic, articulatory, logico-grammatical, and dynamic.

Phonemic aphasias include sensory aphasia, which is "a particular disorder of auditory function—a *type of disturbance of the analysis and synthesis of speech sounds* which arises when the cortical elements of the auditory analyser are impaired" (Luria, 1964a, p. 147). Also considered a type of phonemic aphasia is acoustic-amnestic aphasia in which acoustic hearing may remain normal but defects manifest "themselves primarily in impaired retention of stable audio-speech traces" (Luria, 1964a, p. 151).

Luria distinguishes two types of articulatory or motor aphasias: (1) afferent motor aphasia, which results from kinaesthetic defects in the afferent system which provides directional and correcting guidelines during articulation; and (2) efferent motor aphasia, which results from kinetic defects in the premotor area of the brain and disturbs the sequential organization of the patient's articulation.

Logico-grammatical or semantic aphasia results from a disturbance of the tertiary zones of the parieto-temporal-occipital area of the brain and results in an inability to simultaneously handle the relational synthesis of concepts formed by language.

The final form of aphasia, dynamic aphasia, is a result of frontal lobe damage and appears to be a disturbance of inner speech. In particular, the predicative function of speech is damaged, and the patient is unable to formulate original, spontaneous speech. Disturbed is the "ability to connect words to simple syntagma, and to perceive directly the grammatical form of a word which allows it to enter into a context with other words . . ." (Luria, 1964a, p. 160).

"Neuropsychology in the Local Diagnosis of Brain Damage" (1964b) reviews the history from P. Broca forward of the belief that studying disturbances of higher psychological processes could facilitate the diagnosis of local brain lesions. Luria notes that the isomorphic approaches were doomed to failure because they did not take into consideration the fact that higher mental processes are formed as the result of social-historical development and are "*complex functional systems* based on jointly working zones of the brain cortex" (Luria, 1964b, p. 6).

Consequently, he indicates that higher mental processes may suffer if any link in the structure of this complex functional system is disturbed. However, each link's impairment will result in the higher mental process being disturbed in a particular way, and Luria views it as a basic task of neuropsychology to discover what qualitative changes will be manifested in higher mental processes by damage to which links, or in other words, to evaluate symptoms. In illustration of his position, he presents examples of how the disturbance of writing is affected differently by injury to different areas of the brain, although all might be generalized as writing disturbances.

His basic hypothesis is that

> in the presence of a given local lesion which directly causes the loss of some factor, *all functional systems which include this factor suffer, while, at the same time, all functional systems which do not include the disturbed factor are preserved.* (Luria, 1964b, p. 14)

"Disturbance in the Regulative Role of Speech with Frontal Lobe Lesions" (1964) was co-authored with E. D. Khomskaya, and constitutes a chapter in "*The Frontal Granular Cortex and Behavior*," which is the text of the proceedings of a symposium of the same title held at Pennsylvania State University, August 8–10, 1962. Dr. Luria was unable to attend the conference, but their paper was circulated to the other participants prior to the conference.

The paper begins with a consideration of the problems and hypotheses of the affect of frontal lobe lesion on behavior control, presents research studies investigating various aspects of the problem, and ends by summarizing their research findings:

> The facts that, in massive tumors of the frontal lobes, the vegetative compo-

nents of the orienting reflex are disturbed, and also that it is impossible to stabilize an orienting reaction by means of verbal instruction show that a considerable alteration takes place in the mechanisms underlying the highest forms of regulation of behavior. This would indicate that important destructions of the whole self-regulatory system and especially of the system-selective organization of behavior take place. It results in marked deterioration of the highest forms of attention, as well as in disturbance of the most complicated control of memory processes. (Luria & Khomskaya, 1964, p. 371)

The authors conclude by calling for further objective investigations of the disturbances resulting from lesions to this portion of the brain, and note that compared to other cortical areas such research is still in its very early stages.

"The Programming of Constructive Activity in Local Brain Injuries" (1964) was co-authored with L. S. Tsvetkova, and presents the position that there are two basic forms of constructive activity: (1) the immediate or reproductive form is "directly determined by the perceived pattern; the subject performing the given task need not engage in any deciphering . . ." (Luria & Tsvetkova, 1964, p. 95), and (2) the indirect or productive form involves decoding and recoding by the subject.

Evidence is presented in the article that frontal lobe injuries result in disturbances of the indirect or productive form of constructive activity while parieto-occipital lobe injuries result in problems of spatial orientation that disturb the immediate or reproductive form of constructive activity.

"Eye Movement Mechanisms in Normal and Pathological Visions" (1964) was written in conjunction with E. N. Pravdina-Vinarskaya and A. L. Iarbus [Yarbus], and reviews experiments with a patient whose disturbance of perception was one of quantity rather than size of object. He could perceive only one object at a time. Because drugs could temporarily alleviate the condition somewhat, the authors believe that the symptom is caused by a weakened state of the cortical cells in the visual cortex. However, the long range solution was a mechanical device that gradually shifted control of the patient's reading to the act of kinesthetic tracking.

"Aphasia in a Composer" (1965) was written in conjunction with L. S. Tsvetkova and D. S. Futer, and presents the case history of V. G. Shebalin, a prominent Russian composer, who despite a lesion of the speech areas of the left hemisphere that caused severe sensory aphasia, maintained his musical abilities and continued to compose works that received high acclaim.

The authors observed the composer for three years prior to his death, and concluded that

This case proves that phonematic and musical (prosodic) organization of acoustic perception and memory are included in different systems, and have as their basis different cortical structures. (Luria, Tsvetkova, & Futer, 1964, p. 292)

"Aspects of Aphasia" (Luria, 1965a) reviews acoustic aphasia, afferent motor aphasia, efferent motor aphasia, and semantic aphasia, and presents evidence of the neurological correlates of each.

"Two Kinds of Motor Perseveration in Massive Injury of the Frontal Lobes" (Luria, 1965b) examines the case histories of two patients with massive frontal lobe injuries. Both demonstrated motor impairment, but there were significant differences. Injury to the basal portion of the frontal lobes and the subcortical motor ganglia resulted in motor perseveration, although complicated motor programs were preserved. Injury to the convex area as well as the posterior part of the frontal lobes resulted in "gross impairment in switching from one programme of action to another and inertia of motor stereotypes once they were established . . ." (Luria, 1965b, p. 9). The latter patient exhibited no sign of motor perseveration. It was Luria's conclusion that each syndrome is related to a different cerebral system.

"Brain and Mind" (Luria, 1966a) originally appeared in Russian in 1964, but was translated for a special issue of *Soviet Psychology and Psychiatry,* which constituted a "Handbook of Soviet Psychology Prepared for the XVIIIth International Congress of Psychology." Luria commences the article by reviewing the philosophy of Vygotsky as to what are higher mental processes and how are they developed. He essentially recapitulates what was presented in detail when we defined higher mental processes in our initial chapter.

Then, using the organizational schema of primary, secondary, and tertiary zones in the cerebral cortex delineated in an earlier article, Luria presents his findings of the differing sensations that occur when these zones in the occipital or temporal regions are stimulated by an electric current. The varying complexity of the sensations seems to verify his hypothesis of a hierarchically more complex structure as one proceeds from primary to tertiary zones.

Another pertinent development in Luria's thought on higher mental processes presented in this article is that in addition to the aforementioned zones of the cerebral cortex, the brain itself has three functional systems:

the first maintains the necessary tonus of the cortex; the second receives and processes incoming information; and the third acts as the programming and checking mechanism to ensure the intentional and goal-directed nature of behavior. (Luria, 1966a, p. 67)

The reticular formation and upper brain stem comprise the material base of the first system; the second system is composed of the primary, secondary, and tertiary zones of the cerebral cortex; and the third system derives from the functioning of the frontal lobes of the brain. Thus, Luria's theory reflects an increasingly sophisticated understanding of the neurophysiology underlying higher mental processes.

"Disturbances of Active Visual Perception with Lesions of the Frontal Lobes" (1966) was written in conjunction with B. A. Karpov and A. L. Yarbus, and compares the verbal reports following visual analysis of a complex picture together with eye movements of normal subjects with those of a patient suffering from a large frontal lobe lesion. The authors' conclusion was that active control of eye movements was impaired so that "the *complex process of exploratory, scanning activity is disturbed in lesions of frontal lobes* . . . " (Luria, Karpov, & Yarbus, 1966, p. 212). This, in turn, leads them to the conclusion that the frontal lobes play an important part in the organization or patterning of complex, active cognitive processes.

Higher Cortical Functions in Man (Luria, 1966b) is a book-length work dedicated to Vygotsky's memory originally published in Russian in 1962. In his preface (a second preface was also done by Karl H. Pribram), Hans-Lukas Teuber termed the book a "monumental contribution" to the field of neuropsychology. The book is very comprehensive in its scope, including the historical base of current theory and research as well as summarizing Luria's approximately thirty years (at the time of publication) of investigations of higher mental processes and their neurological correlates.

Basically, the book is organized into three sections. The first section defines higher mental processes and delineates their origin in the brain; the second section discusses how higher mental processes are disturbed by various local brain lesions; and the third section is a presentation of methods of testing mental functioning when the same has been disturbed by brain pathologies. Of particular interest in the last section are two chapters covering tests to be utilized for the investigation of speech functions.

It is in the first section, delineating the origin of higher mental processes in the brain, that we find neurological support for Luria's position on the systemic and developmental formation of the higher mental processes. A cytoarchitectonic analysis or graphic delineation of the neuronal cell structure of the cortical layers of the primary, secondary, and tertiary cortical zones is given, and Luria notes that:

It is the tertiary fields of the cortex that possess the finest neuronal structure, and this may be interpreted as the morphological expression of the particular precision and complexity of the functional differentiation of these
fields, which are responsible for the most highly specialized functional connections and interactions between the analyzers. (Luria, 1966b, pp. 63–64)

Only in man does the overlapping of the boundaries of different analyzers develop to such an extent that these integrative tertiary or overlapping zones "comprise 43% of the total mass of the cortex, ... " (Luria,
1966b, p.28), and "over half of the total surface area of the cortex" (Luria,
1966b, p. 60). The existence of such extensive pluripotentialism negates
the argument that the higher mental processes of humans could be localized in separate, isolated centers in the brain rather than exist as complex
systems.

Luria's developmental stance is supported by the fact that

The peripheral fields of the nuclear zones attain their period of intensive development rather later than do the central fields. In human ontogenesis this
period coincides with the first weeks and months of life. The process of
myelination of the conducting pathways connected with these fields takes
place at correspondingly later periods. The latest of all to mature are the
overlapping zones of the analyzers and the formations of the frontal region;
this process occupies the first few years of life. The connections of these cortical areas are also the last to complete their cycle of development.

The important transformations of cortical organization caused by the
appearance of the second signal system, associated with man's productive
activity, speech, thought, and consciousness, are a specifically human feature. The transformations referred to affect all the groups of cortical fields
that have been under consideration. They are especially marked in relation
to the secondary and tertiary cortical fields. (Luria, 1966b, p. 61)

Narrowing his focus to the higher mental process of spoken language,
Luria discusses the neuronal structure of Broca's area, Wernicke's area,
and how the development of the same reflects "the fundamental role of
spoken language in the entire system of verbal communication" (Luria,
1966b, p. 62).

Human Brain and Psychological Processes (Luria, 1966c) was originally published in Russian in 1963, and is a collection of 10 articles covering
investigations made at various times during the period from 1938 to
1963. Of the collection, three chapters are pertinent to our interests.
"Chapter One—The Human Brain and Psychological Processes" is essentially a recapitulation of arguments reviewed previously, which serve to
reject the position that higher mental processes are situated in isolated, localized areas of the brain.

Chapter Two presents a fascinating rationale for the position that the human brain performs two basic activities: (1) simultaneous synthesis, and (2) successive synthesis. Luria clarifies that, although he is emphasizing the synthesizing aspect of cortical activity, he, in fact, always means analytic-synthetic activity.

Simultaneous synthesis refers to the integration of individual, successive elements into a simultaneous spatial scheme; and the visual, kinetic, and vestibular systems of the brain are considered significant in this process. In contrast, successive synthesis is the synthesis of separate elements into a temporally organized successive series of elements. The motor and acoustic spheres are associated with this activity. In addition, the frontal and frontal-temporal sections of the brain are linked with successive synthesis, an example of which is narrative speech.

Language is a serially organized phenomenon, and the ability to formulate complex, sequential speech is primarily associated with

> The understanding of the grammatical (and especially, syntactic) structure of language, which constitutes in practice the system within which speech takes place. (Luria, 1966c, p. 124)

This, obviously, refers to external speech, but inner speech also becomes involved when its contracted verbal plan is converted into expanded, serially organized narrative speech by motor and/or acoustic analyzers.

"Chapter Six—The Role of Verbal Kinesthesias in Higher Cortical Processes" from *Human Brain and Psychological Processes* (Luria, 1966c) is a presentation of the position of some Soviets that innervation of the speech organs accompanies all but the most highly automatized intellectual operations.

"Impaired Selectivity of Mental Processes in Association with a Lesion of the Frontal Lobe" (1967) was written in conjunction with E. D. Khomskaya, S. M. Blinkóv, and Macdonald Critchley, and presents their studies of a 64-year-old scientist who developed a deep-seated tumor of the mesial parts of the left frontal lobe with an extension into the right frontal lobe. He displayed "frontal lobe syndrome" in that the main defect in his thinking was its lack of organization, because he "was unable to suppress irrelevant associations which were provoked by the situation" (Luria, Khomskaya, Blinkóv, & Critchley, 1967, p. 112).

Although the patient was a man of high intellectual ability, his verbal production demonstrated a loss of what the authors term "selectivity." The case was unusual in that there was a rapid day-to-day deterioration of the patient's condition, which was carefully studied by the authors.

"Neuropsychology and Its Significance for Behavioral Sciences and

Medicine" (Luria, 1967c) appeared in an international journal published in Japan, and recounts how damage to various sections of the brain are manifested in disturbances of mental activity and hence behavior as well as stating the position that higher mental processes are complex functional systems.

"On the Disturbance of Intellectual Operations in Patients with Frontal Lobe Lesions" (1967–68) was co-authored with L. S. Tsvetkova and appeared in *Soviet Psychology*. The article describes the results of their experiments wherein patients were given a written text, asked to read it, and then orally recount it. In addition, they were requested to outline the text. Frontal lobe lesion patients had difficulty with both the recounting and the outlining of the text, while patients with parieto-occipital lesions who exhibited difficulties with both the nominative function of speech as well as its syntactic structure were able to outline the story with comparative ease. The authors conclude that

> Whereas in patients with parieto-occipital lesions the orienting basis of intellectual activity remains intact, and the main defects are associated with disturbances in the ability to formulate the subject verbally, patients with frontal lobe lesions retain this ability, and the main defect is found in a disturbance of the orienting basis of intellectual activity and the ability to program that activity, i.e., to extract a system of ideational relationships as a guide for subsequent exposition. (Luria & Tsvetkova, 1967–68, p. 6)

"Disturbances of the Structure of Active Perception in Lesions of the Posterior and Anterior Regions of the Brain" (1968) was written in conjunction with B. A. Karpov and A. L. Yarbus, and utilizes measurements of eye movements to compare perceptual acts by normal adults, patients with massive frontal lobe lesions, and patients with occipital-parietal area lesions. The latter experienced difficulty with visual spatial synthesis while frontal lobe patients demonstrated difficulty with active orientation efforts.

"The Mechanism of 'Dynamic Aphasia'" (1968) was co-authored with L. S. Tsvetkova, and postulates that dynamic aphasia is a disturbance of "inner speech with its predicative function, which takes place in forming the structure or scheme of a sentence, . . . " (Luria & Tsvetkova, 1968, p. 297). The article reports on their attempts to test this by experiments with 15 patients with dynamic aphasia and 15 normal subjects. The aphasia patients exhibited more difficulty in naming actions than in naming objects, and could not form sentences out of all the separate words necessary to do so. Normal patients had no difficulty with either task. External cues (such as pieces of paper) assisted the subjects in compensating for this loss of the "linear scheme of the phrase . . . " (Luria & Tsvetkova, 1968, p.

302), and the authors concluded that their experiments had proved their hypothesis.

"Frontal Lobe Syndromes" (Luria, 1969a) constitutes a chapter in the *Handbook of Clinical Neurology, Vol. 2,* edited by P. J. Vinken and G. W. Bruyn, and provides a comprehensive consideration of the morphology and functioning of the frontal lobes.

Luria provides such basic information as the fact that the frontal lobes are the youngest portion of the cerebral hemispheres evolutionarily; comprise approximately one third of the total human cerebral cortex; and consist of three main regions: the motor area, the premotor area, and the prefrontal area together with the mediobasal aspects of the frontal region. The complexity of this area of the brain is evidenced by the fact that Layer III of the neocortex in Area 6 of the premotor area contains approximately 207 million pyramidal cells. Because *each* cell may have 2–3,000 synapses, the reader can gain some appreciation of the multiplicity of connections with other areas of the brain of which the frontal lobes are capable.

The most complex zones of the frontal lobes do not complete their physical development until the individual is 7–12 years of age; and the integrative tertiary zones of cortical development are found in the prefrontal region.

A detailed analysis is presented of the morphological, physiological, and clinical data on each of the three regions of the frontal lobes. Of particular interest are the disturbances of higher mental processes and speech that result from lesions in these regions. These have been presented in the reviews of other articles on the frontal lobe syndrome, but this chapter presents the same in more detail and states:

> Analysis of these disturbances shows that they are based on *difficulty in performing complex movements generalized in time.* There is difficulty in denervating one link and moving on smoothly to the next. This disturbance of "kinetic melodies" is the fundamental symptom of a premotor lesion . . . . (Luria, 1969a, p. 731)

With respect to how frontal lobe lesions affect speech, Luria states that

> If the lesion is situated in the inferior portions of the premotor area of the dominant (left) hemisphere, phenomena similar to the disturbances of kinetic melodies described above may also appear in speech and verbal thinking. The patients of this group begin to have difficulty in fluent speech, their speech becomes interrupted, and difficulties arise in the transition from one element of articulation to another. Similar phenomena of the loss of smoothness (and sometimes of perseveration) may also appear in writing. (Luria, 1969a, p. 733)

If the symptoms are severe, one has a case of efferent (or kinetic) motor aphasia.

The symptoms of frontal lobe lesions vary somewhat, of course, depending upon the location of the lesion; however, Luria indicates that there are two main symptoms that occur

> in almost every massive lesion of the prefrontal regions. The first of these symptoms was *a disturbance of the complex forms of active purposive behavior,* and the second *a disturbance of the critical attitude towards the patient's own defects.* Both of these components of the "frontal syndrome" were observed as a rule in all massive lesions of the frontal lobes, although they varied in lesions of the convex and basal portions of the frontal region, and differed depending on the severity of the lesion .... (Luria, 1969a, p. 738)

When such characteristics arise from a lesion of the left prefrontal region, they are manifested in speech activity and verbal thinking and distinguish the aphasia Luria labels dynamic aphasia.

"The Neuropsychological Study of Brain Lesions and Restoration of Damaged Brain Functions" (Luria, 1969b) is a summary of all Soviet research in this area which Luria prepared for *A Handbook of Contemporary Soviet Psychology.* The editors, Michael Cole and Irving Maltzman, basing their commentary on a convention paper presented by D. Bowden to a 1966 symposium sponsored by the American Psychological Association, state that the key concept of a functional cortical system in Soviet brain lesion research can be clarified by remembering the four major postulates underlying Luria's work in this area:

> The first is that the cerebral component of any functional cortical system results from the interaction of a constellation of cerebral areas. Thus, a functional system is localizable in the sense that damage to any one of the areas involved destroys the functional system. Defects will appear in the psychological activities dependent upon this functional cortical system. Second, a given psychological activity, for example, reading, may be performed in different ways, that is, by different functional cortical systems. Thus, a psychological activity is not localizable in the sense that if damage to a structure destroys a functional cortical system upon which reading is based another functional system cannot be developed which would carry out that same activity of reading. Third, the most important adaptive functions that man possesses, such as abstraction, computation, and speech itself, depend upon functional cortical systems which are acquired rather than innate. The fourth major assumption is that the most important determinant of functional cortical systems in man is the organization of the social environment. (Cole & Maltzman, 1969, p. 278)

"Frontal Lobes and the Regulation of Arousal Processes" (1970) was co-authored with E. D. Khomskaya, and appeared in *Attention: Contemporary Theory and Analysis.* The article reports on the results of studies conducted with normal subjects and brain lesion patients in an effort to ascertain the role of the frontal lobes in the regulation of arousal processes or the orienting reflex. The orienting reflex is

> a complex functional system which includes a series of somatic, sensory, vegetative, electrocephalographic, and other components. While having a certain autonomy, all components of the orienting reflex obey common laws: they appear with the presentation of stimuli which are new for the organism; they have a nonspecific character, i.e., they do not depend on the modality of the stimulus; they disappear in proportion to repetition; and reappear with any changes in the experimental situation. Another no less important factor that elicits orienting reactions, is the significance or signal meaning of the stimuli. (Luria & Khomskaya, 1970, pp. 303–304)

The authors demonstrate that, anatomically and neurologically, a number of connections exist between the frontal lobes and those structures of the limbic system and brain stem that are responsible for states of wakefulness, arousal, and the orienting reflex. The latter structures provide the efferent link in the system while the afferent link seems to be located at the cortical level.

The most significant finding of the experiments for our purposes is the fact that in humans one can regulate the orienting reflex by means of speech, which does physiologically modify the same:

> If, by means of speech, stimuli are given signal meaning, a series of changes in the system of the orienting reflex occurs, namely: extinguished orienting reactions reappear and become more intensive (their latent period is shortened, their strength and duration is increased), they do not extinguish any more, and they arise for a wider range of intensities (as a result of the lowering of the threshold of sensation and the elevation of the threshold of the defense reaction). In this situation, the orienting reactions become more discriminating. They are not responsive to any outside nonsignal stimuli. Similar changes in the system of the orienting reflex occurring with the introduction of verbal instructions are observed in all normal subjects who are in an awake state (grownups and children, beginning from 8–10 years of age). (Luria & Khomskaya, 1970, p. 304)

The authors indicate that this regulation of the orienting reflex by means of speech is such an essential characteristic of human mental functioning that it "may serve as an important indicator of the normally functioning brain" (Luria & Khomskaya, 1970, p. 305). The balance of the article recounts their endeavors to test this hypothesis, and their conclusion that the distractibility characteristic of frontal lobe syndrome is due to the absence or weakness of speech's regulation on the orienting reflex process.

"The Functional Organization of the Brain" (Luria, 1970a) appeared in *Scientific American,* and provides a succinct summary of Luria's organizational schema of brain functioning. He also reviews which functional systems arising from which areas of the brain permit the performance of voluntary movement and the writing component of the speech system, and how this information was derived from work with brain injured patients.

"The Structure of Psychological Processes in Relation to Cerebral Organization" (1970) is a short article written in conjunction with E. G. Simernitskaya and B. Tubylevich, which utilizes analyses of writing disturbances in left parieto-occipital patients to support the postulate that psychological processes change their cerebral structure during functional as well as ontogenetic development. For example, a patient unable to write from dictation is still capable of signing his name, which is an act based on kinesthetic stereotypes and controlled by a different area of the brain.

Traumatic Aphasia: Its Syndromes, Psychology and Treatment (Luria, 1970b) was originally published in Russian in 1947 and based in part on Luria's work on sensory aphasia for his second medical degree, Doctor of Medicine, received in 1943. The text was extensively revised and expanded prior to its publication in English, and deals only with aphasias produced by traumatic lesions, which are limited defects in an otherwise healthy, intact brain. Such lesions produce aphasias that are better subjects for study than those involving other more diffuse disturbances, such as those caused by vascular or tumor lesions of the brain. The observations reported are of war-related injuries.

The book constitutes one of the significant basic texts on aphasiology, and is organized into three basic sections: "Part I—General Problems and Topical Syndromes of Traumatic Aphasia," "Part 2—The Neuro-Psychological Examination and the Differential Diagnosis of Traumatic Aphasia," and "Part 3—Rehabilitation of Patients with Traumatic Aphasia."

While others might speak of aphasias in general, Luria presents his own organizational schema. First of all, he groups aphasias into three basic groups according to severity: (1) Total Aphasia is characterized by a total block of production and/or comprehension of speech. The disturbance is severe and lasts at least two or three weeks. (2) Well Expressed Aphasia includes those cases where the symptoms are relatively severe but do not involve a total block of speech activity. (3) Subtle, Slight Aphasia involves cases wherein the disturbance is not always evident at all times. It may appear most strongly only during instances of emotional disturbance or fatigue (Luria, 1970b, pp. 34–35). Because initial trauma to the brain often results in a temporary disturbance of speech activity, Luria is emphatic that judgments with respect to symptoms and severity should be made only during the residual stage, which is the period 2 to 5 months after the trauma.

In addition to grouping by severity, Luria follows the classification schema that was encountered in earlier articles: acoustic aphasia, afferent motor aphasia, efferent motor aphasia, frontal dynamic aphasia, and semantic aphasia.

Of particular interest with respect to the focus of this book is a section wherein Luria, with his usual attention to philosophical bases of research, precedes his presentation of specific types of aphasia with a consideration of "The Structure of Speech Activity." In this brief section, he presents his explanation of when speech phylogenetically became intrinsically linked to thought:

> The isolated words of which verbal speech consisted in its earliest stages of development were capable of reflecting separate signs or primitive concepts, but they could not express even elementary thoughts. The meaning of a word shifted depending upon the situation and was nonexistent outside certain situations. Whereas words possessed a nominative function from the beginning, the predicative function derived only from the concrete setting in which they were uttered. A decisive change occurred when speech went from consisting of individual words to consisting of elementary grammatical sentences, when instead of a single word there arose *a pair or group of words related to one another,* i.e., when the first "syntax" appeared.
>
> The revolution which occurred at this phase in the development of language was truly phenomenal . . . . verbal speech became capable not only of designating an object, but also of formulating a thought. Verbal speech was still bound up with other forms of expression such as gesture and intonation, but with the development of written language thought came to be expressed altogether by means of language and speech became fully capable of performing the predicative function. Speech became an independent system of codes. (Luria, 1970b, p. 83)

Because the development and structure of speech is so complex, Luria maintains that any consideration of its disturbance cannot be simplified and considered to be merely

> disturbances or the speech images of words or . . . the inability to pronounce words. The basic forms of speech disturbances must result from defects in the systems of connections which are concealed behind the word on one hand and in the disintegration of the predicative function of speech on the other. The whole sense of verbal statements resides in this function. Similarly, the cerebral mechanisms which underlie speech processes cannot be at-

tributed to cortical structures which store memory images nor to their associations with "centers of auditory speech" or "centers of articulatory movements." (Luria, 1970b, p. 83)

"The Origin and Cerebral Organization of Man's Conscious Action" (Luria, 1971b) is the text of an evening lecture to the XIX International Congress of Psychology, which met at University College, London, from July 27–August 2, 1969.

Luria commences the lecture by explaining that conscious action has social origins since it is "originally *divided between two persons:* it starts with the mother's command and ends with the child's movement" (Luria, 1971b, p. 37). This, of course, reflects Vygotsky's idea that all higher functions are first interpsychological—originating in relations between individuals. He then proceeds to reiterate the developmental stages of the verbal regulation of behavior or voluntary action, which have been reviewed previously.

Following these introductory remarks, Luria embarks on the real focus of the lecture—the cortical systems that underlie voluntary or conscious action. He states that the frontal lobes of the brain are the cortical areas responsible for conscious action; and he presents research studies by his colleagues and himself in support of that statement. His position is based on the fact that the frontal lobes have been shown to control the level of attentiveness; to control the maintenance of externally originated verbal programs for behavior; and to control the construction of the individual's own strategy, plan, or program for action. Case studies of brain lesion patients are presented to illustrate and support each of these points, and the lecture ends with a call for further research in this area.

The Man with a Shattered World: The History of a Brain Wound (Luria, 1972) is a vivid and poignant account of Zasetsky, a young man who received a bullet in the parieto-occipital area of the brain. The wound was complicated by an inflammation that resulted in adhesions and scar tissue changing adjacent tissue and distorting the normal configuration of the lateral ventricles. The frontal cortex remained intact so that Zasetsky was painfully aware of his defects, and, according to Luria, "fought with the tenacity of the damned to recover the use of his damaged brain. Though in many respects he remained as helpless as before, in the long run he won his fight" (Luria, 1972, p. xx).

Zasetsky was Luria's patient for 25 years, and Luria quotes extensively from the journal that Zasetsky laboriously composed during that time. His dogged efforts to learn again to write, and his painful difficulty in trying to express himself and to link with reality provide powerful verification of Luria's hypothesis that higher mental processes can be restored by reorganization of the brain.

"The Frontal Lobes and the Regulation of Behavior" (Luria, 1973a) constitutes the first chapter in *Psychophysiology of the Frontal Lobes,* which was edited by K. H. Pribram and Luria. In the chapter, Luria reviews the new developments in neuropsychology that have invalidated the classical concepts of brain organization—direct localization and antilocalizationism. The former, of course, held that an isomorphic relationship existed between mental functions and brain structures, while the latter maintained that the brain was a single unit and totally involved in each psychological function.

The frontal lobes in particular have historically been the subjects of conflicting theories, and Luria attributes this to the inadequacy of past approaches to the study of their functioning. Modern theory, however, has developed some hypothesized principles for frontal lobe functioning that have guided Luria's studies, and a summary of his research on the same is presented in this chapter.

Reviewing his research findings on the role of the frontal lobes in the activation processes, verbally programmed behavior, and problem solving activity, Luria notes that "Each human activity starts from definite intention, directed at a definite goal, and is regulated by a definite program which demands that a constant state of cortical tone be maintained" (Luria, 1973a, p. 5). It is his conclusion that the frontal lobes have vital roles in the state of activation that arises when the brain has some task to perform.

In addition, the frontal lobes are vital in the process whereby the orienting reflex is intensified and stabilized as a result of verbal instruction, so Luria concludes that they have a vital role in specifically human forms of attention.

Of particular interest is his evidence that frontal lobe functioning is vital to verbal thought processes:

> the basic thought defect characteristic of patients with lesions of the frontal lobes consists not in the absence of logical codes in them but in the ability to make a goal-directed choice from a number of equiprobable alternatives. (Luria, 1973a, p. 20)

"Towards the Mechanisms of Naming Disturbance" (Luria, 1973c) presents Luria's position that naming is a complex psychological function, and consequently the two previously held explanations for nominal defects are inadequate:

> According to the first, this defect is due to a partial loss of verbal memory traces; according to the second, it is the outcome of a failure of categoriza-

tion, i.e., the object presented for naming cannot be ascribed to its appropriate conceptual class. (Luria, 1973c, p. 419)

Luria commences his argument by noting that functionally a word both designates an object and also includes or codes it into a system of connections that give it meaning. Consequently, there are two groups of psychological processes involved in naming:

First, the subject has to single out some basic features of the object to be named. This necessitates a clear image of the object on the one hand and a well-organized acoustic structure of the appropriate name on the other. Secondly, the coding process must operate normally to provide a clear selective structure of the relevant semantic connections. If one or both conditions are not fulfilled, naming becomes disturbed. (Luria, 1973c, p. 417)

Therefore, defects in naming may result from deficiencies in selectivity that are modality specific or may result from a problem of selectivity at the higher coding level. Luria gives a review of the underlying lesions that precipitate the particular aphasias labeled amnesic aphasia; and summarizes by stating that naming failures result from either visual agnostic or semantic defects, and hypothesizes (noting that as yet he has no proof) that the latter may occur because

there has been a certain equalization of the excitability of a whole network of verbal connections such that the complex semantic matrix of the word has broken down. (Luria, 1973c, p. 420)

The Working Brain: An Introduction to Neuropsychology (Luria, 1973e) is Luria's most comprehensive work on the functional organization of the brain. He includes data derived from his approximately 40 years of research, and states that the book's purpose

is to generalize modern ideas regarding the cerebral basis of the complex working of the human mind and to discuss the systems of the brain which participate in the construction of perception and action, of speech and intelligence, of movement and goal-directed conscious activity. (Luria, 1973e, p. 16)

Of special interest is his chapter on speech wherein Luria states that speech, whether expressive or impressive, has three aspects: one, as a form of social communication, two, "as a tool for intellectual activity, and finally as a method of regulating or organizing human mental processes" (Luria, 1973e, p. 307). He then proceeds to an analysis of impressive or receptive speech and expressive speech together with their underlying brain systems.

Impressive speech is broken into its component stages:

> The first condition for the decoding of incoming speech is the isolation of precise spoken sounds or *phonemes* from the flow of speech reaching the subject. (Luria, 1973e, p. 309)
>
> The next stage in impressive speech is the *understanding of the meaning of a whole phrase* or a *whole connected speech expression.* (Luria, 1973e, p. 311)

These stages, of course, are possible only if certain conditions are met:

> The first condition essential for the decoding of narrative speech is *retention of all the elements of the expression in the speech memory* .... The second essential condition ... is the *simultaneous synthesis* of its elements, and the ability not only to retain all the elements of the narrative speech structure, but also to be able to "survey" it simultaneously and to form it into a simultaneously perceived logical scheme. (Luria, 1973e, p. 311)
>
> The third, and most important condition ... is *active analysis of its most significant elements.* This active analysis is hardly required at all for the decoding of simple phrases and the most elementary forms of narrative speech. However, it becomes an absolutely indispensable condition for decoding the meaning of complex sentences or, more especially, for the understanding of the general meaning and, in particular, the undertone of a complex narrative statement. (Luria, 1973e, p. 312)

In his analysis of expressive speech, Luria begins with the most elementary form, repetitive speech, and indicates that its underlying prerequisite conditions are an accurate auditory perception, a sufficiently precise system of articulation, and the ability to switch from one articuleme to another.

Next in complexity would be the naming of objects, which requires visual perception, integrity of the precise acoustic structure of speech, discovery or selection of the proper meaning and inhibition of irrelevant alternatives, and sufficient mobility of the nervous processes that the individual can switch to another name rather than being locked into a stereotypic perseveration of the same word.

The highest level of expressive speech is implied to be intentional, complex, narrative speech. Luria states that as a whole expressive speech "begins with an *intention* or *plan,* which subsequently must be recoded into a verbal form and moulded into a speech expression" (Luria, 1973e, p. 318). It is his position that this recoding takes place with the participation of inner speech, which has a predicative structure and provides what Luria terms "the linear scheme of the sentence" (Luria, 1973e, p. 319). How this process is accomplished is not enlarged upon in this book, but it is noted that the inferior postfrontal zones of the left hemisphere appear to be involved in this formation, since patients with such lesions are unable to produce spontaneously an elementary verbal expression without external assistance.

The other chapter from this book of particular interest is one entitled, "Thinking." A scientific consideration of the process of thinking became possible when

> In the 1930s, the Soviet psychologist Vygotsky first demonstrated that the process of analysis and generalization, which is the basis of the intellectual act, depends on the logical structure of speech, and that *word-meaning, the basis of ideas, develops in childhood.* (Luria, 1973e, p. 325)

Having realized that "word meaning is the fundamental tool of thinking . . . " (Luria, 1973e, p. 326), psychologists were finally able to consider the psychological structure of thinking holistically. From this base, Luria goes on to distinguish six phases of thinking in general: First, the individual discovers a task that he is motivated to do and "for which he has no ready made (inborn or habitual) solution" (Luria, 1973e, p. 327). Next, one must restrain impulsive responses so that one can perform a process of preliminary investigation. Third, is the discovery of strategy or the selection of one alternative from a number of possible ones and the formulation of a general plan for putting it into effect. The next phase is the discovery of the specific methods and operations that will accomplish the general plan. The fifth phase is problematic, as it is an operative act of thinking rather than a creative one, and it involves the actual solution or answering of the task. This fifth and final phase of thinking consists of the comparison of the obtained results with those originally mandated by the task (Luria, 1973e, pp. 327–329).

Luria then provides a discussion of practical, constructive thinking and verbal-logical thinking together with a consideration of the cortical structures underlying each, which will not be detailed here.

"Aphasia Reconsidered" (Luria, 1977a) is a reprint in *Neurolinguistics* of a 1972 article in *Cortex,* which presents the history of aphasia research as occurring in three stages: The first is the classical approach resulting from 19th century clinical studies which based its schema of the forms of aphasia on the concept of cortical centers having particular roles in human language activity. It is Luria's position that the resultant concepts are now frequently in conflict with modern neurological knowledge.

The second state of aphasia research is that of neuropsychology, which has developed during the last few decades, and which saw as one of its tasks a twofold one of delineating factors and forms of aphasia:

The first task of neuropsychology was to describe carefully speech disorders associated with local brain lesions, and to provide a specification of symptoms and to single out factors underlying the disturbances of speech . . . .

Following this approach we tried . . . to find *partial factors* associated with different zones of the cortex and to understand several forms of aphasia resulting from the operation of such special factors. This approach brought us to a description of certain *basic forms* of aphasia. Classical *sensory aphasia* was described as a result of disintegration of phonematic hearing associated with lesions of the upper parts of the left temporal lobe or as a result of an instability of acoustic traces in cases of lesions of the middle parts of the left temporal lobe. *Motor aphasia* derives either from a breakdown of afferent kinaesthetic schemes associated with lesions of the lower parts of the left retrocentral cortex (afferent or kinaesthetic motor aphasia) or from a breakdown of serial integration of kinetic melodies associated with lesions of the lower parts of the left premotor zone (efferent or kinetic motor aphasia). *Semantic aphasia* derives from breakdown of the simultaneous (quasi-spatial) syntheses associated with lesions of the tertiary temporo-parieto-occipital area, and *dynamic aphasia* is thought of as the result of breakdown of speech programmes associated with lesions of the lower portions of the left frontal cortex and is in part identical with the form of aphasia described by Head as "verbal aphasia." (Luria, 1977a, p. 63)

The third stage of aphasia research, according to Luria, is just beginning. This is the attempt to analyze the neurodynamic mechanisms responsible for the various forms of aphasia.

"Basic Approaches Used in American and Soviet Clinical Neuropsychology" (1977) was co-authored with Lawrence V. Majorski, and based on research that the latter performed with Luria at the Bourdenko Institute of Neurosurgery in Moscow under a grant from the U.S. National Institute of Health's U.S./USSR Health Science Exchange Program.

The article contrasts the Halstead-Reitan Neuropsychological Test Battery, which is a current, quantitative American approach to neuropsychology "with the qualitative syndrome-analysis scheme of clinical investigation used by Soviet neuropsychologists" (Luria & Majorski, 1977, p. 959).

"Brain Disorders and Language Analysis" (Luria, 1977b) is a reprint in *Neurolinguistics* of a 1958 *Language and Speech* article. In this article, Luria notes that the study of various brain lesions permits a componential analysis of language structure, which is impossible in the normal person in whom spoken language is an almost indivisible whole. In addition to presenting the language disorders precipitated by lesions in various areas of the brain covered in our review of previous articles by Luria on aphasia, Luria delineates in detail the neurological reasons why a subject's "communication of relations" may be destroyed while the same subject's ability to "communicate events" remains intact.

"Differences Between Disturbance of Speech and Writing in Russian and in French" (Luria, 1977c) is a *Neurolinguistics'* reprint of a 1960 article in the *International Journal of Slavic Linguistics and Poetics.*

Luria takes issue with the common argument that in cases of aphasia in polyglots the most recently learned language is the one that will be initially affected. His position is that this is true only in instances of pathological change in the overall neurodynamics of the brain; and that in cases of local brain lesions, the language affected is determined by the functional system of the brain that has been impaired.

The article adduces the case of a French journalist who knows French, Polish, German, and Russian. In 1937, he received a war injury that left a shell fragment in the left inferior parietal region of the brain. Nine years after the trauma, he experienced epileptic attacks and underwent surgery to remove all shell and bone fragments. For 6 months following surgery, he could not speak in any language although he understood speech addressed to him.

As expressive speech gradually returned, he displayed similar defects in all languages for both oral speech and in reading. For written speech, a difference between languages emerged, which gives credence to Luria's theory on the systemic, functional organization of the brain that underlies higher mental processes. Russian writing, which is almost completely phonemic, was almost undisturbed. In contrast, French, which he had known far better than Russian, displayed gross errors when he attempted to write it.

> This seeming paradox is fully explained by the fact that the lesion of the inferior parietal system, which carries out the processes of simultaneous visual analysis and synthesis, left successive phonemic analysis wholly intact and by the same token produced no disturbance of phonemic writing, on which the orthography of Russian is based. At the same time it caused substantial disturbance of the simultaneous optic system and hence brought about a considerable disintegration of writing in French, built up on the basis of conventional, non-phonemic orthography. (Luria, 1977c, p. 129)

"A Modern Assessment of the Basic Forms of Aphasia" (1977) was co-authored with J. Thomas Hutton in that the article resulted from a series of lectures that Luria gave to the Moscow Neurological Society and that Dr. Hutton of the University of Minnesota's Department of Neurology adapted to English, providing references and additional explanations where needed.

The article details the clinical characteristics of the "classical" forms of aphasia, and explains, based on the brain structures involved, why the past interpretations of the causes of such aphasia are now known to be inadequate. Luria presents his schema as to the forms of aphasia that we have encountered in previous reviews, and explains why such labels correlate more closely with the underlying neurological facts.

In addition, the following explanation is given for the ambiguity and contradiction that has plagued research on aphasia:

> The theory of aphasia is the most difficult area of neurology. It presupposes the knowledge of several branches of science: neurology, psychology, speech pathology, physiology, and linguistics. If the investigator has no knowledge of any one of these branches, he finds it difficult to do the complex work of analyzing the facts. This is why we had to spend so many years in order to sort this complex problem from the chaos which occurred from the wholly unjustified schematization. (Luria & Hutton, 1977, p. 150)

"L. S. Vygotsky and the Problem of Functional Localization" (Luria, 1978d) previously appeared in English in 1965 and 1967, and was published in Russian in 1966. The article reviews the reasons why Vygotsky's theories of the sociocultural origins and ontogenetic development of higher mental processes cannot coexist with a physiological theory that maintains that the higher functions are localized in specific sites in the brain.

"Neuropsychological Analysis of the Predicative Structure of Utterances" (1978) was co-authored with L. S. Tsvetkova, and was originally published in Russian in 1968. The article presents experimental evidence to support the authors' postulate that dynamic aphasia is a defect of the linear, syntactic scheme of a sentence rather than any type of motor disturbance. In addition, the authors hypothesize that this disturbance is associated with a disturbance of inner speech so that the transition from initial concept to external sentence construction is impeded.

HIGHER MENTAL PROCESSES AND BRAIN ORGANIZATION

In this topical area, Luria provides a very detailed examination of the complex functional systems of the cortex from which the higher mental processes arise. Because of the extreme complexity of the cortical systems and the vast amount of detail that A. R. Luria with his two medical degrees supplies, the following discussion should not and cannot be regarded as anything more than a cursory review of the intricate cortical organization underlying higher mental processes. I have attempted to keep anatomical and neurological terminology as succinct as possible, and a glossary is appended for further clarification, which includes Figure 1—a schematic of the lateral surface of the cerebral hemispheres, cerebellum, pons, medulla oblongata, and spinal cord.

This review moves from the most general view of the brain's organization provided by Luria to a relatively minute view. The most general view of the brain divides it into two sections: the gnostic and the dynamic. The gnostic section of the brain includes the parietal, temporal, and occipital lobes, or all areas of the brain posterior to the Central Fissure of Rolando (Central Sulcus); while the dynamic section of the brain consists of the frontal lobes, which are comprised of the prefrontal, premotor, and motor areas, or all areas anterior to the Central Fissure of Rolando. Essentially, this view of brain organization is a very broad functional one, which separates the brain into the "knowing" (gnostic) section and the "doing/ controlling" (dynamic) section.

Another way of viewing the brain is to organize it according to basic systemic functions. Viewed in this fashion, the brain consists of three blocks or systems. The first and most fundamental of these systems includes the upper brain stem area, and the most significant component of this system is probably the reticular formation. The fundamental function of this system is

> the maintenance of a certain *alert condition* in the cerebral cortex, to make it an apparatus capable of receiving information and regulating active behavior.
>
> This system maintains the cerebral cortex at a working level, but it is not in itself an apparatus to receive information from the outer world and to realize a directed regulation of behavior. This is not an autonomous system. It is constantly under the regulating influence of higher systems of the cerebral cortex, which receive and process information from the external world, and which determine the program of man's dynamic activity. Other sections of the cerebral cortex, more complicated in their structure, fulfill those functions.
>
> The bulk of these sections can be conditionally called the second system (or the second "block") of the brain. They serve to *receive, process,* and *store information* reaching man from the external (and partially from the internal) environment. This system is distributed over the anterior [*sic*] sections (occipital, parietal, and temporal) of the cerebral cortex. I. P. Pavlov called these sections of the cortex the cortical ends of separate analyzers, or, to put it differently, of the instruments ensuring the analysis and synthesis of signals arriving from the external world. (Luria, 1966a, pp. 65–66)

The third system or block of the brain is the anterior portion or the frontal lobes, and this system

> handles the processes of *programming human activity, collating the effect of action with the initial intention, and regulating and controlling mental processes.* (Luria, 1966a, p. 67)

A more morphological view of the brain organizes the neocortex itself into primary, secondary, tertiary zones. This view is most commonly applied to the second block or system in the preceding schema, and describes a structure that is most typical of that region of the cortex (the gnostic section), which includes what Pavlov termed the "sensory analyzers."

In each of them the *primary,* or *projection,* zones occupy first place; here end the fibers that proceed from the peripheral apparatuses—the eyes, skin and ears—and bring information from these instruments to the cerebral cortex. The primary zones of these regions of the brain consist of a highly developed fourth (afferent) layer of minute nerve cells which receive incoming excitations and transmit them both to neighboring cells and to the more complicated secondary zones of the cerebral cortex. The bulk of these zones consists of special nerve cells of the upper layers of the cortex; they receive impulses from the primary cortical areas and ensure a protracted circulation of spheres of excitation within the cerebral cortex. These dynamic systems of excitation, circulating in the cortex and themselves under the constant tonic effect of the reticular formation, form the basis for processing (by analysis and synthesis) of information received, and for storing the "short-term" and "long-term" memory traces evoked by it; . . .
    Above the secondary zones of the cerebral cortex are yet more complex tertiary zones, ... These zones, distributed between the visual, auditory, and general sensory sections of the cortex, mature later than the rest. They consist for the most part of associative neurons, nerve cells with short endings that are based in the second and third layers of these areas. The nerve cells of these sections consolidate the excitations coming to the cortex from the perceptual instruments. This permits complex cognitive processes which require the simultaneous participation of several analyzers. (Luria, 1966a, p. 66)

The most minute structural schema with which we deal in this book is that of the layers of the neocortex itself. It is now widely accepted that the neocortex, that distinguishing feature of the mammalian brain, has six layers of varying thickness according to the region of the brain in which they are located. In some regions, the main layers may have sublayers, while in other regions the main layers may merge into various combinations. For example, in the motor cortex, Layers II through V tend to merge and become almost indistinguishable. To further complicate the matter most layers of the neocortex contain more than one type of cell (Gardner, 1975, pp. 375–378).
    To illustrate how knowledge of the detailed structure of the neocortex provides an objective data base for extrapolation to psychological func-

tioning, the following is an excerpt from Luria's analysis of the neurological features of the secondary zone of the neocortex:

> The most prominent cytoarchitectonic features of the secondary field of the cortical nuclear zones are those elements of their neuronal structure that are adapted for relaying the afferent impulses coming from the subcortex. These impulses come through the granular cells of Layer IV to the large pyramidal cells of the lower level of Layer III . . . . These structural characteristics are responsible for the most powerful system of associative connections of the cortex (the secondary projection-association neuronal complex . . .). As a result of this unique mode of construction, the secondary fields of the nuclear zones play a highly important part in relaying the individual stimuli differentiated by the primary fields and in functionally integrating the nuclear zones of different analyzers and of the groups of impulses arriving from the receptors in the different analyzers. Hence, these fields are mainly involved with the relatively more complex forms of coordinated mental processes associated with detail analysis of the relationship between concrete objective stimuli and with orientation in relation to a concrete spatial and temporal environment. (Luria, 1966b, pp. 49–50).

Given the preceding brief overview of the complexity of the physical organization of the brain, it is understandable that Luria vehemently rejected both the localization and antilocalizationism positions and criticized them repeatedly in his writings. The first position held that higher mental processes could be found in specific, circumscribed locations within the brain, while the latter position proclaimed the dogma that the higher mental processes were a product of the functioning of the brain as a whole, a gestalt totally involved in any higher mental process.

Substantiating Luria's conviction that the brain's cortical organization is that of a complex functional system are his numerous research studies indicating that the cortical organization of a higher mental process is reorganized conjointly with its functional reorganization during developmental stages. These studies were presented in detail in Chapter 5 on cognitive development. A case such as Zasetsky's demonstrates that functional reorganization of the brain is also possible in adults, and can restore at least some of the capabilities that were lost due to brain lesions.

SPOKEN LANGUAGE AND BRAIN ORGANIZATION

A. R. Luria's writings in this topical area demonstrate both that spoken language is a complex functional system in itself, and also that it arises from a "complex functional system of conjointly working cortical zones

... " (Luria, 1966b, p. 35). Thus, introducing a discussion about the possibilities of restoring speech functions following brain lesion, Luria states that

> Human speech is a complex functional system possessing many afferent and efferent links; these links are connected with the functions of a large group of cortical areas occupying a considerable part of the left hemisphere. Disturbance of this "speech zone" can lead to the development of aphasia . . . . These disorders, however, are not identical, and lesions of different parts of this zone, directly affecting one or other aspect of speech, cause structurally different forms of aphasia. (Luria, 1963b, p. 135)

The best organizational scheme for understanding the interactions of these two complex functional systems is a consideration of the forms of aphasia—those disturbances of the system of spoken language precipitated by disturbances of the cortical system. Luria divides aphasia into general categories according to the subsystem of spoken language that is disturbed: phonemic, articulatory, semantic, or dynamic. As becomes obvious in our review of the same, these distinctions are for academic convenience and such separation in practice is often difficult because of the interdependency of the components of the functional system of speech.

These categories are further delineated into six types of aphasia, which Luria considers to be neurologically differentiated types, in contrast to some of the classical labels of aphasia, which, according to him, were based on misconceptions of neurological functioning. Thus, the general class of phonemic aphasia includes sensory aphasia and acoustic-amnestic aphasia. Sensory aphasia results from the "destruction of the posterior third of the upper temporal convolution of the left hemisphere . . . " (Luria, 1964a, p. 147), or Wernicke's area as it is commonly known. The symptoms include a

> disturbance of the understanding of speech, defects in the repetition of words and naming of objects, impairment in writing, and several distinctive defects of the patient's spontaneous speech. (Luria, 1964a, p. 147)

Luria considers sensory aphasia to be caused by a disturbance of the cortical base of the auditory analyzer which, in turn, produces "a *type of disturbance of the analysis and synthesis of speech sounds* . . . " (Luria, 1964a, p. 147). In mild cases, for example, the patient may be unable to distinguish between voiced and unvoiced consonants and therefore is unable to accurately repeat or write dictated words. Speech production may reflect a similar confusion of distinguishing phonemes.

If the pathology does not destroy the secondary zone of the auditory cortex, but rather induces a pathological state of the same, such as a lowering of cortical tone, the defects may

> occur only in special situations, manifesting themselves primarily in impaired retention of stable audio-speech traces.
> Such patients may correctly repeat phonemes similar in sound and they lose their clear differentiation only when the amount of information impinging upon them is increased. . . .
> They repeat separate words easily, but they are unable to repeat a series of three or four words, especially if it is suggested that they maintain a given order. They are often hindered in naming subjects . . . . In connexion with this, they find significant difficulty in developed speech and speech thought, which is greatly disturbed because of the instability of verbal traces. (Luria, 1964a, p. 151)

This type of phonemic aphasia is termed acoustic-amnestic aphasia by Luria.

Motor aphasia is usually linked with a disturbance of Broca's area or the "posterior third of the lower frontal convolution of the left hemisphere" (Luria, 1964a, p. 151). However, Luria labels the condition that results from damage to that area efferent motor aphasia, and distinguishes it from a second type of motor aphasia, afferent motor aphasia. As might be anticipated, the former is a product of disturbances of efferent or motor neurological links in the brain, while the latter arises from defects in the afferent, or sensory links. Motor and sensory are commonly used general terms that are sufficient for some purposes, but neurologically less accurate than efferent and afferent.

All movements have both an efferent and an afferent base neurologically. The distinction between the two is made on the basis of the direction in which a nerve fiber conducts an impulse. This distinction can be made on the level of the individual nerve cell, but for this discussion we define the efferent base as being a nerve fiber which conducts impulses *away* from the cortex, and the afferent base as being a nerve fiber which conducts impulses *to* the cortex. If the efferent base is disturbed, as it is in efferent or kinetic motor aphasia, the patient is unable to make the smooth motor transitions from one articulation to another which are necessary in order to produce a coherent word, and will consequently hopelessly repeat the initial sound.

In afferent or kinaesthetic motor aphasia, the cortical area involved is the post-central part of the cortex, and the afferent or sensory "feedback" elements of the motor system are impaired. Consequently, the patient may produce a "b" for a "p" sound because he is unaware that the articulators are not in the appropriate position to produce the desired sound. In severe cases, the patient is unable to sense any part of the combination of movements required to produce a speech sound (Luria, 1964a, pp. 151–155).

Semantic aphasia is more complex in that it involves not just the word, but also the connected utterance that combinations of the word produce. It is characterized by the disturbance of the logico-grammatical relations, which require a simultaneous synthesis of the meanings of component words. Cortically, it arises from disturbances of the tertiary zones of the parieto-temporal-occipital areas of the brain (gnostic section), and was classically described as a state of alienation between word and meaning (Luria, 1964a, pp. 155–158).

Dynamic aphasia might be considered a type of semantic aphasia in that it can be superficially construed as a disturbance of logico-grammatical relations between words. However, the patient has no difficulty in repeating exactly what the examiner has said or in producing stereotypic expressions. The defect becomes obvious when the patient is called upon to produce spontaneous, narrative speech for which they must originate the structure and/or the goal. It is produced by lesions in the frontal lobes, and Luria hypothesizes that since it is characterized by severe damage to the predicative structure of spoken language, it may be linked to a disturbance of internal speech, which has a predicative nature (Luria, 1964a, pp. 158–160).

As a result of this review of the various types of aphasia, it should be obvious that spoken language cannot be viewed as being localized only in certain circumscribed areas of the brain, but rather exists as a complex functional system built on a complex, interacting system of diffuse cortical components.

7 Neurolinguistics

LITERATURE

"An Objective Investigation of the Dynamics of Semantic Systems" (1959) was co-authored with O. S. Vinogradova, and is the text of a paper presented at a British Psychological Society meeting in 1957. The authors were attempting to establish an objective method of studying the dynamics of semantic systems as manifested by brain functioning, and arrived at a system that measured both vascular and motor aspects of the orienting reaction of the subjects. A second experiment utilized measurement of the defensive reaction (vascular constriction in both head and hand) engendered when the signal word was reinforced by a painful electric current. Subjects included normals, and mild as well as severe oligophrenics.

The results obtained indicate that the semantic system is dominant over sound resemblance. The exceptions were normals under the influence of chloral hydrate, which puts the cortex in an inhibitory state, and both levels of oligophrenics.

With respect to their goal of defining the dynamics and structure of the semantic system, the authors come to two conclusions:

> the words are divided into three groups: (1) *the nucleus of the semantic complex,* to which is related the key word and words in direct semantic proximity to it (they evoke a specific pain reaction); (2) *the periphery of the semantic system* to which are related words linked less directly with the key word (evoking a non-specific orienting reaction); and (3) *neutral words,* which in our experiment did not evoke any specific or orienting reactions.
>
> The correlation of these groups at various stages of the experiments may be different, and if at the beginning of the experiment the nucleus of the semantic system has a relatively generalized character, then later it becomes concentrated and only the key word continues to provoke a specific reaction, while the remaining words, which earlier were included in this nucleus,

113

move into the semantic periphery and begin to evoke only a non-specific orienting reaction. (Luria & Vinogradova, 1959, pp. 99–100)

"Two Basic Kinds of Aphasic Disorders" (Luria, 1973d) begins with the question of whether or not the two basic organizational principles of speech and language identified by deSaussure and Jakobson (paradigmatic and syntagmatic) derive from the same or different cortical systems.

Luria categorizes the brain into the gnostic zones (temporal, parietal, and occipital), which constitute the posterior of the brain, and the dynamic zones (frontal and premotor), which are the anterior portions of the brain. Then, based on an analysis of the cellular structure of the various cortical layers in each of the zones as well as knowledge of their functioning derived from neuropsychology, Luria advances the position that paradigmatic organization of language results from the functioning of the gnostic zones, and syntagmatic organization occurs as a result of the functioning of the dynamic zones. Support of this position is provided by data on the various types of aphasia and their characteristics.

"Towards the Basic Problems of Neurolinguistics" (Luria, 1974d) recounts Luria's rationale for holding that the principle of a direct or isomorphic relationship between language and brain is an untenable one, and that based on the three functional systems of the brain, it should be evident that the relationship is an indirect one.

The unique focus of this article is a consideration of the significance of neurolinguistics in future linguistic research. Luria points out that the most common method for studying linguistic competence has been intuition, and that the most objective research has been done in the area of language development in children by Slobin, Brown, and others. Now, however, the discovery that lesions in various zones of the brain may disrupt either the paradigmatic or syntagmatic organization of language opens new vistas for linguistic research because

> They show how two aspects of language—unseparable in normal speech—
> can be separated by brain pathology, and it is unnecessary to emphasize
> what important perspectives this opens for linguistic science. (Luria, 1974d,
> p. 12)

"Basic Problems of Neurolinguistics" (Luria, 1974a) appeared in *Current Trends in Linguistics,* which was edited by Thomas A. Sebeok. Following some general introductory remarks, Luria presents data obtained by neurolinguistics that contributes to an analysis of the following aspects of speech: phonetic structure, lexical structure, logical-grammatical structure, contiguous or fluent speech, and the pragmatic or regulatory function of speech.

With respect to the phonetic structure of speech, Luria recounts how brain lesions in particular areas of the brain result in deficits in phonemic production and/or comprehension of speech. However, the aspect of phonetic structure for which he hopes neurolinguistics may eventually be able to provide some clarification is that of the different levels of perception of speech sounds—the most elementary being the imitation of sounds, and the more complex being the abstract classification of sounds into specific categories.

Under the consideration of lexical structure, Luria presents neurological research to support his postulate that words have a multidimensional association with each other, and that such associations may be semantic associations, sound associations, or morphological associations. In total, these form a complex verbal network.

Discussing the logical-grammatical structure of speech, Luria explicates the neurological underpinnings for breakdowns in the "communication of events" and the "communication of relations":

> Observations have shown that whereas processes of visual thought, only expressed in the form of speech, form the basis for "communication of events," "communication of relations" involve operations of *inner spatial coordinates,* uniting the correlative elements of a whole sentence into a single simultaneous (quasi-spatial) structure. Such components of simultaneous spatial relationships can easily be seen in the process of understanding such comparative constructions as "a circle underneath a square," . . . "Olga is fairer than Sonya but darker than Katya" . . . "the brother's father" and "the father's brother . . . . "(Luria, 1974a, p. 2584)

In the "communication of relationships," the paradigmatic structure of language is primarily involved, and in the "communication of events," the syntagmatic structure of language predominates.

One of the illustrations he provides of the breakdown of the "communication of relations" is of the case of Zasetsky, which is presented in detail in *The Man with a Shattered World: The History of a Brain Wound* (Luria, 1972).

Contiguous or fluent speech is discussed in view of the cases of dynamic aphasia, and disruptions of the pragmatic or regulatory function of speech are demonstrated as being significant only in those with lesions of the prefrontal or frontal areas of the brain.

In his conclusion, Luria notes that the new field of neurolinguistics presents some difficulties for the would-be practitioner because it requires a skillful level of proficiency in "neurological, psychophysiological, and linguistic knowledge" (Luria, 1974a, p. 2591).

"Basic Problems of Language in the Light of Psychology and Neurolinguistics" (Luria, 1975) appears as a chapter in *Foundations of*

Language Development: A Multidisciplinary Approach, Volume 2 which was edited by Eric and Elizabeth Lenneberg. The article is organized into two basic sections; one of which deals with the structure of the word, and the other with the structure of the phrase.

Noting that each word is a definite sound complex, Luria goes on to discuss the fact that each word contains within it a series of possible meanings from which the user must select one in order to designate something, and that behind each word lies a system of generalizations that changes during ontogenesis.

The question of how a language user makes the choice of the wanted word meaning from all the possible alternatives available to him leads Luria to a discussion of the methods by which this process might be investigated. One method frequently used is to record the enlarged word meanings of the young child, while a variation is to note the various specific meanings of a word to a child at different stages of ontogenesis. Such observations produced Vygotsky's theory

> that the meaning of words develops, and the [*sic*] whereas in early stages the meaning of the word rests on an affective generalization, at later stages the visual image starts to be included with it, and later still, the abstract idea too. The idea that the development that a word undergoes in ontogenesis expresses a profound change in interfunctional relationships, shifting the dominant role from emotional experience to visual memory and then to abstract logical codes, is related to a number of very profound ideas that Vygotsky introduced into psychology. (Luria, 1975, p. 53)

A second method of investigation, used by Luria and Vinogradova (1959) in a study reviewed earlier, is "semantic conditioning." It is viewed as a way of investigating the semantic field of which every word is a component, and it

> involved establishing a conditioned reflex to a particular (test) word, after which tests were made to see what other words with semantic or phonetic similarity would elicit a similar conditioned reflex, and how strong the reaction evoked by such words would be. (Luria, 1975, p. 53)

A variation of this method, also used by Luria and Vinogradova (1959), is to establish a conditioned reflex to pain.

The third method of investigating word choice is neuropsychological investigation or an analysis of the ways in which production and comprehension of spoken language change as a result of lesions in various areas of the brain.

Luria's discussion of the structure of the phrase is divided into a consideration of encoding and decoding. Encoding is a four-step process involving: (1) A motive for the encoding, which results from the various response types—demand, contact, and/or concept. The first two are attributed to Skinner while Luria added the third. (2) A thought precedes the phrase. (3) Inner speech or the transformation of thought to organized speech. (4) The actual production of organized external speech. The decoding process is described as being essentially the reverse of this.

Moving to examples of how neuropsychological investigation contributes to our knowledge of the structures of spoken language, Luria explains that both motive and the structure of the phrase are impaired by damage to the frontal areas of the brain, and proceeds to describe the spoken language production of a dynamic aphasia patient in illustration of this.

Similarly, he notes that it is characteristic of sensory aphasia that the lexical content of speech disintegrates while the general overall structure of speech remains intact. Also, Luria recounts how lesions in the tertiary areas of the lower temporal and temporal-occipital areas of the left hemisphere of the brain lead to a disintegration of the ability to use codes that permit a "communication of relationships." An example of the latter is the case of Zasetsky, which is reported in *The Man with a Shattered World: The History of a Brain Wound* (1972). Luria concludes with an expression of anticipation that neurological investigation will be of great assistance in solving previously insoluble linguistic problems.

Basic Problems of Neurolinguistics (Luria, 1976a) is organized into two general sections. The first is the "Neuropsychological Analysis of Verbal Communication," and the second is entitled, "Aphasia Reconsidered." The former constitutes Luria's most comprehensive presentation of his thoughts on neurolinguistics together with evidence from his brain lesion studies to support his theories. The second section re-examines the various forms of aphasia from more of a linguistic or psycholinguistic perspective than he had utilized in previous considerations of their characteristics.

Noting that linguistics as a field had not realized the necessity of studying "living speech" rather than written speech until the first quarter of the twentieth century, Luria opens the book with a review of the contributions of linguistics and psycholinguistics to the study of the formation of verbal expression with special emphasis upon the works of Chomsky.

Of particular interest for the purposes of this book are his speculations on the intermediary role of inner or internal speech in the process of going from thought to external expanded speech. Thought has no grammatical form, being amorphous according to Luria, so internal speech with its predicative nature is the transitional stage before thought reaches the proper grammatical form of expanded, external speech. Similarly, internal speech is the mechanism that converts subjective "sense" into objective "meaning," which Luria defines in accordance with Vygotsky regarding "meaning" as the system of objective associations represented by the word and reflecting the real phenomena irrespective of the needs to which these associations correspond, . . . [and] "sense" as a subjective selection of the most important aspects of the information given and of its relation to the subject's motives. (Luria, 1976a, p. 8)

Having done his linguistic homework, Luria's explanation of the pathway from thought to speech now reflects a linguistically more sophisticated perspective:

Speech has a definite syntagmatic structure; its formation goes through a series of stages starting from the original plan, continuing through the predicatively constructed "internal speech," and creating first, the semantic record, then the deep-syntax structure of expression and, finally, its surface-syntax structure. (Luria, 1976a, p. 136)

To clarify the above, the semantic record is a representation of the meaning of the sentence; and although Luria does not specifically so state, presumably it will include a consideration of both "sense" and "meaning" in both the encoding the decoding processes.

The encoding and decoding processes involve a number of factors that, according to Luria, are

the motive that impels the speaker to express a certain meaning in words; the content or thought to be incarnated in speech; the system of objective linguistic units in which the thought is incarnated and which play an active role in its precise definition. Finally, ... besides the system of linguistic units, extralinguistic components are also involved in the process of formation and understanding of communication: gestures, facial movements, and intonation, and that besides the text, the whole communication also includes the context, with the aid of which one fragment of the text can be understood against the background of the structure of the text as a while. Finally, there is also no doubt that behind the text of the communication there may be an inner meaning, the result of analysis of the text as a whole, converting the system of meanings incorporated in it into its general meaning. (Luria, 1976a, p. 226)

The complex processes of encoding and decoding into spoken language are tied to the neurophysiological because they are

performed by a complex functional system, made up of several components, and embracing a system of zones of the cerebral cortex working together in close cooperation, each of which is responsible for one particular aspect of this complex process. Local brain lesions of a partcular [sic] zone thus lead to the inactivation (or disturbance) of the corresponding components of the encoding or decoding of communication and they are manifested as different types of disruption of its encoding or decoding. (Luria, 1976a, p. 227)

This rationale is then applied in the second portion of the book when Luria re-examines the linguistic deficiencies of patients suffering from the various types of aphasia.

Neurolinguistics 6: Neuropsychological Studies in Aphasia (Luria, 1977d) is one volume in an international series of books devoted to speech physiology and speech pathology. The book is comprised primarily of various articles on the neuropsychological analysis of aphasia that Luria had published during the prior 30 years. Of the 15 chapters, 9 are articles that have been reviewed previously and consequently are not re-examined here.

Chapters 5 and 7, "A Modern Approach to the Basic Forms of Aphasic Disorders," and "The Neuropsychological Analysis of Transcortical Motor Aphasia," are both concerned with the fact that an increased understanding of neurological functioning negates the classical explanations of many types of aphasia.

Chapter 9, "A Note on the Organization of Fluent Speech in a Semantic Kind of Amnestic Aphasia," is a very brief chapter explaining how a patient, by applying motor automatisms and prosodic organization to written speech was able to laboriously re-learn to write despite his severe aphasia. The case is examined in more detail in *The Man with a Shattered World: The History of a Brain Wound* (Luria, 1972).

Chapter 11, "On Quasi-Aphasic Speech Disturbances in Lesions of the Deep Structures of the Brain," describes the language disorders of a patient with an aneurism of the left thalamus following corrective surgery, and which disorders Luria concludes are due to the lowering of cortical tone.

Chapter 13, "Disturbances of Auditory-Speech Memory in Focal Lesions of the Deep Regions of the Left Temporal Lobe" was co-authored with T. A. Karasseva and presents the case of a patient who demonstrated loss of auditory-speech memory, but did not display any simultaneous disturbance of the acoustic analysis of speech sounds.

Chapter 15, "Disturbances of Grammatical Operations in Semantic Aphasia," is based on a 1946 article published only in Russian. In the article, Luria notes that semantic aphasia patients can understand sentences containing relational words although they cannot explain the meaning of the words individually. He concludes that "Paradigmatic relations are lost if they are not supported by spontaneous syntagmatic verbal usage" (Luria, 1977d, p. 175). This, according to Luria, is one of the main features of semantic aphasia.

Of the 16 chapters comprising Luria's final book, *Language and Cognition* (1982), more than half focus on the structure of language and its cerebral organization. In Chapter 8, "The Syntactic and Semantic Structure of the Sentence," Luria asserts that the sentence is the basic unit of living speech because of its syntagmatic organization. In their simplest form, syntagmatic linkages are limited to subject and predicate; and Luria suggests such relationships are more natural and occur earlier than paradigmatic associations. In support of this claim, he cites classical association experiments that he did some 50 years prior in which young children gave almost completely predicative (syntagmatic) responses while associative (paradigmatic) responses did not begin to appear until adolescent and adult subjects were tested. In the same study, it was also found that response times were much shorter for predicative responses. Consequently, Luria concludes that associative or paradigmatic responses are more artificial and appear later in development.

Chapter 9, "Complex Utterance Forms: Paradigmatic Components in Syntagmatic Structures," contains Luria's examination of not only the fundamental syntagmatic forms utilized to communicate events, but also a review of the paradigmatic devices involved in communicating relationships. Although the forms may be separated for academic convenience, Luria notes that in actual practice both are involved in complex utterances.

All of the chapters in *Language and Cognition* (1982) are relatively brief, and Chapter 10, "Speech Production," consists of only eleven pages. However, it includes Luria's identification of the types of speech utterances, and a delineation of the stages necessary for the transformation of a motive into an expanded speech utterance. Both are discussed later in the section on "Spoken Language and Neurolinguistics."

Chapter 11, "Basic Forms of the Speech Utterance: Oral (Monologic and Dialogic) and Written Speech," is a detailed presentation of the rationale for Luria's claim that "written speech differs from oral speech both in its origin and in its psychological structure" (Luria, 1982, p. 166). An interesting aside on the relationship of oral and written speech is Luria's observation that the novice writer retains many forms from oral speech while one who has mastered the art of writing to the extent that it becomes automatized begins to transfer the rules and forms of written speech into her or his oral speech. Readers of Walter Ong may recall that a similar contagion exists between his oral, script, and electronic stages of the word (Ong, 1967).

Chapter 12, "Comprehension of the Components of a Speech Utterance: the Word and the Sentence," and Chapter 13, "Comprehension of the Sense of a Complex Message: Text and Subtext," are both focused on the decoding process, and emphasize that the basic process involves understanding the meaning and sense of the whole message rather than isolated words and sentences."

Chapter 14, "Language and Discursive Thinking: The Process of Deriving a Conclusion," presents Luria's view that it is "the acquisition of speech [which] makes possible that transition from sensory to rational analysis." (Luria, 1982, p. 199).

The last two chapters in *Language and Cognition* (1982) present Luria's knowledge to date about the cerebral organization of speech production and comprehension based on his research with aphasia patients. In these chapters Luria notes that the psycholinguistic analysis of speech disorders is still in its initial stages.

HIGHER MENTAL PROCESSES AND NEUROLINGUISTICS

While continuing to maintain that any isomorphic relationship between a specific brain structure and a higher mental process is impossible because of the complexity of the physiological/neurological organization of the brain, Luria is predominately concerned in this topical area with the structure of language and the underlying neurodynamics of the same. Consequently, these writings are not germane to the consideration of the characteristics of higher mental processes in general, and are more appropriately considered in the next section of this chapter.

SPOKEN LANGUAGE AND NEUROLINGUISTICS

As a higher mental process, spoken language must be conscious and voluntary in nature, at least in its inception. This criterion is manifested in Luria's classification of speech utterances (Luria, 1982). He declares that involuntary utterances such as affective exclamations and swearing do not require motives. Similarly, the most simple form of dialogic speech, which is simply a response to a question that repeats the question (requiring no creative activity), does not require a motive either. That such responses may remain unimpaired in patients with massive brain lesions of the frontal lobes is further evidence of the absence of motive in their production because Luria's work with aphasia patients indicates that an absence of a motive and the subsequent active attempt to form utterances is one of the distinguishing characteristics of frontal lobe patients.

It is Luria's conclusion that the above forms of speech are not really speech utterances "in the proper sense of the term" (Luria, 1982, p. 148). In other words, they do not constitute examples of spoken language as a higher mental process. In contrast, more complex dialogic speech where the respondent must actively formulate an answer and introduce new information into the conversation, and monologic speech, which is a manifestation of the speaker's own thought, are "true" speech utterances since they do require existence of a motive.

The motive is the initial stage in voluntary speech production, and as noted earlier can be one of three basic types—a demand (Skinner's "-mand"), a desire for informational communication (Skinner's "-tact"), and a desire for a clearer formulation of one's thought, which Luria terms "-cept" for concept, following the schema set up by Skinner (Luria, 1982).

Throughout his work in this topical area, Luria has described the progression from motive to complete utterance as involving at least four stages—motive of the utterance, thought (frequently described as a semantic graph including both theme and rheme), inner speech, and finally, the expanded speech utterance. Having been rather definite about their characteristics in his earlier works, we find him much more tentative about these stages in his final writings in this area (Luria, 1982). Luria is quite candid, in fact, about saying that there is insufficient reliable data to definitively characterize these stages, and that much more investigation is needed. However, he suggests that the initial semantic graph includes the subjective sense of the utterance, which is then converted into a sequentially organized speech utterance via the means of inner speech. Thus, the essential element in the progression from motive to complete external utterance is the transformation of Vygotsky's "sense" into "meaning," and Luria sees inner speech as having the vital role in recoding subjective sense into a syntagmatic schema. So rather than humans having any innate coding mechanism for syntax, it comes into being via the psychological process of inner speech, which has sociocultural origins.

In his work on neurolinguistics, Luria attempted to examine the physical/psychic relationships inherent in spoken language even more closely than he had in his aphasia studies, and there was an attendant shift in focus from the pathological to the linguistic. It was Luria's firm conviction that the fact that the paradigmatic (vertical) and syntagmatic (horizontal) organizations of spoken language, which are inseparable in normal speech, can be separated in cases of brain pathology opened new perspectives for linguistic science.

On the most general level of organization, Luria noted that the gnostic or "knowing‛ posterior area of the brain reflects its pathologies in deterioration of the paradigmatic organization of spoken language, while the pathologies of the dynamic or "doing/controlling" areas of the brain are manifested in disturbances of the syntagmatic structure of speech (Luria, 1974d, p. 12).

This statement that the two systems of structural organization involve differential cortical systems is supported by the fact that patients with severe disturbances of the paradigmatic system do not usually demonstrate any involvement of the syntagmatic system. Their basic subject-predicate associations and prosodic organization remain intact although there may be no nominal content. Similarly, patients with disturbances of the syntagmatic structure of spoken language do not, as a general rule, display any impairment of the paradigmatic organization. An interesting, but incidental, point in Luria's discussion of such aphasias was his observation that temporal lobe or acoustic aphasia patients (disturbance of paradigmatic system) tend to relate their case histories using all verbs while motor aphasia patients (disturbance of syntagmatic system) tend to relate their disease history using nouns, with verbs omitted (Luria, 1973d, pp. 61–63).

In the normal human, however, the two organization systems co-exist and

> Every word included in an expression . . . not only introduces the object or action it denotes into a system of hierarchically (paradigmatically) organized concepts, but at the same time introduces it into a system of expanded (syntagmatic) verbal expression.
>
> Investigations undertaken by many different psychologists have clearly shown that such syntagmatic connections appear very early. The present writer showed long ago that syntagmatic groups (such a "house burns," "dog barks") arise much earlier and take place much more easily than "associatively" organized paradigmatic connections: inclusion in a common category ("sun"—"moon"), subordination ("dog"—"animal") and so on (Luria, 1927). [1928c]
>
> Clearly the presence of these syntagmatic groups is just as important a condition for the production of fluent expanded speech as the introduction of a given lexical unit into a certain system of hierarchically constructed paradigmatic relations and the significance of these "syntagmatic groups" in the production of expanded verbal expression derives from the fact that all speech, being a means of communication, is a system of syntagms (whole expressions) rather than a complex of lexical units (words); it was this that led eminent thinkers such as Hughlings Jackson (1866) [sic] to say that "to speak is to propositionize," and A. A. Potebnya (1882, 1888) [sic] to postulate that the unit of speech is not so much the word as the real combination of words, the syntagm, the embryo of the proposition.
>
> It is these two factors—the "paradigmatic" relation between individual lexical meanings that forms the concept and is the act of "simultaneous synthesis" of individual elements of information, and the "syntagmatic" combination of single words into verbal expressions, manifested as the "serial organization of speech processes" (Lashley, 1951)—that are the two most general psychophysiological conditions essential for the conversion of thought into speech and for the expansion of verbal expression.
>
> The role of both these factors of verbal communications differs in differ-

ent types of communication; in the first, which Svedelius (1897) at that time called "the communication of relationships" ("Socrates→man," "birch→tree"), the process of placing the object into a class or, in other words, the paradigmatic factor, arranging the elements of communication in hierarchically constructed simultaneous schemes, is predominant; in the second form—"communication of events" ("house burns," "dog barks") there is a totally different psychological process and the syntagmatic connections, the units of coherent expression are clearly predominant. (Luria, 1976a, pp. 34–35)

The encoding and decoding processes of spoken language that occur within the paradigmatic system do so within the multidimensional association complex that lies behind the word. Basically, these associations are of three types:

a) *semantic associations,* according to which words which are part of the system of one total concept and words designating objects which make up one total situation are associated with each other. Thus, the word *loshad'* (horse) can be linked with the words *korova* (cow), *ovtsa* (sheep), *sobaka* (dog) through the category of "domestic animals" and with the words *volk* (wolf), *medved'* (bear), *lissa* (fox) through the more general category of "animals"; with the word *oves* (oats), *seno* (hay), through the category of "food"; with the words *ekipazh* (vehicle), *telega* (cart) through the category of "work" etc.

b) *sound associations,* by which a word is linked with other words similar in sound. Thus, the word *koshka* (cat) can be linked with the words *kroshka* (crumb), *kryshka* (cover), *kruzhka* (mug), or the word *skripka* (violin) with the word *skrepka* (clamp).

c) *morphological associations,* by which a word can be linked to other words similar in morphological structure. Thus, the word *tele-tayp* (teletype) can be linked to compound words *tele-graf* (telegraph), *tele-fon* (telephone), *mikro-fon* (microphone), etc. which are morphologically similar. (Luria, 1974a, pp. 2573–2574)

In the normal, healthy person the semantic association (situational and conceptual) dominates, but this changes as a result of disturbances of the normal neurological processes such as chemicals, extreme fatigue, or infections and also as a result of pathological conditions of lesions or cortical under-development. The experiments of Luria and Vinogradova verified the fact that normally the semantic system is dominant. Utilizing an experimental method that measured vascular components of the orienting reaction of the patient to a word to which a conditioned reaction has been established, they identified three categories of words within the semantic system of association:

(1) *the nucleus of the semantic complex,* to which is related the key word and words in direct semantic proximity to it (they evoke a specific pain reaction); (2) *the periphery of the semantic system* to which are related words linked less directly with the key word (evoking a non-specific orienting reaction); and (3) *neutral words,* which in our experiment did not evoke any specific or orienting reactions. (Luria & Vinogradova, 1959, p. 99)

An interesting consequence of the dominance of the semantic system is Luria's hypothesis that the reason we all have difficulty in recalling surnames or family names is because such words have no semantic association within our lexical system, and we have to rely on the weaker morphological or sound associations (Luria, 1947a, p. 2574).

This marvelously intricate organizational structure of spoken language may, despite its complexity, be inadequate to convey "sense" or the affective aspect of the semantic component of spoken language for the individual. Consequently, it is beneficial that spoken language continues to retain some of its sympractic origins:

Whereas written speech, in which there is no interlocutor, is always monologic and cannot be supported by extralinguistic (sympractic) aids—knowledge of the situation, facial expression, gestures,—in spoken (especially dialogic) speech this limitation is absent: in this case information can be transmitted by extralinguistic aids, and incomplete expansion, ellipsis, the participation of intonation, and so on, can exist. (Luria, 1976a, pp. 36–37)

In addition, spoken language is closer in nature to the individual's internal speech in which,

with its contracted structure and predicative function, sense predominates over meaning, and the transition from thought and internal speech to external verbal communication is largely connected with the process of transition from subjective motives and senses to meanings that are extended, objective, and accessible for transmission as information. (Luria, 1976a, p. 25)

Thus, spoken language can more facilely convey the subjective nuances of intended meaning than can the more constrained written mode.

In contrast, the "meaning" aspect of the semantic component of language is an objective reflection of generalized relationships that exist in reality; is socially and culturally formed; and is manifested in the codes of language:

The codes of language are constructed at different levels; they are organized into hierarchical systems of elements on the basis of certain cues (in other words, they have a definite paradigmatic structure). A disturbance of ability to acquire and use these codes may arise independently of disturbances of the syntagmatic organization of coherent expression and it is most frequently associated with lesions of the posterior cortical areas of the left hemisphere . . . .

The paradigmatic system of language, formed by oppositions of a more or less complex type, can be studied at the levels of its phonemic, lexical and semantic organization.

The phonemic organization of language is based on a system of acoustic and articulatory oppositions, without which it would be impossible to use the codes of the language.

In different languages the assortment of features on which these oppositions are based varies; some oppositions exist in all languages, others are used in only certain languages (Jakobson, 1941–1942). For instance, the vowel-consonant contrast exists in all languages, whereas the opposition of nasal and nonnasal consonants or between long and short vowels is used in only some languages. However, the presence of a strict paradigmatic organization of the phonological level of linguistic codes is equally essential to all languages. The secondary zones of the sensory and sensomotor cortex play an essential role in the cerebral organization of this level and the syndrome of "phonemic disintegration," that arises in lesions of these zones, was well described in the French literature many years ago.

The lexical or, more precisely, the morphological organization of language is concerned with the meaning of its words and it forms the basis of the system of concepts which the language uses.

In languages such as Russian, most words have a root and a system of additional components (prefixes, suffixes, and inflections); these components not only distinguish the essential features of an object or action described, but they also place it in a certain category; it is this function of speech that is essential for concept formation . . . .

Naturally this lexical-morphological organization of speech is based on a system of "paradigmatic" contrasts, which this time is concerned not with the phonemic (acoustico-articulatory), but with the semantic features of words.

The word "chernil'nitsa" (inkstand) does not simply denote an object, but immediately places it into a whole system of comparisons . . . .

In the same way changes in the prefix in the verbs "prikhodit'" (to come), "u-khodit'" (to go away), "azkhodit'" (to go visit often), "pod-khodit'" (to approach), as well as changes in words affecting features denoting number, time, or state form a highly complex system of codes enabling phenomena designated by the words to be organized, their essential features distinguished, and the phenomena placed into particular categories.

Clearly in all these cases the lexico-morphological system of codes formed in the language in the course of tens of thousands of years does not simply permit particular objects and actions, qualities and relations, to be named but it automatically undertakes for us the highly complex task of picking out the necessary features, placing the objects or actions into certain categories, and contrasting the phenomenon named with others not possessing the particular feature or included in other categories.

Such a semantic organization, which is incomparably more complex than the simple assigning of a word for a particular object, evidently leads to even more complex forms of cognitive activity that depend less on sensomotor processes and are perhaps effected by other cortical functional systems.

We must now consider the last and, evidently, the most complex level of organization of the codes of language—the semantic level.

Psychologists are well aware that words with the same lexico-morphological organization and denoting the same object . . . may have quite different meanings.

The word "ugol" (charcoal, carbon), by which the housewife understands the substance required for heating the stove, but which the charcoal burner uses to denote the material he makes, is placed by the chemist in a large and abstract category of substances designated by the letter C and including such widely different articles as charcoal, anthracite, or diamond . . . .

The phenomenon I have described has been called either the "meaning" or "semantic organization," or sometimes the "internal form of words." The discovery that at the different stages of the child's development a word not only possesses a range of associations that differs in its width, but also conceals different psychological processes, was made by L. S. Vygotskii [Vygotsky] more than forty years ago . . . .

It will be obvious that this level of semantic organization of language also uses a complex hierarchical system, or in other words, it has a complex paradigmatic structure; . . .

I have enumerated the principal levels of paradigmatically organized codes of language that must of necessity be used whenever verbal communication is encoded. (Luria, 1976a, pp. 95–97)

The preceding quote delineates the paradigmatically structured objective system of codes into which the expressive process of spoken language must be encoded, and from which the impressive process of spoken language must be decoded. Consequently, the process element of spoken language is inextricably tied to its structural dimension in the normal, healthy individual. But Luria's study of the pathological spoken language functioning of the aphasic patient permitted him to separate the normally inseparable, and he could then trace the cortical underpinnings of the various codes. The results demonstrated that the higher mental process of spoken language arises from "a complex functional system of conjointly working cortical zones . . . " (Luria, 1966b, p. 35), and that various cortical systems underlie the various codes of spoken language:

For instance, the acquisition and use of phonemic linguistic codes requires the participation of the secondary parts of sensory and sensomotor subdivisions of the speech areas, but this is quite unnecessary for the acquisition and use of lexical and semantic codes.

On the other hand, the acquisition and use of lexicomorphological and semantic codes requires the participation of the most complex, tertiary zones of the cortex, adjacent to areas responsible for the reception, processing, and storage of visual and auditory information; these zones are concerned with the organization of complex forms of perceptual activity and have an absolutely essential role in the more elementary forms of external, acoustic speech. (Luria, 1976a, pp. 98–99)

The developmental stages of the encoding and decoding processes of spoken language were covered earlier, and therefore are not recapitulated in detail here, but only summarized. The three basic developmental stages of encoding activity are: (1) repetitive speech, (2) naming objects, and (3) intentional, complex, narrative speech (Luria, 1973e, pp. 318–319); the latter stage of which requires the existence of the more general developmental stage of internal speech from the sequence of (1) external speech, (2) egocentric speech, and (3) internal speech (Vygotsky & Luria, 1930, p. 465).

Decoding activity or impressive speech has a minimum of two stages: (1) the isolation of phonemes, and (2) the comprehension of the whole connected utterance (Luria, 1973e, pp. 309–311). The comprehension stage includes a reverse of the four-stage progression from motive to expanded utterance that was delineated earlier. In addition, however, these stages can occur only if the individual also has the neurological capacity for analysis and synthesis of the perceived elements and a sufficient level of memory to maintain these elements while the analysis and synthesis proceeds (Luria, 1973e, pp. 311–312).

An examination of how these characteristics of spoken language impact upon the development of intellect or higher mental processes is presented in Chapter 8—"Functional Relationships Between Higher Mental Processes and Spoken Language."

8 Functional Relationships Between Higher Mental Processes and Spoken Language

All of the theories and research of A. R. Luria evolved from his goal of developing an objective theory of the human mind. Initially, when he focused on the mind-body dichotomy, spoken language was for him merely a means of reflecting, via the free-association method, the conflict between the emotions and the intellect over which would control the body. As Luria's work progressed and his thought developed, his primary goal still remained an adequate explanation of the functioning of the human mind, but the role of spoken language in his theories changed from one of merely *giving form* to mental processes to a role of *forming* higher mental processes. He argues that "mind" is impossible without its synergetic relationship with spoken language, and that both arise from the physical reality of the human brain and human society. An understanding of such a mind/spoken language relationship is particularly significant for any theorist attempting explanations or predictions about the phenomenon of human communication. To clarify that relationship, this chapter presents the essence of Lurian theory—eight lawful relationships between higher mental processes and spoken language. Each statement of relationship is followed by a brief review of the evidence supporting the same.

Relationship #1:

> Spoken language is the means by which higher mental processes derive their sociocultural origins.

Elementary processes are biologically determined, and higher mental processes emanate from sociocultural origins (Vygotsky, 1978). Yet, the two are interdependent in that the elementary processes of humans and other higher animals produce signalization—the most general and fundamental activity of the cerebral hemispheres. Signalization is an involuntary process, the passive reflection of naturally occurring connections among naturally occurring stimuli. Humans, however, build upon this reflexive

129

process and step beyond it in that they are capable not only of altering naturally occurring connections, but of creating new stimuli and connections. Vygotsky believed that only humans have this ability, and that it is accomplished by means of the tool and the sign. Tool use leads to a change in objects, and manifests an external orientation by the user. In contrast, sign use does not change objects since it is internally oriented, and aimed at changing the individual himself or herself. It is the combined usage of tool and sign in psychological activity that defines higher mental processes for Vygotsky (Vygotsky, 1978); and both Vygotsky's and Luria's work (et passim) present the dominant role of the sign in shaping human intellect.

Phylogenetically, tools and signs were both invented and perfected over the long course of human history. Vygotsky and Luria take a similar developmental approach to ontogenesis. Psychological activity with its combined usage of tool and sign is not innate; rather, such functioning is gradually acquired by the child through social interaction. Vygotsky and Luria hold that

> Every function in the child's cultural development appears twice; first, on the social level, and later, on the individual level; first, *between* people (interpsychological), and then *inside* the child (intrapsychological). This applies equally to voluntary attention, to logical memory, and to the formulation of concepts. All higher functions originate as actual relations between human individuals. (Vygotsky, 1978, p. 57)

The interaction between child and adult exemplifies the social component of the sociocultural origins, and that interaction is accomplished by means of spoken language—that system of signs that "carries within it the generalized concepts that are the storehouse of human knowledge" (Luria, 1979, p. 44). Hence, the social and the cultural sources of higher mental processes become inextricably united in the vehicle of spoken language. The importance of the social source is emphasized by Luria's comment that "a lack of oral communication with others cannot avoid producing a natural retardation in intellectual development" (Luria, 1963a, p. 19), since interaction is essential for the genesis of intellect. Gradually, during ontogenesis, these social origins of speech are converted into the functional dimension of spoken language "as a form of social communication" (Luria, 1973e, p. 307); yet, the social continues to be bound to the cultural.

Cultural conditions can have importance throughout the lifespan in that "the social circumstances in which a child grows up will inevitably leave their mark on the mechanisms underlying complex psychological processes, not just on the content of those processes" (Luria, 1974b, pp.

49–50). This postulate was supported by Luria's work in the 1930s with peasants in a remote area of central Asia (Luria, 1976b). The data was suppressed, but finally presented in *Cognitive Development: Its Cultural and Social Foundations* (1976b). It was Luria's premise that people internalize their cultural level of development via the developmental progression of word meaning associations inherent in spoken language: (1) affective associations, (2) concrete image associations, and finally, (3) verbal-logical associations. He found that the illiterate people of Uzbekistan were characterized by concrete, situational thinking and were incapable of the abstract, formal reasoning that typifies other cultures whose language skills have developed beyond the stage of primary orality. The study provides an exemplar of the fact that the speech system of an oral culture is always dominated by the sympractic dimension of spoken language. As his theory anticipates, Luria found a similar structuring of elementary processes, but a difference in the organization of higher mental processes because of "the way the various thought operations are structured among people whose cultural history has not supplied them with a tool such as writing" (Luria, 1979, p. 45).

At first it may appear that Luria's view of the sociocultural origins of higher mental functioning is very deterministic. However, intervention is possible since spoken language is the most easily influenced of the higher processes according to Luria. As a result, speech's participation in the formation of mental connections can be manipulated, and "significantly accelerated by training" (Luria, 1957b, p. 118). This idea was demonstrated in Zaporozhet's research, which accelerated the acquisition of syllogistic reasoning (Luria, 1982); and in a study with identical twin boys in which levels of mental development were heightened by special speech training (Luria & Yudovich, 1959).

The pedagogical implications of the sociocultural origins theory and research, according to Luria, are that one must vary one's teaching according to the different levels of socialization engendered by different social environments.

The theoretical stance of mind's sociocultural origins embodied in speech fueled Luria's vehement rejection of "locationalist" approaches to neurological functioning throughout his long career. Such origins combined with his concept of higher mental processes evolving through developmental stages could not logically coexist with any physiological theory which maintained that higher functions were localized in specific sites in the brain; and Luria's theory always meets the criterion of logical self-consistency.

Relationship #2:

> Spoken language is the initial and basic developmental stage of the speech
> system, which is always a factor in the formation of higher mental processes.

Ten representatives from the USSR attended the Ninth International
Congress of Psychology held at Yale University September 1–7, 1929. Included in that number was Luria who presented a paper co-authored with
Vygotsky entitled, "The Function and Fate of Egocentric Speech" (1930).
They indicate that the stage of childhood speech that Piaget termed "egocentric" does not merely accompany behavior but rather has an organizing function. Further, instead of simply disappearing as it is replaced by
more socialized verbal behavior, Vygotsky and Luria maintain that egocentric speech has an active role:

> On the strength of our experiments we consider it possible to change the tra-
> ditional schema of the verbal evolution of explicit speech, vi., external
> speech—internal speech, into external speech—egocentric speech—
> internal speech. We thus consider egocentric speech as one of the most im-
> portant processes having a specific function in the evolution of the cultural
> behavior of the child. (Vygotsky & Luria, 1930, p. 465)

The first stage of external speech includes the spoken language of others in the child's social environment as well as utterances by the child.
Thus it is the stage that spawns the social origins of social language. The
child's external speech is initially imitative and then evolves into egocentric speech, which serves a special function by aiding the child in organizing his or her behavior, and is characterized by its "coding for self" nature. Such speech is gradually internalized and becomes internal or inner
speech. However, in the process of that internalization its character is
modified somewhat so that its most distinctive feature becomes its predicative nature. Internal speech is also characterized by its ellipsis, synthesis of meaning, and silence. Periodically, Luria refers his reader to the
Vygotsky's writings for a more explicit explanation of the general developmental stages of spoken language since Luria presumes a familiarity by
the reader with these stages and does not discuss them in great detail.

Written speech is another possible stage of the speech system that influences the formation of higher mental processes, but it is not required for
the existence of the same. If written speech develops, it affects higher
mental processes only as a result of the fact that internal speech is susceptible to its influence:

the functional and structural features of written speech . . . have . . . one important aspect; they inevitably lead to a considerable development of *inner speech*. Delaying the direct revelation of speech connections, inhibiting them and showing increased requirements for the preliminary speech act not being revealed at once by training, written speech produces such a rich development of inner speech as could not have a place in the earlier phases of development. Therefore, neuro-pathologists are not working at random when, desiring to investigate the possibilities of inner speech, they turn to the nature of the written speech of their patients. (Luria, 1961d, p. 738)

Even in oral cultures, however, the child's mental functioning does not begin from nothing, but draws upon the resource of the spoken language that significant others bring to the initial stage of the child's speech system, and uses that wellspring to spawn categorical thought.

Relationship #3:

Spoken language is a determining factor in the developmental stages of higher mental processes.

For Luria, the sociocultural origins of higher mental processes mandate that such processes are acquired in a developmental manner rather than being found ready-made in the infant, and their evolution includes a qualitative shift when

elementary direct forms of activity are replaced by complexly organized functional systems shaped on the basis of association of the child with adults in the course of the child's education. These functional systems are complex in structure and are implemented with the direct participation of language. As language is, to begin with, the major means of human intercourse, it has at the same time become one of the principal tools for shaping man's mental activity and regulation of his behavior. It is specifically as a consequence of this that complex forms of psychological activity, which are gradually implemented with the participation of the second signal system, acquire new characteristics and begin to function in accordance with new laws that replace many of the rules followed in the elaboration of the elementary conditioned reflexes of animals . . . . (Luria, 1963d, p. 18)

Thus the elementary, sensory systems in the child's brain, which are originally affective in nature, are gradually changed by the influence of spoken language. This transformation has such an impact on the child's mental development that Luria considers it a basic task of psychology to trace how the elementary, direct forms of association which initially have an emotional-active character gradually become conditioned by speech; how this verbal behavior becomes separated from overall behavior into a special activity depending on a system of language; and how on the basis of these complex forms of verbal associations new forms of mental activity, which are social in their origin and speech-conditioned in their structure, begin. (Luria, 1969c, p. 128)

The mental associations or connections between objects that are typical of higher mental processes thus derive their complexity from the fact that they are engendered by the speech system, and as a result, Luria states that they have unique characteristics in contrast with mental connections in animals: (1) Speech-formed connections form immediately while mental connections in animals must be formed gradually over time. (2) Speech-formed links provide their own reinforcement, and have no need for any external reinforcement, while the conditioned associations of animals are soon extinguished unless they receive external reinforcement. (3) Speech-formed associations can be modified immediately while those produced through conditioning in animals are very difficult to reshape.

The plasticity or mobility of human mental connections exists because the word preserves within itself all the possible levels of association. Consequently, the problem solving activities supported by speech-formed mental connections have the ability to use whatever level of relations or associations is appropriate for the task at hand—elementary and visual, or complex and abstract (Luria, 1961d, p. 728).

An illustration of how the acquisition of speech-formed mental connections impacts on the developmental stages of concept formation is presented by Luria in "Speech Development and the Formation of Mental Processes" (1969c), which appeared in *A Handbook of Contemporary Soviet Psychology* edited by Michael Cole and Irving Maltzman:

In the earliest stages of development, grouping geometric figures into one whole designated by a single word is very difficult. In response to this task the child simply selects all figures which fall within his gaze, uniting into one conglomerate set all those blocks which he sees. The word still does not play the role of a unifying sign, and grouping does not continue beyond the limit of this random, syncretic approach to objects . . . . Such syncretism without preliminary orientation to attributes and without preliminary analysis constitutes the earliest stage of thinking, in which the word does not play a substantial role but is subordinated to the influence of immediate impressions.

. . . there follows a second stage which has a distinct and internally regular structure. Attempting to select all objects which are designated by one artificial word, the child makes a preliminary analysis of the group of objects placed before him and singles out certain attributes. However, this signal attribute is far from obligatory and may change from trial to trial . . . .

Only in the next stage, which is formed under the influence of systematic training, is there substantial change. The word, changing its structure, is given a new, important meaning in the execution of the task. In this stage which, according to Vygotskii, is attained only during adolescence, the word becomes freed from the influence of direct impressions. It abstracts now one, now another attribute and synthesizes them into a complex of attributes. The process of classification acquires a complex character mediated by the word. The selection of each figure is determined not by direct impression, but by a stable preserved system of attributes abstracted with the aid of the word and shared by the objects selected in the required group. Generalizations underlying the word lose their concrete character. A system of abstract meanings becomes the guiding criterion for further intellectual operations. The word becomes the basic instrument of thinking, and thinking acquires a mediated character. (Luria, 1969c, pp. 134–135)

To clarify and summarize, there are three developmental stages for concept formation: (1) syncretic unification, which is accomplished through immediate sensory impressions, (2) situational unification, which occurs as a result of visual operations, and (3) abstract unification, which is accomplished through the mechanism of spoken language's stage of internal speech.

Attainment of the final stage is characterized by speech becoming so pervasive in the thinking of the individual that it is utilized even when the requirements of the task do not mandate it. Thus, when humans who have achieved this level of mental functioning are

faced with a certain *problem,* they always find their bearings by using the abstracting and generalizing, analyzing and synthesizing power of language. It is important to note that this is so even when the experiment is concerned with relatively simple, perceptible connections; when speech does not replace the signals presented and is not mentioned in the subject's verbal report after the experiment. (Luria, 1957b, pp. 120–121)

In fact, Luria argues that after reaching this stage when internal speech is the means of forming mental connections, spoken language becomes so dominant in the formulation of new mental connections in humans that any disturbance or lessening of this characteristic serves as an indicator of a pathological change in human mental functioning (Luria, 1957b, p. 124), and he supports this argument with evidence from his own research with various types of mental pathologies.

To summarize, once the internal speech stage of spoken language becomes a component in the development of any mental process, Luria maintains that it then makes a qualitative shift to the level of a higher mental process with the attendant consequences that its capacity for functioning is greatly enlarged, and the mental connections underlying the process become more stable and controllable.

Relationship #4:

> Spoken language reorganizes the cortical zones that underlie higher mental processes.

This reorganization of the cortical zones occurs in both phylogenetic and ontogenetic human development. In looking at the cortical reorganization that resulted in the human race from the influence of spoken language, Luria notes that it impacted particularly on the secondary and tertiary cortical fields:

> It is only in man, in the peripheral segments of the nuclear zones of the analyzers and of the motor cortex, that structural and functional differentiation into highly specialized, distinct areas, concerned with the analysis and integration of stimuli of especial importance to the various aspects of speech, took place. For instance, a special area in the posterior segment of the peripheral field of the auditory cortex (Wernicke's "center") is concerned with the analysis and integration of the receptive elements of spoken language or phonemes, and an area in the peripheral fields of the visual cortex is concerned with the analysis and integration of the visual elements of receptive language. In areas of the inferior segments of the parietal region, situated next to the curaneokinesthetic zone and in direct contact with the sensory "centers" of the arm, lips, tongue, and larynx, the analysis and integration of cutaneokinesthetic reception fundamental to articulation takes place. A certain portion of the periphery of the motor cortex, the inferior segments of the premotor zone (Broca's "center"), is the seat of the neurodynamic processes involved in the synthesis of the individual sounds of spoken speech into complex successive units. In another portion of the premotor zone, adjoining the motor "centers" of the upper limb (in the posterior segment of the mid-frontal gyrus), are located the cortical mechanisms for the programming and performance of the complex systems of successive movements and motor skills . . . .

> As a result of the segregation of specialized speech areas of the cortex in the peripheral fields of the nuclear zones, the neuronal structure of the central fields of these zones becomes perfected and capable of perceiving the elements of speech and differentiating their sensory and motor components with a high degree of precision. This process is particularly conspicuous in the central auditory field.

. . . These progressive structural changes reflect the fundamental role of spoken language in the entire system of verbal communication.

The upshot of the qualitative transformation undergone by the overlapping zones of the analyzers in the frontal portion of the cortex following the formation of the second signal system is that all of man's conscious mental processes, governing his actions, involve the participation of the system of verbal communication and, indeed, are under its domination . . . . (Luria, 1966c, pp. 61–63)

A cursory review of human brain structure is in order to facilitate an understanding of the above quote for the reader without neurological training. The cerebral cortex is morphologically a complex hierarchical system comprised of primary, secondary, and tertiary zones. All zones not only receive stimuli, but also produce multilevel excitation in the central nervous system. All zones are also subject to the tonic influence of the reticular formation.

The primary or "extrinsic" zones receive afferent (carrying toward, usually to the central nervous system) fibers, which, via the nuclei of the thalamus, have a direct connection to outside stimuli. Similar in organization are the secondary or "projectional-associative" zones, which overlay the primary zones. However, they are characterized by more complexly developed cellular formation in the second and third layers of the cortex (neocortex usually has six layers) which provides them with the capacity for more systemic and complex operation of the analyzer in question.

The tertiary or "intrinsic" zones are referred to by Luria as "overlapping zones" since they are less modally specific and serve to integrate several analyzers for the performance of complex functions. They receive stimuli from both the nuclei of the thalamus and from other primary areas of the cerebral cortex. It is unique to the human brain that a high percentage of it is comprised of tertiary zones, and Luria suggests that this is due to the evolutionary influence of spoken language.

The cortical base underlying higher mental processes is also transformed during ontogenetic or individual development:

The structural variation of the higher mental functions at different stages of ontogenetic (and, in some cases, functional) development means that their cortical organization likewise does not remain unchanged and that at different stages of development they are carried out by different constellations of cortical zones . . . . The essential thing to remember . . . is that this change in the character of localization (or, more accurately, cortical organization) of the higher mental functions is strictly regular, conforming to a pattern ascertained by Vygotskii [Vygotsky] (1960, pp.390–391) . . . .

Observations have shown that the relationships between the individual components of the higher mental functions do not remain the same during successive stages of development. In the early stages, relatively simple sensory processes, which are the foundation for the higher mental functions, play a decisive role; during subsequent stages, when the higher mental functions are being formed, this leading role passes to more complex systems of connections that develop on the basis of speech, and these systems begin to determine the whole structure of the higher mental processes. For this reason, disturbance of the relatively elementary processes of sensory analysis and integration, necessary, for example, for the further development of speech, will be decisively important in early childhood, for it will cause underdevelopment of all the functional formation for which it serves as a foundation. Conversely, the disturbance of these forms of direct sensory analysis and integration in the adult, in whom the higher functional systems have been formed, may have a more limited effect, compensated for by other differentiated systems of connections. This concept implies *that the character of the cortical intercentral relationships does not remain the same at different stages of development of a function and that the effect of a lesion of a particular part of the brain will differ at different stages of functional development.* (Luria, 1966b, pp. 36–37)

This cortical reorganization engendered through spoken language is indirectly demonstrated by the fact that the human brain after the internalization of speech is capable of two types of integrative or analytic-synthetic activity: (1) simultaneous synthesis, and (2) successive synthesis.

The first of these forms is the integration of the individual stimuli arriving in the brain into *simultaneous, and primarily spatial, groups,* and the second is the integration of individual stimuli arriving consecutively in the brain *into temporally organized successive series.* (Luria, 1966c, p. 74)

These activities are supported by different cortical systems. Simultaneous synthesis results from the functioning of the visual, kinetic, and vestibular systems that orient the body in space. Successive synthesis is a product of the motor and acoustic systems, which are also the systems primarily concerned with spoken language. Narrative speech is considered by Luria to be an excellent example of successive synthesis in that it is temporally ordered, and comprised of serially organized elements.

Relationship #5:

Spoken language is the means by which more elementary sensory systems of the brain are consciously controlled by higher mental processes.

Even in Luria's early writing (1932a), he implies that spoken language is somehow involved in the control of the elementary subcortical systems although, at that time, no neurological knowledge existed to support his rather vague postulate that speech was the primary mechanism in the "functional barrier," which organized excitations and thus kept them from being transferred directly to the motor systems and initiating uncontrolled actions.

Later in his career, Luria's premise became more specific and he declared that internal speech, a developmental stage of spoken language, is a process that is *"characteristic of the development of almost all the higher forms of mental activity"* (Luria, 1961 a, p. 35). Internal speech is an inherent part of higher mental processes because it is the source of the mental associations that make higher functioning possible. Luria often refers to these mental associations as "temporary links" reflecting the fact that they are susceptible to change while mental associations or links formulated under the direction of instinct are rigid and inflexible.

As noted previously, because the mental associations or links of humans have their genesis in internal speech and because they are always mediated by the verbal system, they are much more complex than the mental associations of animals and have unique characteristics. These unique qualities include immediate formation, provision of innate reinforcement, and the capacity for instant modification.

This participation of a stage of spoken language (internal speech) in the formation of mental connections is so pervasive in human mental activity that Luria indicates frequently that human pathologies are defined by its absence.

The internalization of spoken language to form internal speech is also accompanied by an internalization of the verbal principles that are inherent in its structure. These principles, derived from the paradigmatically and syntagmatically structured code systems of spoken language, become organizing patterns for action and for understanding action so that

> The inability verbally to formulate the principle of the motor reactions, which is characteristic of oligophrenic children, confirms the fact that in these cases the system of the verbal connections really does not take part in the formation of motor reactions. (Luria, 1961a, p. 135)

As spoken language gains dominance over behavior, it reverses the occurrence sequence of action and speech so that voluntary behavior evolves in three developmental stages: (1) practical action, (2) action followed by external speech, and the final stage, (3) contracted speech or internal speech leads action (Luria, 1957b, p. 118). The latter stage reflects the achievement of higher mental functioning.

Throughout his work, Luria continued to amass evidence that not only were higher mental processes located physically above the lower processes—neocortex versus subcortical—but that they also occupied a position of functional dominance. One area of research supporting this position that cortical level functioning dominates the subcortical was Luria's work with Parkinson's disease patients (1959b, 1960b, 1961a, and 1967d), which demonstrated that it is possible to transfer the control of defective involuntary (subcortical) motor behaviors to the voluntary (cortical) motor areas so that the subject can still perform the desired action, since the pathology has left the cortical areas intact.

Parkinsons' disease patients are characterized by the fact that:

> The injured subcortical apparatus excites repeated tonic responses, and the pathologically perseverating tension of all muscles is an obstacle to the execution of the instruction. It is easy to imagine such a difficulty in carrying out voluntary movement if one briefly tenses all the muscles in one hand and then tries to move it without relaxing the tension. (Luria, 1959b, p. 455)

However, if the origin of the motor act is shifted from the automatic movement realm governed by the subcortical motor apparatus to the conscious movement domain of the cortical motor areas, the patient is able to carry out the required movements. This may be accomplished by

> attaching a symbolic function to his movements. He is asked to reply to the experimenter's questions by beating out the necessary numbers with his finger. If we then ask him, "How many wheels on a car?" or "How many points on a compass?" we see that the same patient who failed in the previous experiment and could not automatically strike the table with his fingers even two or three times, easily begins to do so, switching his movements into his speech system and subordinating them to the complex dynamic constellations of cortical connections. (Luria, 1959b, p. 455)

Even when both the neocortex and subcortical levels have been physiologically weakened, as in the case of cerebroasthenic children, the neocortex or cortical level will still dominate the subcortical and can be used to assist in the latter's defective functioning. In one experiment comparing the verbal and motor reactions in such children, Luria presented the children with insignificantly different color and time duration signals. Using only a motor response, the children did not distinguish between the signals. In contrast, when required to give an oral response labeling the signal as "dark" or "light" and "long" or "short," the children differentiated easily between the signals. The dominance of the verbal organization was demonstrated by the fact that the motor responses also became accurate when they were combined with the verbal response.

An example of the domination of the cortical over the subcortical in normal humans through the means of internal speech is illustrated by the fact that the reflexive "orienting reflex" to new stimuli in an individual's environment can be reinstituted or prolonged merely by attaching verbal significance to a stimulus. The orienting reflex

> includes a series of somatic, sensory, vegetative, electrocephalographic, and other components. While having a certain autonomy, all components of the orienting reflex obey common laws: they appear with the presentation of stimuli which are new for the organism; they have a nonspecific character, i.e., they do not depend on the modality of the stimulus; they disappear in proportion to repetition; and reappear with any changes in the experimental situation. (Luria & Komskaya, 1970, pp. 303–304)

The orienting reflex is an involuntary response that humans share with other species. However, Luria and Khomskaya found that in humans one can regulate the orienting reflex by means of speech, which physiologically modifies the functioning of the same:

> If, by means of speech, stimuli are given signal meaning, a series of changes in the system of the orienting reflex occurs, namely: extinguished orienting reactions reappear and become more intensive (their latent period is shortened, their strength and duration is increased), they do not extinguish any more, and they arise for a wider range of intensities (as a result of the lowering of the threshold sensation and the elevation of the threshold of the defense reaction). In this situation, the orienting reactions become more discriminating. They are not responsive to any outside nonsignal stimuli. Similar changes in the system of the orienting reflex occurring with the introduction of verbal instructions are observed in all normal subjects who are in an awake state (grownups and children, beginning from 8–10 years of age). (Luria & Khomskaya, 1970, p. 304)

Luria and Khomskaya indicate that this regulation of the orienting reflex by means of speech is such an essential characteristic of healthy human mental functioning that it "may serve as an important indicator of the normally functioning brain" (Luria & Khomskaya, 1970, p. 305). In fact, Luria states that the dominance of speech-mediated systems of mental connections over the direct sensory ones can be an indicator of pathology (if the level drops), which is as reliable as the more basic physiological indicators of pathological mental functioning:

> specific criteria for various pathological conditions are to be found not only in general patholophysiological indicators (changes in force, mobility, and equilibrium of neural processes) but also in changes in interaction between

the two aforementioned levels of neural processes. (Luria, 1967d, pp. 413–414)

Relationship #6:

> Spoken language is the customary source of auxiliary stimuli (*"stimuli artificially introduced into the situation"* (Vygotsky, 1966, p. 24), which produce the mediated structure of higher mental processes.

Earlier, when defining higher mental processes, it was noted that they always have a mediate structure. In other words, something always acts as a mediating factor between the stimuli of the environment and the response of the organism, and this mediation is possible only through auxiliary stimuli. An example given in the earlier discussion was that of a person tying a knot in his or her handkerchief to remember something that has nothing to do with handkerchiefs. A clearer portrayal of how the use of auxiliary stimuli evolves during development is given by Luria in his observations of developmental stages in children given memory tasks:

> (1) The child is not in a state to perform the task by the complicated auxiliary means. He is incapable of connoting the objects offered as the auxiliary means and fails to remember a series of words "with the aid" of cards; such is the *preinstrumental* stage of development.
>
> (2) The child begins to attempt to use the objects offered as the means for attaining the object, but does it clumsily, without attempting to establish a rational connection between the task and the auxiliary means, looking at the latter as a sort of magic . . . . This phase is characterized by a purely formal attitude to the method adopted, a blind faith in its efficacy though it is thoroughly inadequate. This phase (which we have observed in children of five to seven though it may appear in later years) we can call the magical or the *pseudoinstrumental* phase.
>
> (3) Finally, much later we observe the *real instrumental* stage in the development of the child, the main features of which are the complicated structure of acts of behavior, the ability to adapt one's self to difficult tasks by using adequate means and the outer auxiliary stimuli. It is precisely this part of behavior which develops most in a schoolboy and the modern civilized man, and is of utmost significance. (Luria, 1928a, pp. 503–504)

The whole process, however, attains a higher level of efficiency when the auxiliary stimuli are internally generated via internal speech, and the child is no longer dependent upon the resources of the external environment. The complexity of mental connections or associations possible is increased tremendously by the fact that the word preserves in itself all systems of connections inherent in it, beginning with the very elementary and visual and ending with the very complex and abstract; and . . . depending on the different tasks, dominating connections can be established either by this or other systems of connections. Without this, any plastic thinking could not be possible and the person using the system of most abstract relations for the solution of more concrete everyday problems, always risked finding himself in the position in which a schizophrenic patient in whom the second signaling system is severed from the first and behavior loses its sensible and expedient character [*sic*]. (Luria, 1961d, p. 728)

Consequently, once developed, speech-formed connections are the prevalent source of auxiliary stimuli for humans, yet they acquire a range of choices with such connections. They can, if they wish, choose to utilize the more elementary level connections of the visual or phonetic systems rather than the complex connections of the semantic level.

The ramifications of the mediated structure that results when auxiliary stimuli render higher processes indirect rather than being direct stimulus-response reactions to the environment are presented in the discussion of the next relationship.

Relationship #7:

Spoken language is the means by which the individual becomes capable of conscious and voluntary processes.

In *The Nature of Human Conflicts* (1932a), Luria defined voluntary behavior as "the ability to create stimuli and to subordinate them; or in other words, to bring into being stimuli of a special order, directed to the organization of behavior" (Luria, 1932a, p. 401). Consequently, even in his early work we see evidence of a perceived relationship between auxiliary stimuli created by the individual and volitional control of the individual's actions. The implication is that volition cannot exist without the existence of auxiliary stimuli.

Even as a reflex, the motor act has a beginning and a conclusion. The latter is based on the fact that

Many outstanding neurophysiologists have repeatedly pointed out that the regulation of action requires a system of "feedback" afferentations which give a signal for the discontinuance of the action after its accomplishment; and they have also stated that without such a system of signals, arising from the effect of the action, movement cannot become controllable. (Luria, 1961a, p. 63)

Given this need for afferent feedback to end action, Luria and his colleagues hypothesized that it might be possible to utilize a contravening movement by the young child in response to verbal instructions as the afferent signal to end diffuse motor impulses:

> Experiments on these lines performed by S. V. Yakovleva yielded very interesting results: in 50 percent of all the children tested at eighteen months to two years, and in 75 percent of children at the age of two to three years, this change in the instructions resulted in the complete disappearance of accidental intersignal pressures of the bulb and produced clear cut reactions co-ordinated with the conditioned signal . . . on the other hand the removal of the sanctioning afferentation led, in the overwhelming majority of children, to the recovery of the original diffusiveness of the motor reactions. (Luria, 1961a, p. 66)

In these examples, the auxiliary stimuli were introduced into the situation by the experimenters, and Luria calls the outcome *"the first and simplest model of a voluntary movement in a very young child"* (Luria, 1961a, p. 66). Gradually, through developmental stages, Luria maintains that the initiation of afferent feedback to end action changes in locus from the external source of the adult to the child himself or herself. The final development stage is then voluntary action or behavior that is a higher mental process since it has sociocultural origins, evolves through developmental stages, is conscious as well as voluntary in nature, with the speech system playing a part in its development:

> voluntary action arises in the process of the child's relationships with the adult, and passes through a number of successive stages in its development. Originally taking the form of the fulfillment by the child of the adult's verbal instruction, it is gradually—with the development of the child's own speech—transformed into a system of self-regulating in which the decisive role is played first by external and subsequently by internal speech, the chief mechanism of voluntary action. (Luria, 1960a, p. 139)

This paradigm together with the sociocultural origins supported Vygotsky's conviction that all the higher psychological functions of humans are voluntary in nature rather than merely reflexive, which he considered to be a limitation of the mental functioning of other higher animals. In fact, he noted that it is voluntary activity rather than intellect which distinguishes humans from other higher life forms.

Another example of the development of the volitional nature of a higher mental process is provided in Luria's description of the evolution of voluntary attention, which, in turn, becomes a component in the higher mental process of active perception:

> If the mother shows the child an object at the same time saying "this is a cup," this object is distinguished from the remaining objects and as a signal becomes a strong component of the complex of stimuli acting on the child. The cup begins to attract the child's attention, which at this time remains "involuntary" in its form but social in its content.
>
> However, when the growing child, forming his behavior in intimate interaction with the adult, himself begins to *point* to the proper object, to change its position in space, to note its additional signal sign or simply to call it by a specific word, the child produces in the environment those changes which in the future begin to act on him as a type of "feedback" and which, thereby, begin to attract his attention. In this case we have a new structure in organization of attention, which, remaining reflex in its nature, acquires, however, the quality of a mediated act and becomes in the original scientific sense of this word *voluntary attention.*
>
> Under "voluntary attention" (as, however, even under any complex "voluntary" function) we should, consequently, understand such a reflex act as social according to its genesis and mediated according to its structure and with which the subject *begins to submit to changes themselves produced by him in the environment and in this way to master his own behavior.* (Luria, 1961d, p. 748)

As well as illustrating the social origins characteristic, the above example of voluntary attention also demonstrates how spoken language can act as a mediating factor between the individual and the environment; and there is again the implication that volition cannot occur without the prior existence of auxiliary stimuli.

Soviet psychology considers rational consciousness to be the highest form of mental activity. Consequently, this perspective dominates in Soviet research (Luria, 1961d) while the subconscious occupies a very subordinate role in Soviet studies. Rational consciousness itself, however, evolves through developmental stages. Initially, animal or sensory consciousness is mere wakefulness or the passive "reflexion of objective reality" (Luria, 1967a, p. 469). Secondly, such consciousness may develop into a "complex activity which has a semantic and systemic structure" (Luria, 1967a, p. 469), and thus combines sensory and rational levels. The latter stage constitutes uniquely human consciousness and is an attributional aspect of higher mental processes. It includes the active alteration of connections in both external and internal reality as well as volitional self-awareness.

A truly *objective* and abstract consideration of self, however, is possible only when the speech system's developmental stage of written speech evolves from the prior stages of spoken language, and provides logical thought with the mechanism whereby the self and its functioning can be objectified. In support of this, Luria found that the illiterate people of Uzbekistan were generally incapable of analyzing their own psychological functioning or the subjective qualities of their personalities (Luria, 1976b, pp. 144–160).

Such objective self-awareness is a further enrichment of the second developmental stage of consciousness. The augmentation is possible, but not inevitable, since it depends on the developmental level of the culture's speech system. The second stage of consciousness, with or without this objectivity, is always necessary for voluntary behavior; and the interdependency of spoken language, consciousness, and volition for Luria is demonstrated in his statement that "the unconscious element in our behavior may quite accurately be called 'the unverbalized element' " (Luria, 1978e, pp.140–141).

On the neurological level, Luria notes that the frontal lobes of the brain are the cortical areas responsible for conscious action. His position is based on the fact that the frontal lobes with their prevalence of tertiary zones have been shown to control the level of attentiveness; to control the maintenance of externally originated verbal programs for behavior; and to control the construction of the individual's own strategy, plan, or program for action. His case studies of brain lesion patients are usually presented to illustrate and support each of these points and a succinct presentation of the same was given in an evening lecture to the XIX International Congress of Phychology, which met at University College, London, from July 27–August 2, 1969 (Luria, 1971b).

Relationship #8:

> Spoken language is a component in the complex functional systems of other higher mental processes. ·

The initial step in explicating this relationship is to define what constitutes a "complex functional system" for Luria. To begin with, functions are not inflexible, inevitable processes of activity; rather the term refers to a

> complex adaptive activity (biological at some stages of development and social-historical at others), satisfying a particular demand and playing a particular role in the vital activity of the animal. A complex adaptive "func-

tion" such as this will usually be executed by a group of structural units and
... these will be integrated into a functional system. The parts of this system
may be scattered over a wide area of the body and united only in the execution of their common task (for example, respiration for locomotion). Between these parts there is a pliable yet strong temporary connection, uniting
them into one system and synchronizing their activity. This "functional system" works as a complete entity, organizing the flow of excitation and co-
ordinating the activity of the individual organs. (Luria, 1963b, p. 36)

Since spoken language impacts both phylogenetically and ontogenetically on the cortical organization of the brain as noted earlier, it is a factor in setting up the complex cortical systems underlying the functioning
of all higher mental processes. A mental as well as physical relationship of
spoken language to the complex functional systems of higher mental processes results from the fact that internal speech, a developmental stage of
spoken language, is a mental process necessary for the normal development of higher mental activity. Internal speech is also an inherent part of
developed higher mental processes because it is the source of the mental
associations that make their functioning possible. Luria frequently calls
these mental associations "temporary links," referring to the fact that they
can be altered easily while mental associations formed via conditioning or
instinct are inflexible.

As a result of this genesis in internal speech and their mediation by the
verbal system, human mental associations are much more complex than
the mental associations of animals, which *are* derived from instinct or
conditioning. Their unique qualities were noted earlier, but to review the
same briefly, include the fact that they form immediately, provide their
own reinforcement, and can be modified immediately if one wishes to
do so.

This participation of internal speech in the formation of mental associations or connections is such a salient characteristic of human mental activity that Luria continually maintains that its absence is an indicator of
pathology. Thus, the specific feature that characterizes the higher mental
activity of oligophrenic (mentally retarded children)

consists in the fact that the speech system does not here participate so actively in the formation of new connections as in normal children of the same
age. (Luria, 1961a, pp. 132–134)

The internalization of spoken language to form inner speech includes
an internalization of the verbal principles inherent in its structure. Consequently, these principles, derived from the structured code systems of
spoken language, become organizing patterns for action and for understanding action.

As mentioned earlier, when comparing verbal and motor reactions in cerebroasthenic (cortically weakened) children, Luria found their speech responses to be much more stable and organized than their motor responses, which indicated to him that inherent in the child's speech was an organizing factor. In his experiments, these children were presented with insignificantly different color and time duration signals. The children's motor responses indicated no differentiation while their verbal responses accurately distinguished between the stimuli. The motor response became accurate only when accompanied by the verbal response, thus demonstrating the dominance of verbal organization when verbal and motor responses were combined.

The plasticity or mobility of human mental connections exists because the word preserves within itself all the possible levels of association. As a result, the problem-solving activities supported by speech-formed connections have the ability to use whatever level of relations or associations is appropriate for the task at hand—elementary and visual, or complex and abstract (Luria, 1961a, p. 728). Luria postulates that words have a multidimensional association with each other and that such associations in order of dominance may be phonetic (auditory) associations, morphological (visual) associations, or semantic associations. In total these associations form a complex verbal network that constitutes the paradigmatic or vertical structure of language.

Luria maintains that the semantic associations always dominate in a healthy individuals's waking consciousness, and that phonetic and visual associations remain incidental and inhibited. This was demonstrated in experiments conducted with O. S. Vinogradova. One of the experiments utilized measurements of the defensive reaction (vascular constriction in both head and hand) engendered when the signal word was reinforced by a painful electric current. Subjects included normals, and mild as well as severe oligophrenics (retarded children).

The results obtained indicated that the semantic system is dominant over sound associations in normals. Exceptions were normals under the influence of chloral hydrate, which puts the cortex in an inhibitory state, and both levels of oligophrenics.

When spoken language becomes a component in any mental process, it is transferred to the level of a higher mental process and its capacity for functioning is greatly enlarged. In addition, the mental connections underpinning the function or process become much more stable. An example of this influence is memory. Not only is the activity stabilized and expanded, but the new higher level of memory is capable of augmenting defective functioning on the part of the lower mnemonic processes:

> Local lesions deep in the brain, like those located in the posterior (temporal, parietal and occipital) zones of the hemispheres, give rise only to elemen-

tary disturbances of memory that can be compensated by a transfer to a higher level of semantic organization. (Luria, 1976c, p. 24)

If spoken language is a component in the complex functional system that comprises any higher mental process, then any decrement in spoken language's development should also precipitate a deficit in the higher mental process of which it is a part. For example, in normal development, the memory functions that make possible the development of abstract thought can do so because the mental connections that such functions store for later recall are based on semantic associations. Semantic associations permit the individual to move himself or herself from the concrete sensory level in logical thought to the abstract. However, if the memory traces or connections are preserved through perceptual associations, the higher mental process of logical thought of which they are a component is automatically affected.

Such a situation is typical of a developmental stage of adolescence, but it was also exemplified by Luria's case study of S., the man who was dominated by his visually-based memory. In normal development, however,

> this soon ceases to be a problem for the adolescent, . . . for he shifts from thinking in concrete terms to dealing with abstractions; the role graphic images once played in his thinking is replaced by certain accepted ideas about the meaning of words. His thinking becomes verbal and logical in nature, and graphic images remain on the periphery of consciousness, since they are of no help in understanding abstract concepts. (Luria, 1968, pp. 132–133)

In the case of S., abstract thought was never possible, since his memory was forever constrained to sensory connections.

In summary, spoken language is such an essential component in the complex functional systems of other higher mental processes that

> speech cannot be treated in isolation from other psychological activities and . . . the acquisition of language plays a decisive role in the organization of all higher psychological functions, perceptual and motor, thus establishing a higher level of human behavior. (Luria & Simernitskaya, 1977, p. 175)

OVERVIEW OF RELATIONSHIP

As stated earlier, Luria had originally perceived of spoken language as *giving form* to mental processes. He had combined free-association with a simultaneous motor response because he conceived of verbal and motor

responses as being a unitary system, which would reflect the conflict between the intellect and the emotions. Thus, the underlying mental processes were merely given form by the verbal and motor responses.

Luria's view of the role of spoken language began to change, however,
when he was exposed to the theories of L. S. Vygotsky. Luria describes the
influence as follows:

> My own work was permanently changed by my association with Vygotsky
> and by the ingenious studies of our students. . . . I was still conducting stud-
> ies using the combined motor method, but as exemplified in *The Nature of
> Human Conflicts,* the focus in my work began to change. Although I had
> begun with an interest in studying the dynamic course of emotions,
> Vygotsky saw in my research a model for studying the relation between
> complex voluntary movements and speech. In particular, he emphasized
> the way in which speech served as an instrument for organizing behavior.
> (Luria, 1979, pp. 51–52)

Vygotsky's interest in such higher psychological functions produced an
attendant interest in neurology, and resulted in Vygotsky's enrollment in
medical school. The observations Vygotsky made at the neurological clinic began with cases of aphasia. Both Vygotsky and Luria (who had also en-
rolled in medical school) found that they needed a better comprehension
of linguistics, since the state of neurology at that time was not adequate to
explain the aphasic behavior they were encountering. Luria explains,

> My interest in linguistic phenomena grew naturally out of early research
> using the combined motor method and Vygotsky's theory, which empha-
> sized language as a key tool, unique to human beings, for mediating their in-
> teractions with the world. But a serious study of language as a highly organ-
> ized system of human behavior began in earnest only after I had begun work
> on the problem of the neuropsychology of sensory and semantic aphasia.
> (Luria, 1979, p. 165)

Luris indicates that it was also the reading of the neurologists, Potzl,
Head, Gelb, Goldstein, and others which led him to realize that he must
understand the way information is stored in the brain and how people
construct summaries of detailed events. To do this, he turned to a study of
Trubetskoy, Vinogradov, Svedelius, and other linguists, and his perception of the relationship of higher mental processes and spoken language
began to give an increasingly active role to spoken language.

> One of the distinctions which began to appear in linguistics with the work of
> de Saussure in the 1920s and which I came to use heavily in the 1940s owing

to the work of Roman Jakobson was the difference between the "paradigmatic" aspects of language, which refers to the placing of words and the things they denote into categories, enabling people to use language to make comparisons and generalizations, and the "syntagmatic" aspect of language, which enables people to join words together into coherent expressions. The paradigmatic function of speech allows the codes of language to be used to separate out significant cues in the environment, and it also makes it possible to take whole categories of cues into consideration at a single moment, which is what we do when we use categories. The paradigmatic function of speech is intimately related to the basic motives that direct activity. It links our intentions to our thoughts.

In trying to understand the cortical organization of language, we must recognize the existence of both the categorizing and the intention-fulfilling functions which intermingle in every utterance. Moreover, recognizing that they carry out different, if related, functions, we can expect their cortical organization to be different. Looking back into the history of neurology, we can see that as early as 1913 Pick was pointing to the syntagmatic function when he sought to determine how condensed thought patterns can be expanded into smooth, sequentially organized statements, and Jackson's reference to the "propositionizing" aspect of speech showed that he too recognized the importance of this function.

Working with this distinction, which was anticipated and used by Vygotsky in *Thought and Language* and in his preliminary articles on brain localization, we found the anticipated difference in the brain localization of syntagmatic and paradigmatic language functions. (Luria, 1979, p. 169)

Luria goes on to note that the gnostic or posterior portion of the brain processes the paradigmatic structure of language while the dynamic anterior area of the brain is the material base for language's syntagmatic structure. Such a concatenation of the neurological and the linguistic was made possible by the 2 years of linguistic study Luria undertook in an effort to increase his tools for understanding the human mind, and the role of spoken language in its development. Anything more than a superficial or fragmentary understanding of mind requires a number of such tools, according to Luria. For this reason, he advocated a knowledge of tools provided by such fields as neurology, psychology, speech pathology, physiology, speech communication, and linguistics. The tunnel-vision of the "specialist" was viewed by Luria as being incapable of the theoretical scope mandated by the complexity of mental functioning.

The role of spoken language in Luria's theory of mind expanded throughout his career until it reached the proportions presented in this chapter. In essence, Luria presents spoken language as the mechanism by which human functioning makes the qualitative shift from the purely physiological to the more complex, abstract level of higher mental processes that continue to have a physiological base.

It is my conclusion that all the multifaceted aspects of the relationship between higher mental processes and spoken language presented in Lurian theory could be condensed into a single term, *means*. Spoken language or speech is both the *means* by which higher mental processes *have form* or are expressed, and through the internalization of spoken language as internal speech, spoken language also becomes the *means* by which higher mental processes *are formed* in ontogenesis. Thus Bacon's proposition (which Vygotsky once used as a book motto) could have been referring to the function of spoken language in the creation and expression of higher mental processes: "Nec manus nuda, nisi intellectus sibi permissus, multum valent: instrumentis et auxilibus res perticitur. [Neither bare hand, nor intellect by itself, are worth much: things get done with the aid of tools and means.]" (Leontiev & Luria, 1968, p. 342).

Epilogue:
Critique and Commentary

The primary purpose of this book is to acquaint the reader with the quintessence of Lurian theory as well as with the scope of his work. A secondary purpose is to provide a sort of "reader's guide" to the Lurian corpus. Suggesting that a newcomer to Luria read the corpus without benefit of a category system and/or a glossary for guidance is an almost certain guarantee of frustration due to Luria's diversity of subjects and his sometimes specialized language. Consequently, it is hoped that this text may render the task less formidible for students approaching Luria for the first time, and that it may facilitate the investigations of more knowledgeable scholars who wish to focus on a particular topical area. The wealth of insight that Luria's writings can provide is too valuable to be lost simply because of logistical problems in acquiring it.

In support of the text's primary purpose, it has been my experience that the majority of American scholars seem to have constrained their knowledge of Luria to a focus on either aphasiology or the verbal regulation of behavior, thus ensuring a disregard of his core theory and its range. This book was engendered by that experience and my conviction that Lurian theory constitutes a general theory of such scope and validity that any scholar of either human intellect or spoken language would benefit from a consideration of Luria's assertions about the mind/speech relationship in formulating her or his own theory.

Given those reasons for publication, I was reluctant to dilute Luria's thought with too much commentary in the text since that might divert the reader's attention to an analysis of my critique rather than of Luria's theory. Therefore this epilogue is my forum for evaluating Luria's theory using metatheoretical criteria, and for reviewing what I consider to be the theory's implications for spoken language scholars.

METATHEORETICAL CRITERIA

Theory construction in actual practice is never as pedestrian nor as pristine as theory-building textbooks present it. Yet, I think we can gain some perspective on the quality of Lurian theory by applying metatheoretical criteria to it. A general theory, such as Luria's, has a broad range or scope in that it attempts to cover all instances of a phenomenon rather than merely explaining limited aspects of it under certain conditions. Louis Hjelmslev (1971) provides us with three criteria by which to judge the quality of a general theory in his *Prologomena to a Theory of Language.* In order of priority, a good general theory must be: (1) logically self-consistent, (2) exhaustive in dealing with the phenomenon, and (3) parsimonious or as simple as possible.

In meeting the first criterion, Luria excels. Producing a theory that does not contradict itself begins with the theorist's epistemological assumptions or world view, and the appropriateness of that perspective for the questions being addressed by the theory. Behavioristic theories of meaning, for example, originate from a world view that is inadequate to accommodate the phenomenon they are attempting to explain. In contrast, Luria's perspective, developed in conjunction with Vygotsky, views humans as active organisms that achieve their mental potential via a developmental process resulting from an interaction with their sociocultural milieu. This development, of course, is dependent on the material base of a healthy, human brain, and made possible by the symbol system of spoken language. I find this perspective to be of sufficient breadth to deal with the explanations and/or predictions about human mental functioning attempted by Luria.

The timing and placement of Luria's career also may have influenced his construction of a logically self-consistent theory. One of the strengths of Soviet psychology has been its emphasis on a consideration of philosophical problems, and Marxist-Leninist philosophy has some advantages as an attempt to answer the old problem of the nature of the psyche and its relationship to the material world. As Payne (1968) notes, this philosophy rejects Cartesian dualism and espouses a moderate materialism that recognizes that psychic events are not material. It is also a relatively well articulated philosophy, which facilitates its application. This philosophy combined with the proximity of Luria's early career to the 1917 Revolution, and his participation in the "troika" (Luria, Vygotsky, and Leontiev), which attempted to redefine psychology in keeping with the revolution's Marxist-Leninist ideals, may have forced a consideration of world view in formulating his theory that other times and environments might not have mandated.

The Soviet emphasis upon philosophy may have encouraged a well-developed world view, but it also resulted in a political climate that sometimes fostered illogical premises and curtailed research pursuits, as when Luria's investigations of the oral culture of Uzbekistan were suppressed, or when his twin research was terminated. However, the shifting political environment never restructured Luria's theoretical foundations. He simply shifted to another avenue of investigation that was compatible with his theory, yet viable in the current climate. An exemplar was his response to the 1950 edict that Soviet psychology had to be faithful to both the "Classics" and Pavlovian theory.

To unite the basic reductionism of Pavlov with the moderate materialism of Marxism-Leninism is an almost impossible task since the two are essentially incompatible world views (Payne, 1968). Luria solved the problem by assimilating what he considered to be Pavlov's legitimate tenets on the physiological level, and using them in pursuing the origins of voluntary behavior via the combined motor method. This approach was a viable investigation of Vygotsky's thesis that psychology should resolve the problem of interaction between lower and higher mental functions as well as his premise that speech is a psychological tool that shapes consciousness (Kozulin, 1984). Pavlovian theory was adequate in Luria's opinion to explain lower mental functions, and the combined motor method resembled Pavlovian conditioning experiments. This solution was particularly ingenious, according to Cole (1979), because of its focus on speech. As an elderly man, Pavlov had begun to speculate on whether conditioning could account for human language, and had made it quite clear that this was the one area in which his theory was incomplete. Consequently, Luria's research on voluntary behavior met the demands of the political environment without forcing any inconsistencies in his own theoretical framework.

As might be anticipated, Luria frequently criticized his Western collegues for their atheoretical approach to research. He seemed genuinely astounded by the absence of a developed theory in some researchers, and suggested that such an omission lead them into erroneous assumptions and nonproductive studies. A typical example of this are his comments regarding many of the participants at an international symposium on brain and consciousness (Luria, 1967a).

Some theorists with a developed theory are criticized for being too rigid, and consequently not open to the discovery of new ideas or the consideration of new evidence. Luria, despite his well articulated theory, did not become dogmatic in his response to either new discoveries or new theories. In fact, he was sometimes criticized by fellow Soviets for being too open to Western ideas while some Western critics have denigrated his willingness to incorporate others' theories too readily. Yet, every new idea, such as Chomsky's deep structure, is added to Lurian theory via assimilation, not accommodation. In other words, the concept is preserved, but its attendant rationale is modified so that it augments Luria's theory and is compatible with it.

I found Luria's fidelity to a theoretical paradigm served an organizing function rather than one of perpetuating a closed mind. The organizing capacity of a theory is particularly valuable in dealing with multifaceted behavior, especially a behavior so complex as mental functioning. The research process is facilitated when the researcher can follow the guidelines of an organized theory rather than simply hoping that somehow some pattern will emerge. Luria's work demonstrates that theory also encourages continual progression in the development of knowledge, rather than sporadic, almost accidental advancement. The characteristics of higher mental processes and spoken language delineated in Chapter 1 were extrapolated from work throughout Luria's career of over 50 years, yet all are logically consistent with the theoretical foundations that Luria and Vygotsky had developed in its first decade.

The second criterion of being exhaustive in dealing with the phenomenon of mental functioning is one of Luria's strengths. To my knowledge, no theorist has ever dealt with the phenomenon of human mind across a domain comparable to Luria. He covers the physiological/neurological mind, the developing mind, the pathological mind, and the mind as shaped by varying sociocultural environments. Despite the amazing scope of his theory, there are still omissions. Some areas are not covered because of what Luria considered to be their minimal importance, and other areas would have been probable extensions of his theory if time and technology had permitted them. Evidently, emotional aspects of human mental functioning were not seen as pertinent by Luria, since after his early investigations of reason versus emotion for control of the human organism, no interest was shown in the emotional side of mind. That such neglect was deliberate is also implied by Payne's (1968) criticism of Soviet psychology in general for not dealing with the affective aspects of mental functions.

There is ample evidence that Luria was a very empathetic and personable clinician, but none that he considered emotion an appropriate area of study. It would have been theoretically consistent for Luria to have examined the cognitive labeling of affective states, or human emotions that depend upon mediation by the speech system for their existence or recognition. Yet, he never did. The most plausible explanation for such an omission is that evidently Luria continued to consider affective states examples of lower mental functioning à la his early work (Luria, 1932a), and therefore not relevant to a theory focusing on higher mental processes.

Spoken language in its function as a form of social communication, and the phylogenesis of spoken language seem to be omitted from Luria's investigations simply because of a lack of interest on his part rather than any theoretical irrelevance. He occasionally makes a token reference to the position of the "Classics" that spoken language resulted from a need to communicate engendered by social forms of labor, but it is always a formulaic aside without real significance in his discussion. It would have been interesting to learn his reaction to Susanne Langer's (1972) idea that spoken language arose from the human brain's receptiveness to stimuli.

An aspect of Luria's theory that he would certainly continue to pursue if he were still alive is the attribute of inner speech. The process of inner speech is essential to Lurian theory, and yet its functioning is probably the most vague explanation in his theory. No doubt, this is due to the difficulty in investigating it with any precision. Some have accused Luria of reification in his presentation of inner speech, but a close review of his writings demonstrates that Luria was never so foolish as to presume a concrete structure for inner speech. Throughout his career, Luria was a vehement anti-locationalist, and in his later work, such as *Language and Cognition* (1982), he was very explicit in talking about inner speech as a process rather an entity having any material morphological characteristics.

In conjunction with inner speech, Luria's discussion of the progression from thought to external utterance never deals with the origins of the initial step—motives. It seems plausible to me that "-mand" and "-tact" could be spawned by purely physical origins, but how would Luria have explained the motive that was his own creation, "-cept" or the desire for a more clear formulation of thought? No indication is provided, so I can only speculate that Luria would have maintained that a self-awareness of any of the three motives cannot exist until the internalization of spoken language makes possible the shift from animal to human consciousness. Hence, motives too would have sociocultural origins.

Dealing extensively with the phenomenon is one of Luria's assets, but it also results in repetitiveness. In preparing this book, apparent redundancy was somewhat of a problem. I think this results from Luria's attention to nuances and detail. He utilizes the same study several times, and interprets it each time in light of his expanding knowledge to illustrate various points as the theory continues to build. His studies with retarded children, which were utilized to discuss memory, verbal regulation of behavior, and cortical tone, are an example. The same study may be referenced, but his understanding of the phenomenon of mental functioning is being expanded just a bit more with each new examination and review of the study.

The third criterion of being parsimonious is very important and very difficult when a theorist is dealing with a phenomenon as complex as mental functioning. I find Luria's style of thinking and writing to be generally succinct. He frequently uses almost formulaic expressions which condense his presentations, but do present some difficulties for the reader who is not familiar with the detailed interpretation of those formulas. When he writes about the structure and neurology of the brain, it would certainly be possible to bury the reader in incredible detail and abstruse terminology, however, I found Luria's discussion in many instances to be more clear than my neurology texts in graduate school. Some of this clarity may be due to the fact that Luria was extremely proficient and skillful in the use of language. Generally, someone who loves language and enjoys its variety is more masterful in expressing complex, abstract concepts than the individual who wields language in a perfunctory manner, insensitive to the many possible shades of meaning.

The theory itself is a parsimonious theory in that there are only eight statements of relationship between the two main theoretical units. There is the possibility, of course, that these could be compounded greatly if one attempted to push for more specific propositions in the pursuit of empirically testable hypotheses. Yet, I think the eight lawful relationships are a fair representation of the substance of the theory, and reflect Luria's organized, parsimonious treatment of the symbiotic relationship between spoken language and higher mental processes.

Similar to the concise treatment of the units' relationship is Luria's description of the units. Higher mental processes are presented with seven general characteristics while spoken language embodies that same seven plus seven more. Given theoretical units of such complexity, it is a testimony to Luria's fulfillment of the criterion of parsimony that their description is that simple rather than requiring pages of minutia. Thus, it is my conclusion that Luria does an outstanding job of keeping his theory as simple as possible, especially given the complexity of the phenomenon.

Using Hjelmslev's criteria, I find Luria's theory to be an excellent general theory. However, that does not mean that he has said all there is to say on the topic of mental functioning. A fourth standard for judging theory, which did not originate with Hjelmslev but provides a nice segue to move to a consideration of the implications of Luria's theory for spoken language scholars, is what Littlejohn (1983) refers to as a theory's heuristic value. This refers to a theory's potential for generating research to investigate its premises as well as additional theory relevant to the phenomenon. The scope of Luria's theory and the logical consistency with which it was formulated make it an excellent resource for further research and theorizing. It is a frequent source of frustration to me that American spoken language scholars appear, in general, to be unfamiliar with this resource.

IMPLICATIONS FOR SPOKEN LANGUAGE STUDY

In addition to the areas of further research and theorizing that have already been discussed, Lurian theory has pedagogical implications with respect to the preparation of scholars for spoken language study and for the domain of the specific academic discipline of speech communication. We would have to expand the preparation of students for spoken language study in order to utilize Luria's theory as fully as possible. Luria rejected any particular educational specialization as being adequate to understand mental functioning; and similarly, I think students should have at least a basic understanding of anatomy, neurology, psychology, speech communication, anthropology, sociology, and linguistics.

The basic understanding of anatomy is necessitated by the fact that spoken language is built on a functional base of the more elementary sensory systems of the brain. A knowledge of neurology is mandated by spoken language's existence as a stimulus, and by the dynamic status of its "conjointly working cortical zones" (Luria, 1966b, p. 35) in the neurological realm. Both fields provide spoken language study with an objectively verifiable data base, and the knowledge to examine it.

Spoken language's status as a human behavior, which according to Luria underlies all other human behavior, necessitates the study of psychology. In addition, the fact that one of the functions of spoken language is its existence as a form of social communication together with its social origins also calls for some familiarity with current speech communication studies. A need to know the basics of anthropology and sociology results from Luria's premise that spoken language is cultural as well as social in its origins, and the fact that social conditions continue to have a role in its development since it is an associative higher mental process. Linguistic study is required since any comprehension of the encoding and decoding process of spoken language cannot progress beyond the level of rather elementary speculation unless the investigator has some knowledge of the paradigmatic codes and the syntagmatic organization by which such codes are connected into complete, meaningful utterances. In summary, Luria's presentation of spoken language as a complex functional system constructed on a base of material complex functional systems mandates that the acquisition of knowledge and skills to adequately investigate its character and functioning cannot be as simplistic as study of a single academic major. Yet, speech communication could come close if it would expand its focus to include all of Luria's spoken language functions.

Utilizing memory as his specific example, Luria indicated that when spoken language becomes a component in a mental process, its capacity is significantly enlarged, and the mental connections underpinning it become much more stable (Luria, 1976c). In a somewhat analogous position, I think that the incorporation of Luria's theory regarding the relationship between higher mental processes and spoken language into the current discipline of speech communication would result in a similar enlargement of the capacities of the discipline and a stabilization of its underpinnings. In addition, such an assimilation of Lurian theory would provide a base for unifying the applied and theoretical aspects of the field, since his theory encompasses the interests of both. Tying current considerations of the functions and consequences of symbolic interaction to a theory which also considers the physiological/neurological functioning of spoken language could provide the objective, concrete data base desired by some theorists seeking to emulate the hard sciences.

Incorporation of Luria's theory into spoken language study as it is generally constituted in speech communication would also serve to expand the capacities of the discipline's various areas of study. For example, studying the social origins of all higher mental processes should expand the domain of interpersonal communication. It could grow as an area of study from its usual concern with adult social interaction to being concerned as well with the influences of interpersonal communication on the development of higher mental processes with an emphasis on the characteristics of spoken language manifested in various relationships and subsequent mental functioning.

That area of speech communication usually labeled nonverbal communication could gain additional cognitive credence if it were given roots in the characteristic that spoken language always retains an element of the sympractic (extralinguistic) activity so important to primitive languages rather than seeking a parity with verbal language. The area could thus be integrated into an expanded, holistic approach to spoken language study based on Lurian theory.

Spoken language is the most readily influenced of the higher mental processes (Luria, 1957b; Luria & Yudovich, 1959), and this characteristic has implications for the performance areas of speech communication such as public speaking, oral interpretation, debate, persuasion, argumentation, etc. It suggests the desirability of a return to an emphasis on these performance aspects similar to that of the classical period, not because performance is an art to be developed for its own sake nor for practical application in business (although one could support such positions), but rather because such performance skill-building is one means of increasing the adequacy of external spoken language and concomitantly influencing inner speech and subsequently other higher mental processes.

The field of speech communication theory has in the past been primarily concerned with spoken language's function as a form of social communication. The area would be expanded considerably if theorists would also focus on Luria's other functional characteristics of spoken language—that it is a tool for intellectual activity, and that it is a method of organizing or regulating mental processes. The mental processes so organized then, of course, serve to control human behavior. Consequently, the domain of speech communication theory could be extended from a focus basically on the transmission of information to one that incorporates all human activity mediated by spoken language. According to Luria, this would include all conscious and voluntary activity within the purview of speech communication theory.

The applied area of speech communication would also be enlarged to include pedagogy on a general level. For example, one practical application of the study of spoken language could be to influence normal development. The child has no capacity for self-direction according to Lurian theory until the acquisition of spoken language, which then mediates between the child and the direct stimulus. Consequently, prior to spoken language acquisition, pedagogic activity is constrained to the level of conditioning. Once volition and human consciousness are achieved by means of spoken language, one could then proceed to utilize spoken language training to facilitate and even accelerate the mental development of the child. Luria maintained that the teaching process must provide for mental development rather than the mere absorption of knowledge (Luria, 1961d), and held that "The participation of a verbal system in the formation of new connections can be significantly accelerated by training" (Luria, 1957b, p. 118). This capacity of spoken language exists because the mental associations or "temporary links" of humans have their genesis in internal speech rather than continuing to be mechanically formed as are the temporary links formed by conditioning in animals (Luria, 1961a).

Since human mental associations are derived from a stage of spoken language (internal speech), and since one characteristic of spoken language is that it is the most readily influenced of all the higher mental processes, it is logical to anticipate that spoken language training would influence the development of higher mental processes. Luria and Yudovich's twin experiment demonstrated that such an expectation has validity in practice, at least with children (Luria & Yudovich, 1959).

Given such results, it is a significant implication that one practical application of Lurian theory would be the implementation of spoken language training as a regular and required part of the normal academic regimen from preschool forward. Such training, one anticipates, should improve the child's performance in all academic areas that require the application of mental processes mediated by inner speech. Similarly, spoken language training could and should be utilized to compensate for any deficiencies of the child's sociocultural environment. Luria's research (1933, 1974b, & 1976b) demonstrates that sociocultural circumstances influence higher mental processes not just at their origination, but continue to influence their dynamics as well as their content throughout life.

In addition, since Luria (1933, 1976b) indicates that higher mental processes continue to be susceptible to the influence of the speech system in adulthood, one might anticipate that continuing education and other programs directed at the adult should be concerned with the role of spoken language in mental development, and should make use of its characteristics in maximizing their efforts.

Before proceeding to a consideration of the practical application of spoken language study for cases of anomalous development, it should be noted that such study may have implications for the fields of neurology and psychology. The synergistic relationship between higher mental processes, spoken language, and their cortical base presented in Luria's work implies that an increased understanding of the composition and functioning of one of the three components, spoken language, should serve to increase our understanding of human behavior and neurological functioning just as neurological/psychological knowledge has provided insights into the character and functioning of spoken language.

Luria presented evidence that cases of anomalous mental development can be assisted by a knowledge of the characteristics of spoken language (Luria, 1959b, 1959d, 1960a, 1960b, 1961a, 1961b, 1961c, 1963a, 1963b, *et passim*). His studies with Parkinson's disease exemplifies this aid since he found that patients were able to eliminate the perseverating muscle tension by providing a symbolic function for their movements. The possibility of utilizing the speech-mediated level of motor control would probably not have been considered without Luria's postulate that spoken language has the capacity to control the more elementary systems of the brain. This postulate was also supported by Luria's (1960b) discovery that cerebroasthenic children with their generally weakened physiological state of the cortex could compensate for defects in motor control by directing such activities with the semantic aspect of spoken language.

Even the severely retarded, i.e., oligophrenic children, can derive benefits from the study of spoken language. Luria noted that the speech-formed mental associations of the oligophrenic child are even less mobile than his or her motor reactions (Luria, 1963c). However, his study of the developmental states of the mental process of generalization: (1) syncretic unification, (2) situational unification, and (3) abstract unification (Luria, 1961d) lead him to the hypothesis that if the children were incapable of the final stage of generalization because of defects in speech-formed mental associations, then a practical approach would be to attempt to augment the second or concrete, situational stage of development to assist

words . . ." (Luria, 1964a, p. 160). Generally results from lesions to lower portions of left frontal cortex.

Dystropia—Malnutrition.

Edema—"Abnormal collection of tissue fluids, causing swelling." (Zemlin, 1968, p. 540)

EKG—Electroencephalogram. Recording the electrical activity of the brain.

Efferent—Carrying or bearing. Used as carrying from the central nervous system outward. Frequently used as synonymous with motor.

Efferent motor aphasia—Speech defects are manifested as distrubance of the sequential organization of articulation. Generally results from lesions in lower parts of left premotor zone.

Endothelium—"A form of epithelial tissue that lines the walls of the blood vessels." (Zemlin, 1968, p. 540).

Galvanic skin response—Refers to the psychogalvanic reflex which is based on fact that a reflex increase in sweating occurs during emotional states. "If a mild current is passed through the hands, the flow of current increases as the sweating increases. . . . Thus, the reflex response can be measured in a way that tends to furnish objective evidence of emotional reaction" (Gradner, 1975, p. 428). Via conditioning, this reflex can be tied to a stimulus that would not normally elicit such a response.

Ganglion—"An enlargement or mass of nerve tissue containing nerve cells, ..." (Gardner, 1975, p. 433). Usually located outside of the central nervous system.

Granule cells—Smallest of all neurons.

Gray matter—So called in contrast to white matter because it contains mainly cell bodies and fibers that are not myelinated.

Gyrus—"A fold in the cerebral cortex; a convolution." (Zemlin, 1968, p. 542)

Histology—A science which studies the structure of tissues.

Hippocampus—"A part of the brain next to the temporal horn of the lateral ventricle." (Gardner, 1975, p. 433)

Inferior—"The lower of two parts. Situated below or underneath." (Zemlin, 1968, p. 542)

Kinesthesia—The sense of movement of muscles, and the perception of weight, resistance, and position." (Zemlin, 1968, p. 543)

Kinetic—Involving motion.

Lesion—"Any morbid change in tissues due to disease or injury." (Gardner, 1975, p. 433)

Lobe—General parts of the brain, most of which are separated by sulci. Each cerebral hemisphere has a frontal, temporal, parietal, and occipital lobe.

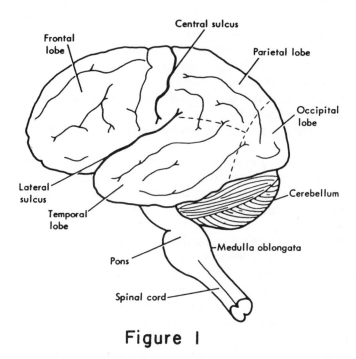

Figure I

"Meaning"—Luria uses it as Vygotsky did to refer to objective associations or denotations.

Mesial—Middle. The mesial plane divides the body into right and left halves as does the sagittal plane.

Morphology—Study of the structure and form of animals.

Myelination—Formation of a fatty sheath on the axon of a nerve.

Neocortex—The new cortex, which is also known as the isocortex. It is the newest type of cortex evolutionarily, and is unique to mammals. Usually multilayered, normally with six layers.

Neurolinguistic—Used by Luria to refer to a field of study that investigates the neurodynamics underlying linguistic structures.

Neuropsychology—Used by Luria to refer to field of study that correlates human behavior with brain anatomy/neurology.

Oligophrenia—Type of severe mental retardation that "develops as a rule after inflammation, intoxication, or trauma affecting the child's brain even at the fetal stage, at the time of birth, or in very early childhood" (Luria, 1959b, p. 458).

Orienting reflex—Term which originated with Pavlov and describes a reflex that consists of "turning the eyes, and then the head toward this stimulus, the cessation of all other, irrelevant forms of activity, and the occurrence of a clearly defined group of respiratory cardiovascular and psychogalvanic responses . . . ." (Luria, 1973e, p. 258).

Paradigmatic—Term refers to the hierarchical, vertical dimension of lan-

166

guage or its scheme for storage. Based on associative connections which may be phonetic, morphological, or semantic in nature.

Parkinson's disease—Degenerative disease characterized by muscular rigidity and tremor. Results from degeneration of a subcortical area of the brain.

Posterior—Dorsal. "Toward the back, or away from the front." (Zemlin, 1968, p. 547)

Primary zone—Those areas of the cortex to which the afferent paths project. These areas are modally specific.

Psychometric tests—Luria uses this term to refer to one-time psychological tests such as the IQ test.

Pyramidal cells—One of two basic types of nerve cells found in the neocortex. They have a conical-shaped body.

Reticular formation—Forms the central core of the brain stem, and comprises much of the central portion of the medulla oblongata. Comprised of a diffuse mixture of gray and white matter which contains many types of neurons. Has an important role in conscious states and attention.

Sagittal—The sagittal plane divides the body into right and left halves. Parasagittal refers to any plane parallel to the mid-sagittal plane but away from the mid-line.

Secondary zone—System of cortex surrounding the primary zones that is neurologically constructed to be less modally specific than primary zones, and thus serves a synthesizing function (Luria, 1973e, pp. 68–69).

Semantic aphasia—Speech defects manifested in inability to simultaneously handle the relational synthesis of concepts formed by language. Generally results from lesions to tertiary zones of temporo-parieto-occipital areas.

Semantic conditioning—Consists of establishing a conditioned reflex to a particular word (Luria, 1975, p. 53).

"Sense"—Luria uses it as Vygotsky did to refer to subjective associations or connotations.

Sensory aphasia—Speech defects that are a "type of disturbance of the analysis and synthesis of speech sounds which arises when the cortical elements of the auditory analyser are impaired" (Luria, 1964a, p. 147). Generally results from lesions to the upper part of the temporal lobe.

Signalization—Vygotsky's term which refers to passive reflection of naturally occurring ties or associations in objective reality. In Pavlov's schema, it would refer to the First Cortical System which includes the special senses such as sight, smell, etc.

Signal systems—Refers to Pavlov's schema of dividing mental functioning into three signal systems: Subcortical, First Cortical, and Second Cortical. The subcortical signal system includes reflexive activity; the first cortical signal system includes the passive reflection of reality via the special senses; and the second cortical signal system includes the creation of stimuli via spoken language.

Signification—Vygotsky's term which refers to the active creation of artificial stimuli. In Pavlov's schema, it would refer to the Second Cortical Signal System.

Simultaneous synthesis—According to Luria, one of two types of analysis-synthesis of which the human brain is capable. It consists of the integration of individual successive elements into a simultaneous spatial scheme. Luria states that the visual, kinetic, and vestibular systems are associated with this process.

Successive synthesis—One of the two types of analysis-synthesis of which the human brain is capable according to Luria. It consists of the integration of separate elements into temporally organized, successive series of elements. Luria states that the motor and acoustic systems are associated with this activity.

Sympractic—Refers to the extralinguistic aids that spoken language utilizes to convey meaning such as gesture, intonation, facial expression, etc.

Synesthesia—Describes state in which a stimulus elicits various subjective, sensory sensations. For example, if the word "gate" evoked a specific taste, a specific smell, a specific color, etc.

Synsemantic—Refers to communication in which linguistic means are the only conveyors of meaning, i.e., written speech.

Syntagma—Any linguistic unit or group of units that is syntagmatically or serially organized, i.e., word, phrase, or clause (Bolinger, 1975, p. 27).

Syntagmatic—Term refers to the horizontal structure or organization of language. Luria utilizes it to also refer to the subject-predicate association in language.

Tertiary zones—Also called the overlapping zones. They are responsible for enabling several sensory analyzers to work in concert, and are specifically human structures. Their function is the integration of stimuli; and they respond to general features such as number of components, type of spatial arrangement, etc., which the secondary and primary zones are incapable of doing (Luria, 1973e, p. 73).

Thalamus—A major part of the diencephalon.

"Troika"—Russian term for a team of three horses.

Unilateral—Involving only one of the cerebral hemispheres.

Ventricle—Small cavity or chamber. The lateral, third, and fourth ventricles contain structures that produce cerebrospinal fluid.

Wernicke's area—Posterior third of the superior left temporal gyrus (Luria, 1973e, p. 303).

White matter—So called because contains large numbers of myelinated fibers that are whitish in appearance.

Bibliography

Bolinger, D. (1975). *Aspects of language* (2nd ed.). New York: Harcourt Brace Jovanovich.

Buhler, K. (1934). *Sprachtheorie*. Jena: Fischer. (In German).

Chomsky, N. (1975). *Reflections on language*. New York: Pantheon Books.

Cole, M. (1978). Introduction. In M. Cole (Ed.), *The selected writings of A. R. Luria*. White Plains: M. E. Sharpe.

Cole, M. (1979). Epilogue: A portrait of Luria. In A. R. Luria, (M. Cole & S. Cole, Eds.), *The making of mind: A personal account of Soviet psychology*. Cambridge: Harvard University Press.

Cole, M., & Maltzman, I. (Eds.). (1969). *A handbook of contemporary Soviet psychology*. New York: Basic Books.

Critchley, M. (1978). In memoriam: A. R. Luria. *Brain and Language, 5*(1), v–vi.

Dance, F. E. X. (1979, July). *A taxonomy of primitive terms for a speech theory of human communication*. Unpublished taxonomy.

Dance, F. E. X., & Larson, C. E. (1972). *Speech communication: Concepts and behavior*. New York: Holt, Rinehart & Winston.

El'konin, D. B. (1954). Features of the intereaction of the first and second signal systems in children of preschool age. *Izv. Akad. Pedag. Nauk. RSFSR, 64*. (In Russian).

Feigenbaum, E. A. (1970). Information processing and memory. In D. A. Norman (Ed.), *Models of human memory*. New York: Academic Press.

Gardner, E. (1975). *Fundamentals of neurology: A psychophysiological approach* (6th ed.). Philadelphia: W. B. Saunders.

Gray, J. A. (1966). Attention, consciousness and voluntary control of behavior in Soviet psychology: Philosophical roots and research branches. In N. O'Connor (Ed.), *Present-day Russian psychology*. Elmsford, NY: Pergamon Press.

Hjelmslev, L. (1971). *Prologomena to a theory of language.* (F. J. Whitfield, Trans.). Madison: University of Wisconsin Press.

Jackson, J. H. (1932). Notes on the physiology and pathology of language. In *Selected writings of John Hughlings Jackson.* London: Hodder & Stouton.

Jakobson, R. (1942). *Kindersprache, aphasie und allgemein lautgesetze.* Uppsala: Almqvist & Wiksell. (In German).

Karpov, B. A., Luria, A. R., & Yarbus, A. L. (1968). Disturbances of the structure of active perception in lesions of the posterior and anterior regions of the brain. *Neuropsychologia, 6,* 157–166.

Karpova, S. N. (1955). Realization of the verbal component of speech by a preschool child. *Vop. Psikhol., 4.* (In Russian).

Kozulin, A. (1984). *Psychology in utopia: Toward a social history of Soviet psychology.* Cambridge: The MIT Press.

Langer, S. K. (1972). *Mind: An essay on human feeling (Vol. II).* Baltimore: The John Hopkins University Press.

Lashley, K. S. (1951). The problem of serial order in behavior. In L. A. Jeffress (Ed.). *Cerebral mechanisms in behavior.* New York: Wiley.

Leont'ev, A. N. (1959). *Problems in development of the mind.* Moscow: Press of the Akad. Ped. Nauk. RSFSR. (In Russian).

Leont'ev, A. N. (1961). The social nature of human mental activity. *Vop. Filos, 1.* (In Russian).

Leontiev, A. N., & Luria, A. R. (1968). The psychological ideas of L. S. Vygotskii. In B. B. Wolman (Ed.), *Historical roots of contemporary psychology.* New York: Harper & Row.

Leontyev, A., Luria, A. R., & Smirnov, A. (Eds.). (1966). *Psychological research in the U.S.S.R., Vol. 1.* Moscow: Progress Publishers.

Littlejohn, S. W. (1983). *Theories of human communication. (2nd ed.).* Belmont, CA: Wadsworth.

Lubovskij, V. I. (1956). Some peculiarities of higher neural activity of normal and abnormal children. In A. R. Luria (Ed.), *Problems of the higher neural activity of the normal and abnormal child* (Vol. 1). Moscow: publisher unknown. (In Russian).

Luria, A. R. (1928a). The problem of the cultural behavior of the child. *Journal of Genetic Psychology, 35,* 493–506.

Luria, A. R. (1928b). Psychology in Russia. *Journal of Genetic Psychology, 35,* 347-355.

Luria, A. R. (1928c). [1927 date cited in quoted text.] *Speech and intellect in the child's development.* Moscow: publisher unknown. (In Russian).

Luria, A. R. (1929). A book review of the journal of psychology, pedology and psychotechnics. Series A; Psychology, K. H. Korniloff (Ed.), 1928, *1*(1), p. 196. Series B: Pedology, Salkind (Ed.), 1928, *1*(1), p. 199. Series

C: Psychophysiology of Labor and Psychotechnics, Spielrein (Ed.), 1928, *1*(1), p. 96. *Journal of Genetic Psychology, 36,* 491-496.

Luria, A. R. (1930a). A book review of M. Bassov, general principles of pedology, Moscow; Leningrad, 1928. *Journal of Genetic Psychology, 37,* 176-178.

Luria, A. R. (1930b). The new method of expressive motor reactions in studying affective traces. *Ninth International Congress of Psychology— Proceedings and papers—New Haven, September 1-7, 1929.* Princeton: The Psychological Review.

Luria, A. R. (1931). Psychological expedition to Central Asia. *Science, 74*(1920), 383–384.

Luria, A. R. (1932a). *The nature of human conflicts.* W. H. Gantt (Ed. & Trans.). New York: Liveright.

Luria, A. R. (1932b). Psychological expedition to Central Asia. *Journal of Genetic Psychology, 40,* 241-242.

Luria, A. R. (1933). The second psychological expedition to Central Asia. *Science, 78*(2018), 191–192.

Luria, A. R. (1934). The second psychological expedition to Central Asia. *Journal of Genetic Psychology, 44,* 255-259.

Luria, A. R. (1935a) L. S. Vygotsky. *Character and Personality, 3,* 238-240.

Luria, A. R. (1935b). Professor L. S. Vygotsky (1896-1934). *Journal of Genetic Psychology, 46,* 224-226.

Luria, A. R. (1935c). Russia. *Character and Personality, 3,* 350-351.

Luria, A. R. (1936–1937). The development of mental functions in twins. *Character and Personality, 5,* 35–47.

Luria, A. R. (1950). *Essays on the psychophysiology of handwriting.* Moscow: Izd. Adad. Pedag. Nauk. RSFSR. (In Russian).

Luria, A. R. (1956). *Problems of the higher neural activity of the normal and abnormal child* (Vol. 1). Moscow: publisher unknown. (In Russian).

Luria, A. R. (1957a). Appendix I—psychopathological research in the U.S.S.R. In B. Simon (Ed.), *Psychology in the Soviet Union.* Stanford: Stanford University Press.

Luria, A. R. (1957b). The role of language in the formation of temporary connections. In B. Simon (Ed.), *Psychology in the Soviet Union.* Stanford: Stanford University Press.

Luria, A. R. (1958a). Dynamic approach to the mental development of the abnormal child. *Journal of Mental Deficiency Research, 2,* 37–52.

Luria, A. R. (1958b). [1958a date cited in quoted text.] *Problems of the higher neural activity of the normal and abnormal child* (Vol. 2). Moscow: publisher unknown. (In Russian).

Luria, A. R. (1959a). The directive function of speech in development and dissolution: Part I: Development of the directive function of speech in early childhood. *Word, 15*(2), 341–352.

Luria, A. R. (1959b). The directive function of speech in development and dissolution: Part II: Dissolution of the regulative function of speech in pathological states of the brain. *Word, 15*(3), 453–464.

Luria, A. R. (1959c). Disorders of "simultaneous perception" in a case of bilateral occipito-parietal brain injury. *Brain, 82,* 437–449.

Luria, A. R. (1959d). Experimental study of the higher nervous activity of the abnormal child. *Journal of Mental Deficiency Research, 3,* 1–22.

Luria, A. R. (1960a). Experimental analysis of the development of voluntary action in children. In H. P. David & J. C. Brengelmann (Eds.), *Perspectives in personality research.* New York: Springer.

Luria, A. R. (1960b). Verbal regulation of behavior. In M. A. B. Brazier (Ed.), *The central nervous system and behavior: Transactions of the third conference February 21, 22, 23, and 24, 1960, Princeton, N.J.* New York: Josiah Macy, Jr. Foundation.

Luria, A. R. (1961a). *The role of speech in the regulation of normal and abnormal behavior.* J. Tizard (Ed.). New York: Liveright.

Luria, A. R. (1961b). The genesis of voluntary movements. In N. O'Connor (Ed.), *Recent Soviet psychology.* New York: Liveright.

Luria, A. R. (1961c). An objective approach to the study of the abnormal child. *American Journal of Orthopsychiatry, 31*(1), 1–16.

Luria, A. R. (1961d). Speech development and the formation of mental processes. *Psychological science in the U.S.S.R., vol. 1.* Washington, D.C.: U.S. Joint Publication Research Service No. 11466, pp. 704–787.

Luria, A. R. (Ed.). (1963a). *The mentally retarded child: Essays based on a study of the peculiarities of the higher nervous functioning of child-oligophrenics.* Oxford: Pergamon Press.

Luria, A. R. (1963b). *Restoration of function after brain injury.* Elmsford, NY: Pergamon Press.

Luria, A. R. (1963c). The role of speech in the formation of temporary connections and the regulation of behaviour in the normal and oligophrenic child. In B. Simon & J. Simon (Eds.), *Educational psychology in the U.S.S.R.* Stanford: Stanford University Press.

Luria, A. R. (1963d). The variability of mental functions as the child develops (based on a comparative study of twins). *Soviet Psychology and Psychiatry, 1*(3), 17–21.

Luria, A. R. (1964a). Factors and forms of aphasia. In A. V. S. DeReuck & M. O'Connor (Eds.), *Disorders of language: Ciba foundation symposium.* Boston: Little, Brown.

Luria, A. R. (1964b). Neuropsychology in the local diagnosis of brain damage. *Cortex, 1*(1), 3–18.

Luria, A. R. (1965a). Aspects of aphasia. *Journal of Neurological Sciences, 2,* 278–287.

Luria, A. R. (1965b). Two kinds of motor perseveration in massive injury of the frontal lobes. *Brain, 88,* part 1, 1–12.

Luria, A. R. (1966a). Brain and mind. *Soviet psychology and psychiatry, 4*(3–4), 62–69.

Luria, A. R. (1966b). *Higher cortical functions in man.* New York: Basic Books.

Luria, A. R. (1966c). *Human brain and psychological processes.* New York: Harper & Row.

Luria, A. R. (1967a). "Brain and conscious experience": A critical notice from the U.S.S.R. of the symposium edited by J. C. Eccles (1966). *British Journal of Psychology, 58*(3 & 4), 467–476.

Luria, A. R. (1967b). Kurt Goldstein and neuropsychology. *Neuropsychologia, 5,* 311–313.

Luria, A. R. (1967c). Neuropsychology and its significance for behavioral sciences and medicine. *Psychologia: An International Journal of Psychology in the Orient, 10*(1), 1–6.

Luria, A. R. (1967d). The regulative function of speech in its development and dissolution. In K. Salzinger & S. Salzinger (Eds.), *Research in verbal behavior and some neurophysiological implications.* New York: Academic Press.

Luria, A. R. (1968). *The mind of a mnemonist: A little book about a vast memory.* New York: Basic Books.

Luria, A. R. (1969a). Frontal lobe syndromes. In P. J. Vinken & G. W. Bruyn (Eds.), *Handbook of clinical neurology, Vol. 2.* Amsterdam: North-Holland Publishing.

Luria, A. R. (1969b). The neuropsychological study of brain lesions and restoration of damaged brain functions. In M. Cole & I. Maltzman (Eds.), *A handbook of contemporary Soviet psychology.* New York: Basic Books.

Luria, A. R. (1969c). Speech development and the formation of mental processes. In M. Cole & I. Maltzman (Eds.), *A handbook of contemporary Soviet psychology.* New York: Basic Books.

Luria, A. R. (1970a). The functional organization of the brain. *Scientific American, 222*(3), 66–78.

Luria, A. R. (1970b). *Traumatic aphasia: Its syndromes, psychology and treatment.* The Hague: Mouton.

Luria, A. R. (1971a). Memory disturbances in local brain lesions. *Neuropsychologia, 9,* 367–375.

Luria, A. R. (1971b). The origin and cerebral organization of man's conscious action. *XIX International Congress of Psychology: Proceedings—London, July 27–August 2, 1969.* London: Henry Ling.

Luria, A. R. (1972). *The man with a shattered world: The history of a brain wound.* New York: Basic Books.

Luria, A. R. (1973a). The frontal lobes and the regulation of behavior. In K. H. Pribram & A. R. Luria (Eds.), *Psychophysiology of the frontal lobes.* New York: Academic Press.

Luria, A. R. (1973b). The quantitative assessment of levels of wakefulness. *Soviet Psychology, 12*(1), 73–84.

Luria, A. R. (1973c). Towards the mechanisms of naming disturbance. *Neuropsychologia,* 1973, *11,* 417–421.

Luria, A. R. (1973d). Two basic kinds of aphasic disorders. *Linguistics, 115,* 57–66.

Luria, A. R. (1973e). *The working brain: An introduction to neuropsychology.* New York: Basic Books.

Luria, A. R. (1974a). Basic problems of neurolinguistics. In T. A. Sebeok (Ed.), Vol. 12, Part II, *Current trends in linguistics.* The Hague: Mouton.

Luria, A. R. (1974b). A child's speech responses and the social environment. *Soviet Psychology, 13*(1), 7–39.

Luria, A. R. (1974c). Speech and intellect among rural, urban, and homeless children. An empirical study edited by A. R. Luria: Foreword. *Soviet Psychology, 13*(1), 5–7.

Luria, A. R. (1974d). Towards the basic problems of neurolinguistics. *Brain and Language, 1,* 1–14.

Luria, A. R. (1975). Basic problems of language in the light of psychology and neurolinguistics. In E. H. Lenneberg & E. Lenneberg (Eds.), *Foundations of language development,* Vol. 2. New York: Academic Press.

Luria, A. R. (1976a). *Basic problems of neurolinguistics.* The Hague: Mouton.

Luria, A. R. (1976b). *Cognitive development: Its cultural and social foundations.* Cambridge: Harvard University Press.

Luria, A. R. (1976c). *The neuropsychology of memory.* Washington: V. H. Winston & Sons.

Luria, A. R. (1977a). Aphasia reconsidered. *Neurolinguistics, 6,* 61–66.

Luria, A. R. (1977b). Brain disorders and language analysis. *Neurolinguistics, 6,* 21–44.

Luria, A. R. (1977c). Differences between disturbance of speech and writing in Russian and French. *Neurolinguistics, 6,* 118–129.

Luria, A. R. (1977d). *Neurolinguistics 6: Neuropsychological studies in aphasia.* Amsterdam: Swets & Zeitlinger B. V.

Luria, A. R. (1978a). The development of constructive activity in the preschool child. In M. Cole (Ed.), *The selected writings of A. R. Luria.* White Plains: M. E. Sharpe.

Luria, A. R. (1978b). The development of writing in the child. In M. Cole (Ed.), *The selected writings of A. R. Luria.* White Plains: M. E. Sharpe.

Luria, A. R. (1978c). Experimental psychology and child development. In M. Cole (Ed.), *The selected writings of A. R. Luria.* White Plains: M. E. Sharpe.

Luria, A. R. (1978d). L. S. Vygotsky and the problem of functional localization. In M. Cole (Ed.), *The selected writings of A. R. Luria.* White Plains: M. E. Sharpe.

Luria, A. R. (1978e). Paths of development of thought in the child. In M. Cole (Ed.), *The selected writings of A. R. Luria.* White Plains: M. E. Sharpe.

Luria, A. R. (1978f). Psychoanalysis as a system of monistic psychology. In M. Cole (Ed.), *The selected writings of A. R. Luria.* White Plains: M. E. Sharpe.

Luria, A. R. (1979). *The making of mind: A personal account of Soviet psychology.* M. Cole & S. Cole (Eds.). Cambridge: Harvard University Press.

Luria, A. R. (1982). *Language and cognition.* J. V. Wertsch (Ed.). New York: Wiley.

Luria, A. R., & Artem'eva, E. Yu. (1978). Two approaches to an evaluation of the reliability of psychological investigations (reliability of a fact and syndrome analysis). In M. Cole (Ed.), *The selected writings of A. R. Luria.* White Plains: M. E. Sharpe.

Luria, A. R., & Hutton, J. T. (1977). A modern assessment of the basic forms of aphasia. *Brain and Language, 4,* 129–151.

Luria, A. R., & Karasseva, T. A. (1968). Disturbances of auditory-speech memory in focal lesions of the deep regions of the left temporal lobe. *Neuropsychologia, 6,* 97–104.

Luria, A. R., Karpov, B. A., & Yarbus, A. L. (1966.) Disturbances of active visual perception with lesions of the frontal lobes. *Cortex, 2*(2), 202–212.

Luria, A. R., & Khomskaya, E. D. (1962). An objective study of ocular movements and their control. *Psychologische Beitrage, 6*(3–4), 589–606.

Luria, A. R., & Khomskaya, E. D. (1964). Disturbance in the regulative role of speech with frontal lobe lesions. In J. M. Warren & K. Akert (Eds.), *The frontal granular cortex and behavior.* New York: McGraw-Hill.

Luria, A. R., & Khomskaya, E. D. (1970). Frontal lobes and the regulation of arousal processes. In D. I. Mostofsky (Ed.), *Attention: Contemporary theory and analysis.* New York: Appleton-Century-Crofts.

Luria, A. R., Khomskaya, E. D., Blinkov, S. M., & Critchley, M. (1967). Impaired selectivity of mental processes in association with a lesion of the frontal lobe. *Neuropsychologia, 5*(2), 105–117.

Luria, A. R., Kiyashchenko, N. K., Moskovichyute, L. I., Faller, To. O., &

Fillippycheva, N. A. (1978). Syndromes of mnemonic disorders accompanying diencephalic tumors. In M. Cole (Ed.), *The selected writings of A. R. Luria.* White Plains: M. E. Sharpe.

Luria, A. R., & Klimovskiy, M. (1970). On the organization of short-term memory by modality. *Soviet Psychology, 8*(3–4), 257–263.

Luria, A. R., & Majorski, L. V. (1977). Basic approaches used in American and Soviet clinical neuropsychology. *American Psychologist, 32,* 959–968.

Luria, A. R., Pravdina-Vinarskaya, E. N., & Iarbus [Yarbus], A. L. (1964). Eye-movement mechanisms in normal and pathological vision (simultaneous agnosia and optical ataxia). *Soviet Psychology and Psychiatry, 2*(4), 28–39.

Luria, A. R., Pribram, K. H., & Khomskaya, E. D. (1964). An experimental analysis of the behavioral disturbances produced by a left frontal arachnoidal endothelioma (meningioma). *Neuropsychologia, 2,* 257–280.

Luria, A. R., & Simernitskaya, E. G. (1977). Interhemispheric relations and the functions of the minor hemisphere. *Neuropsychologia, 15,* 175–178.

Luria, A. R., Simernitskaya, E. G., & Tubylevich, B. (1970). The structure of psychological processes in relation to cerebral organization. *Neuropsychologia, 8,* 13–19.

Luria, A. R., Sokolov, E. N., & Klimkowski, M. (1967). Towards a neurodynamic analysis of memory disturbances with lesions of the left temporal lobe. *Neuropsychologia, 5,* 1–11.

Luria, A. R., & Tsvetkova, L. S. (1964). The programming of constructive activity in local brain injuries. *Neuropsychologia, 2,* 95–108.

Luria, A. R., & Tsvetkova, L. S. (1967–1968). On the disturbance of intellectual functions in patients with frontal lobe lesions. *Soviet Psychology, 6*(2), 3–6.

Luria, A. R., & Tsvetkova, L. S. (1968). The mechanism of "dynamic aphasia." *Foundations of Language: International Journal of Language and Philosophy, 4*(3), 296–307.

Luria, A. R., & Tsvetkova, L. S. (1978). Neuropsychological analysis of the predicative structure of utterances. In M. Cole (Ed.), *The selected writings of A. R. Luria.* White Plains: M. E. Sharpe.

Luria, A. R., Tsvetkova, L. S. & Futer, D. S. (1965). Aphasia in a composer. *Journal of the Neurological Sciences, 2,* 288–292.

Luria, A. R., & Vinogradova, O. S. (1959). An objective investigation of the dynamics of semantic systems. *British Journal of Psychology, 50*(2), 89–105.

Luria, A. R., & Yudovich, F. Ia. (1959). *Speech and development of mental processes in the child.* J. Simon (Ed.). London: Staples Press.

Malinowski, B. (1930). The problem of meaning in primitive languages. In C. K. Ogden & I. A. Richards (Eds.), *The meaning of meaning.* (3rd ed.). London: Harcourt, Brace.

Meshcheryakov, A. I. (1956). *Disturbance of the interaction of the two signal systems in the formation of simple motor reactions in cases of brain lesions.* Dissertation, Department of Psychology, Moscow University. (In Russian).

Meshcheryakov, A. I. (1958). The mechanisms of abstraction and generalization processes in mentally retarded children. In A. R. Luria (Ed.), *Problems of the higher neural activity of the normal and abnormal child* (Vol. 2). Moscow: publisher unknown. (In Russian).

Morozova, N. G. (1948). Development of the attitudes of preschool children to a verbal task. *Izv. Akad. Pedag. Nauk. RSFSR, 14.* (In Russian).

Nazarova, L. K. (1952). Role of speech kinesthesis in writing. *Sovet. Pedag., 6.* (In Russian).

Ong, W. J. (1967). *The presence of the word: Some prolegomena for cultural and religious history.* New Haven: Yale University Press.

Pavlov, I. P. (1949). *Complete collected works.* (Vol. 3). Moscow: Izd. AU SSSR. (In Russian).

Payne, T. R. (1968). *S. L. Rubinstejn and the philosophical foundations of Soviet psychology.* Dordrecht, Holland: D. Reidel.

Pevzner, M. S. (1956). Clinical characterization of the basic variants of defects in oligophrenia. In A. R. Luria (Ed.), *Problems of the higher neural activity of the normal and abnormal child* (Vol. 1). Moscow: publisher unknown. (In Russian).

Potebnya, A. A. (1888). *Some notes on Russian grammar* (2nd ed.). Khar'kov. (In Russian).

Pribram, K. H., & Luria, A. R. (Eds.). (1973). *Psychophysiology of the frontal lobes.* New York: Academic Press.

Radzikhovskii, L. A., & Khomskaya, E. D. (1981). A. R. Luria and L. S. Vygotsky: Early years of their collaboration. *Soviet Psychology, 20*(1), 3–21).

Reitman, W. (1970). What does it take to remember? In D. A. Norman (Ed.), *Models of human memory.* New York: Academic Press.

Scheerer, Ed. (Ed.). (1980). Luria memorial issue. *Psychological Research, 41*(2–3).

Shiffrin, E. M. (1970). Memory search. In D. A. Norman (Ed.), *Models of human memory.* New York: Academic Press.

Skinner, B. F. (1957). *Verbal behavior.* New York: Appleton-Century-Crofts.

Slobin, D. I. (1966). Soviet psycholinguistics. In N. O'Connor (Ed.), *Present-day Russian psychology.* Oxford: Pergamon Press.

Sokolov, A. N. (1972). *Inner speech and thought.* (D. B. Lindsley, Ed., G.

T. Onischenko, Trans.). New York: Plenum Press.

Smirnov, A. A. (1948). *The psychology of memorizing.* Moscow-Leningrad: Press of the Akad. Ped. Nauk RSFSR. (In Russian).

Smirnov, A. A. (1966). *Problems in the psychology of memory.* Moscow: Prosvescheniya. (In Russian).

Svedelius, C (1897). *L'analyse du langage.* Uppsala. (In French).

Tikhomirov, O. K. (1978). The formation of voluntary movements in children of preschool age. In M. Cole (Ed.), *The selected writings of A. R. Luria.* White Plains: M. E. Sharpe.

Ukhtomskii, A. A. (1945). *Essays on the physiology of the nervous system.* Collected works (Vol. 4). Leningrad: publisher unknown. (In Russian).

Vygotskii, L. S. (1956). *Collected psychological investigations.* Moscow: Izd. Akad. Pedag. Nauk. RSFSR. (In Russian).

Vygotskii, L. S. (1960). *Development of the higher mental functions.* Moscow: Izd. Akad. Ped. Nauk RSFSR. (In Russian).

Vygostky, L. S. (1929). The problem of the cultural development of the child. *Journal of Genetic Psychology, 36,* 415–434.

Vygotsky, L. S. (1962). *Thought and language.* E. Hanfmann & G. Vokar (Eds. & Trans.). Cambridge: MIT Press.

Vygotsky, L. S. (1963). Learning and mental development at school age. In B. Simon & J. Simon (Eds.), *Educational Psychology in the U.S.S.R.* Stanford: Stanford University Press.

Vygotsky, L. S. (1966). Development of the higher mental functions. In A. Leontyev, A. R. Luriya, and A. Smirnov (Eds.), *Psychological research in the U.S.S.R.* Moscow: Progress Publishers.

Vygotsky, L. S. (1977). The development of higher psychological functions. *Soviet Psychology, 15*(3), 60–73.

Vygotsky, L. S. (1978). *Mind in society: The development of higher psychological processes.* M. Cole, V. John-Steiner, S. Scribner, & E. Souberman (Eds.). Cambridge: Harvard University Press.

Vygotsky, L. S. & Luria, A. R. (1930). The function and fate of egocentric speech. *Ninth International Congress of Psychology: Proceedings and papers—New Haven, September 1–7, 1929.* Princeton: The Psychological Review Company.

Wertsch, J. V. (1982). Editor's introduction. In A. R. Luria, (J. V. Wertsch, Ed.), *Language and cognition.* New York: Wiley.

Zemlin, W. R. (1968). *Speech and hearing science: Anatomy and physiology.* Englewood Cliffs, NJ: Prentice-Hall.

Zinchenko, V. P., Leont'ev, A. N., Lomov, B. F., & Luria, A. R. (1974). Parapsychology: Fiction or Fact? *Soviet Psychology, 12*(3), 3–20.

Zivin, G. (Ed.). (1979). *The development of self-regulation through private speech.* New York: Wiley.

Author Index

Subject Index